Revolutionary Prophecies

Jeffersonian America

CHARLENE M. BOYER LEWIS, ANNETTE GORDON-REED,
PETER S. ONUF, ANDREW J. O'SHAUGHNESSY, AND
ROBERT G. PARKINSON, EDITORS

Revolutionary Prophecies

The Founders and America's Future

Edited by
Robert M. S. McDonald
and Peter S. Onuf

University of Virginia Press / Charlottesville and London

University of Virginia Press
© 2021 by the Rector and Visitors of the University of Virginia
All rights reserved
Printed in the United States of America on acid-free paper

First published 2021

9 8 7 6 5 4 3 2 1

LIBRARY OF CONGRESS CATALOGING-IN-PUBLICATION DATA

Names: Revolutionary prophecies (Conference) (2013 : St. Louis, Missouri) |
  McDonald, Robert M. S., 1970– editor. | Onuf, Peter S., editor.
Title: Revolutionary prophecies : the founders and America's future / edited by
  Robert M. S. McDonald and Peter S. Onuf.
Description: Charlottesville : University of Virginia Press, 2020. | Series: Jeffersonian
  America | Includes bibliographical references and index.
Identifiers: LCCN 2020039801 (print) | LCCN 2020039802 (ebook) |
  ISBN 9780813944494 (cloth) | ISBN 9780813945002 (ebook)
Subjects: LCSH: United States—Politics and government—1783–1789. |
  Revolutionaries—United States—Biography. | Founding Fathers of the United
  States. | United States—History—Confederation, 1783–1789. | United States—
  History—Constitutional period, 1789–1809. | Nationalism—United
  States—History—18th century. | National characteristics, American—
  History—18th century.
Classification: LCC E302.5 .R48 2013 (print) | LCC E302.5 (ebook) | DDC
  973.3092/2—dc23
LC record available at https://lccn.loc.gov/2020039801
LC ebook record available at https://lccn.loc.gov/2020039802

Cover art (left to right): Gilbert Stuart, portrait of George Washington, c.1796–1803,
oil on canvas (Clark Art Institute, clarkart.edu); Gilbert Stuart, portrait of John
Adams, c.1800–1815, oil on canvas (Everett–Art/Shutterstock); John Trumbull,
portrait of Alexander Hamilton, 1804–6, oil on canvas (The Met, www.metmuseum
.org); Gilbert Stuart, portrait of James Madison, c.1821, oil on wood (Everett–Art/
Shutterstock)

In memory of Lance Banning

Contents

Preface

This volume traces its origins to a June 2013 conference bearing the same title. It took place in the shadow of the famous 630-foot St. Louis "Gateway Arch," which, in shimmering stainless steel, celebrates the westward expansion of the United States. The monument, on land not far from the pre-Columbian metropolis of Cahokia, occupies ground once claimed by Spain and then purchased by Thomas Jefferson as part of a vast tract from France. St. Louis served as the launch pad for the 1804–6 expedition of Meriwether Lewis and William Clark, who helped chart the new, nearly transcontinental world over which the United States in 1803 had gained possession. What better location to consider the founding generation's hopes, fears, ambitions, and anxieties for and about America's future?

St. Louis was a fitting location for another reason. It served as the birthplace of the distinguished academic career of the late Lance Banning, who in 1971 received his Ph.D. from Washington University. A professor at the University of Kentucky for more than three decades, his first book, *The Jeffersonian Persuasion: Evolution of a Party Ideology* (1978), broke new ground by helping to extend the republicanism of the American Revolution forward in time to the Early Republic. He sustained his focus on the Jeffersonian Republicans' political thought, especially that of James Madison, in articles appearing in the *William and Mary Quarterly* and *Virginia Magazine of History and Biography* as well as in his 1995 books *Jefferson and Madison: Three Conversations from the Founding* and *The Sacred Fire of Liberty: James Madison and the Founding of the Federal Republic.* In later years he turned his attention to crafting an elegant survey of the rise of the first party system, *Conceived in Liberty: The Struggle to Define the New Republic, 1789–1793* (2004), and editing *Liberty and Order: The First American Party Struggle* (2004), which leverages primary documents to explore the contest between Republicans and their Federalist rivals. At the time of his death in 2006, he was compiling a book of previously published essays, a "greatest hits" collection, that Todd Estes, his former doctoral student, pushed to completion as *Founding Visions: The Ideas, Individuals, and Intersections That Created America* (2014).

All of the contributors to this volume knew Lance Banning, and they dedicate it to his memory. Some were once his students. All consider themselves his friends. One of the things we appreciate most is his capacity for careful, close analysis and independent thought. Estes, a contributor to this volume, remembers his first meeting with the man who was his dissertation adviser. He "didn't know then" but "would learn quickly that Lance has a trademark conversational style. When the person he is conversing with is speaking, Lance usually cocks his head to one side and looks off into space, staring intensely at some far-off point, and listens to what is being said. Then, when the speaker has finished, he often pauses—for what can seem to the uninitiated like several minutes—before he speaks himself." This, Estes is quick to point out, is because Banning "listened carefully to what I would say, thought with equal care about what he wanted to say, and then—only then—did he speak."

This degree of deliberation seems present in all of Banning's scholarly judgments. "Lance had no academic axe to grind or agenda to push," remembers Dave Nichols, another former graduate student. This held true whether, as at the start of his career, he was leading historiographical trends while a student of J. G. A. Pocock and an informal mentor of contributor Drew McCoy, or toward the end of it, when he broke with many scholars of the Early Republic by expressing misgivings about the new conventional wisdom that Jefferson had engaged in a long-term relationship with Sally Hemings, his late wife's half-sister—and also his slave. Whether he was wrong or right in these specific stands, no one who gathered at St. Louis questioned Banning's intellectual independence, honesty, or courage. All these qualities, together with his diligence and dedication as a teacher, mentor, and colleague, were his hallmarks.

The "Revolutionary Prophecies" conference, the fourth Sons of the American Revolution (SAR) Annual Conference on the American Revolution, represented a continuation of the National Society of the SAR's efforts to encourage historical research—one of the purposes specified in the charter it received from Congress in 1889. Joseph W. Dooley served as conference director and also as the SAR's 2013–14 president general; without Joe's many efforts, the gathering would not have been possible. Among those in attendance were Barbara Oberg and the late John Murrin, each of whom offered perceptive and constructive comments on many of the essays. The conference relied on the generous support of the George Washington Endowment Fund of the National Society of the SAR; the Mount Vernon Ladies' Association; Arlington Blue Top Cabs; The WinSet Group, LLC; the California Society SAR Ladies Auxiliary; David N. Appleby; Mr. and Mrs. John H. Franklin Jr.; Joseph R. Godfrey, Ph.D.; Stephen A. Leishman; S. John Massoud; Eugene D. Melvin; Samuel C. Powell, Ph.D.; Timothy E. Ward; and the George Washington Chapter and the George Mason Chapter, both of the Virginia Society SAR.

After the conference, the collegial team of professionals at the University of Virginia Press—including Ellen Satrom, Mark Mones, Helen Chandler, and Charlie Bailey—helped to transform this collection of papers into a cohesive and coherent book. This was our final project with our old friend Richard Holway, who retired as senior executive editor, and our first with new friend Nadine Zimmerli, who recently took the reins as history and social sciences editor. Frank Cogliano and Brian Steele, our formerly anonymous peer reviewers, offered helpful critiques that improved the book considerably. So did the corrections and suggestions of Margaret A. Hogan, our copyeditor and fellow historian.

Revolutionary Prophecies

Introduction

PETER S. ONUF AND ROBERT M. S. MCDONALD

When Thomas Jefferson responded to Washington, D.C., mayor Roger Weightman's letter asking him to attend ceremonies marking the fiftieth anniversary of American independence, his life spanned eighty-three years into the past—and only ten days into the future. Yet on June 24, 1826, when he wrote to decline Weightman's "kind invitation," noting that "it adds sensibly to the sufferings of sickness, to be deprived" of the opportunity to join the celebration, he did not dwell on the actions of the members of the Continental Congress, who in 1776 made "the bold and doubtful" choice "between submission or the sword." Instead, he imagined how the decision to declare independence and fight for liberty would shape human history in the decades and centuries to come: "May it be to the world, what I believe it will be, (in some parts sooner, to others later, but finally to all,) the signal of arousing men to burst the chains under which monkish ignorance and superstition had persuaded them to bind themselves, and to assume the blessings and security of self-government." Thanks to the American Revolution, he wrote, "all eyes are opened or opening to the rights of man. The general spread of the light of science has already laid open to every view the palpable truth, that the mass of mankind has not been born with saddles on their backs, nor a favored few, booted and spurred, ready to ride them legitimately, by the grace of God."[1]

Jefferson's letter continues to inspire. Who could fail to tap a foot to the drumbeat cadence of the steady march of individual rights? Who would hesitate to cheer liberal democracy's conquest of tyranny? A world once dominated by kings, emperors, dictators, and other despots now is led largely by elected presidents and parliaments. But Jefferson's letter to Weightman also reminds us that a prediction necessarily reflects the perspective of the prognosticator. Presumptions about the audience for whom a prediction is intended, as well as the vices and virtues of the time and place from which it emerges, often mean that prophecies reveal more about the present than the future.

On July 4, Weightman had Jefferson's letter published in his city's two daily newspapers. After Jefferson's death on the fiftieth anniversary of the ratification of his Declaration of Independence—an almost impossible coincidence that seemed positively providential following the revelation that John Adams, Jefferson's partner in the cause of American autonomy, had died on the Fourth as well—the reprinting of the letter in papers throughout the nation must have stirred nearly all Americans. Nearly all—except those, about one-sixth of the total population, who had been born with metaphorical saddles on their backs. Enslaved Americans remained among the "others" for whom Jefferson's prediction of liberation offered only "grounds of hope."[2]

The future Jefferson envisioned for his fellow Americans and for people everywhere on the new nation's fiftieth birthday was not the same future Americans—speaking through his Declaration—had envisioned in 1776. Times had changed and perspectives with them. The membership and boundaries of the union of rebellious Anglo-American colonies that revolutionary statesmen declared into existence were not yet clearly defined. Other British colonies rebuffed American entreaties and chose not to abjure their allegiance to George III; the same was true for large numbers of loyalists, or "Tories," living in the seceding, self-constituted states. The bonds that attached patriots to the so-called Common Cause were often tenuous, disguising conflicting interests and agendas. In theory, consent could not be coerced—although, in practice, belligerent patriots did not hesitate to "persuade" (or intimidate) recalcitrant neighbors by any means necessary. In many respects, the Revolution was more like a civil war than a war of national liberation.

The Revolution was also a war among the peoples of North America. Most Indian nations hoped to sit out the war; some even joined forces with the Americans. But the widely shared presumption was that the "merciless Indian Savages"—as Jefferson characterized them in the Declaration—were counter-revolutionary, internal enemies.[3] This was clearly the case with enslaved people as well. Jefferson could only imagine doing justice to this "captive nation" by deporting them to a place where they could have a future in a "country" of their own.[4] Nor could the planter-patriarch—or most other men—imagine women exercising equal rights in the new American republic. Patriotic wives and mothers belonged in their homes, preparing future generations to make their way in the world.[5]

Jefferson's July 4 prophecy testified to his enduring faith in America's great experiment in republican self-government. Shining a bright, retrospective light on the new nation's beginnings, the octogenarian offered his countrymen a dazzling vision of their future. This was a message that patriotic Americans were eager to hear in an expansive (if short-lived) "era of good feelings" and "spread-eagle" nationalism.[6] But Jefferson could only look forward so hopefully on the eve of his death by overlooking a deeply troubled past. More than once, the union he cherished had nearly collapsed, as it eventually would in the not-too-distant future. His inspiring narrative brought patriots together, affirming their national identity. But it also cast conflicting narratives and alternative prophecies into the shadows. The essays in this volume can only hint at the range and complexity of the ways in which men and women of the founding generations imagined their future—and made our history.

Revolutionary Americans' historical consciousness reflected converging conceptions of themselves as a people and of the North American continent as their homeland. Situating themselves in space and time, Americans looked in different directions as they envisioned the future. In a memorandum to President George Washington, Alexander Hamilton positioned the United States with Canada on "our left" and Latin America on "our right" as he looked toward Europe for models of American greatness. But Jefferson gazed westward to the future. Like most Americans, he found Thomas Paine's prophecy compelling: "We have it on our power to begin the world over again."[7]

On the eve of independence, Paine insisted that "there is something very absurd, in supposing a continent to be perpetually governed by an island."[8] It was unnatural for Britain, a small, circumscribed island with limited resources, to give rule to a great continent with boundless prospects. Americans were blessed with a bountiful supply of fertile land; as settlers cultivated raw terrain into fertile farms, it would make them a prosperous and powerful people. Yet neither Paine nor Jefferson turned away from Europe, for they both saw free and unfettered access to European markets as the key to future greatness. American independence would initiate a progressive revolution in commerce and diplomacy. "Westward the course of empire," Bishop George Berkeley famously exclaimed in 1722, setting the stage for continental expansion.[9] The future would be enacted on the far frontiers of settlement. The progress of civilization was marked by movement across space: the continent was a *tabula rasa,* or blank slate, with "room enough for our descendants," Jefferson promised, "to the thousandth and thousandth generation."[10]

Patriots conjured up new temporal and spatial horizons for the men and women who constituted a new American people. The Revolution launched a "new order of the ages," a "world turned upside down." The term "revolution" traditionally suggested circular movement, like the progress from one day to another, season to season, year to year; the rise and fall of classical republics and modern dynasties followed the same inevitable pattern. Rulers changed but the basic conditions of human life for their subjects persisted, time out of mind. The American Revolution promised to change everything, liberating a newly self-conscious and self-governing people from the thralldom of foreign despotism. As the circle became a line, the people could envision a future for their grandchildren's grandchildren, stretching across the generations to a distant, western horizon. The sovereign people could now claim the kind of immortality that was once the exclusive prerogative of monarchy and aristocracy. As American republics banished the last vestiges of feudalism, crown lands became the people's patrimony.

The first great modern republic was, in Jefferson's words, something "new under the sun."[11] Old World monarchies were imprisoned by the past. Founders of royal houses reached beyond the grave to impose their despotic rule—the past's dead hand—across future generations. "Wars and contentions," Jefferson wrote to Jean, Comte Diodati-Tronchin, in 1807, "fill the pages of history." But the "silent course of happiness" in enlightened America "furnishes nothing for history to say."[12] The new nation owed nothing to the past. No longer entangled in a perpetual state of war with Britain's imperial rivals, the United States would live in peace with the world and with each other. For Jefferson, American independence repudiated the kind of history told by David Hume and other "Tory" historians to justify and perpetuate dynastic rule. With sycophants silenced, the voices of ordinary people would be heard, telling their own stories and making their own history.

Ordinary Americans first found their voices in the Declaration of Independence. The Declaration did not declare a fact. It was instead a kind of prayer—a revolutionary prophecy—that would only be fulfilled if a spirited people sustained its commitment to the Common Cause. The Declaration's opening paragraphs set forth the "self-evident" principles that justified the break with Britain and authorized Americans to think of themselves as a people. Subsequent paragraphs recited colonists' grievances against King George III, providing a unifying national narrative of recent, otherwise disconnected events in the various provinces. Americans conceived of themselves as a people when they identified with each other across provincial boundaries, recognizing that "all men are created equal."[13] The respective provinces and their histories were not erased when "Americans" enlisted in the continental Common Cause. Quite to the contrary, popular political and military mobilization fostered a broad conception of diversity-in-unity, *e pluribus unum,* based on equal rights and reciprocal recognition. A shared sense of the past enabled Americans to look forward to a shared national future. When they did so, they began to think about "history" itself in radical new ways.

American nationalism drew inspiration from British sources.[14] The precocious development of nationalist sentiment in metropolitan Britain paved the way for proto-nationalist mobilization on the imperial periphery.[15] Before their Revolution, Anglo-Americans exulted in a greater British identity manifest in their enthusiasm for the Glorious Revolution and allegiance to the Hanoverian succession. Constitutional controversies eroded that identification as colonists resisted imperial policies which threatened to subvert their equal rights as Englishmen within the empire. When the insular British Parliament claimed sovereign authority over a domesticated crown and throughout the empire, American patriots reluctantly concluded that they must be a separate people, if they were to be a people at all. "We might have been a free & a great people together," Jefferson lamented in his rough draft of the Declaration, "but a communication of grandeur & of freedom it seems is below their dignity." Americans would be a free and independent people, not servile subjects of a despotic king. "The road to glory & happiness is open to us too," Jefferson concluded, and "we will climb it in a separate state."[16]

The constitutional arguments that propelled colonists toward the break with Britain were grounded in the past, drawing deeply on the histories of particular colonies and their relationship to the imperial metropolis to counter parliamentary sovereignty claims. From the increasingly alienated perspective of Anglo-American patriots, Parliament's consolidation of authority only made sense in a geographically specific British context, not in the colonies. If the Americans invoked the "rights of man" when they rejected Parliament's sovereignty and withdrew their allegiance to the Crown, they did so in response to British denials that *their* histories mattered.[17] When had Americans ever acknowledged Parliament's right to suspend or vacate colonial charters? What right did Parliament have to interfere in the colonies' internal affairs and violate their (customary) constitutions? As Jefferson insisted in his 1774 *Summary View of the Rights of British America,* American colonists were the true creators of their own colonies: the imperial connection thus depended on their continuing consent. "For themselves they fought" for survival in the American wilderness; "for themselves they conquered, and for themselves alone they have right to hold." The American enterprise had not been sponsored by the king; their "country" "had been acquired by the lives, the labors and the fortunes" of the colonists and their forbears. Far from rejecting history, Americans turned to the past as they created their new nation and imagined its future.[18]

The "long train of abuses" cited in the Declaration of Independence marked the emergence of a new national historical consciousness, building on, synthesizing, and abstracting fundamental principles from their provincial histories. Those separate histories now flowed into a single narrative. Political and military mobilization eroded the jurisdictional hierarchy of the imperial old regime, collapsing the distance between the higher authority of the central government and its distant provinces. The logic of equal rights was leveling. With the diffusion of authority, local events took on continental significance. The pain inflicted on Boston by Parliament's Intolerable Acts of 1774 in retaliation for the Tea Party was felt across the continent.[19] Jefferson's *Summary View* invoked the terms "America" and "Americans" more than thirty-five times.[20] His catalogue of grievances evoked a community of suffering that imaginatively obliterated provincial boundaries. Declaring themselves to be a people or nation, "Americans" began to think of the continent as their homeland. For ordinary citizens making critical choices, popular sovereignty was no fiction. Every American was an agent of change, playing a vital role in the demolition of the monarchical old regime and the construction of its republican successor.

The essays in this collection explore the historical consciousness of Americans caught up in the Revolution and its aftermath. By focusing on how various individuals and groups envisioned their future, we can better understand how they understood their past and present circumstances. Nation-making was world-changing. Revolutionary Americans knew they were making choices that would redirect the "course of human events."

The early American federal republic was a work in progress. The boundaries of the country were contested and indeterminate, subject to the vagaries of war and diplomacy. The revolutionaries called their rudimentary government "continental," evoking both the existential imperative of inter-colonial unity and the aspiration to extend their "empire of liberty" across far frontiers. America was, at first, less a "country" seeking to secure a place in the world than a grand speculative project. The 1783 Peace of Paris secured extraordinarily generous boundaries for the Americans, unleashing a flood of settlers and speculators; maps and surveys framed an expansive cartographic image of a nation in the making. New state constitutions enabled citizens to visualize their futures within recognized boundaries, while the federal Constitution created a capacious framework for an expanding union of self-governing state-republics.

America was a modern-day promised land. But Americans recognized that its promises would only be fully redeemed at some future date. The mass mobilization of young men disrupted families, fostering generational identity and a genealogical consciousness.[21] Risking their lives, "sons of liberty" acted collectively as a generation to secure their families' welfare. If they survived, these sons would be good fathers to their own children and good husbands to their wives; if they did not, their countrymen would assume the sacred obligation to support their surviving families. Patriotic widows would step into the breach, sacrificing everything on behalf of their children's future. Jefferson's conception of generational stewardship (or "usufruct") evoked this sense of obligation: the country was the people's great estate, and each generation was an "independent nation," morally obligated to its successors. The sovereignty of the "living generation" was foundational to Jeffersonian constitutionalism, providing a framework for renewing and fulfilling the Revolution's promises to the American people and to the world.[22]

Jefferson and his fellow patriots were obsessed with the epochal, world-historical significance of the Revolution, confident that other victims of oppression would follow the Americans' lead and cast off the shackles of monarchical despotism. Writing from Paris in August 1789, Jefferson exulted in the first tremors of revolutionary upheaval in France. "I will agree to be stoned as a false prophet if all does not end well in this country," he wrote

Diodati. "Nor will it end with this country," for this "is but the first chapter of the history of European liberty."[23] Jefferson would prove a poor prophet, but his historical consciousness was in tune with the times. Hereafter "history" would be inscribed in a new "book," its chapters revealing the unfolding narrative of nation-making in a global context.

Reviving the "Spirit of 1776" on the Fourth of July became a civic ritual for patriotic Americans, signifying their ongoing commitment to the union. But visions of a glorious American future antedated the break with Britain. Indeed, it was the British connection that inspired those visions. The leading revolutionaries were all originally British imperial patriots with exalted ideas about the colonies' role in the empire's future. Benjamin Franklin's *Observations Concerning the Increase of Mankind* (1755) projected the exponential growth of the Anglo-American population. Demography was destiny in an era when political economists still linked prosperity and power to a rising population. Within a century, Franklin predicted, "the greatest Number of Englishmen will be on this Side the Water."[24] A young John Adams struck a similarly prophetic note (probably after reading Franklin) when he assured a correspondent that America would eventually, inevitably, replace Britain as a hegemonic power. "Such heady dreams were in the cultural air," J. Patrick Mullins writes, as Britain mobilized its forces—including large numbers of Americans—to vanquish its French rival in the great war for North American empire that culminated triumphantly in the 1763 Peace of Paris.[25] Territorial expansion and demographic growth now converged. Britain's empire, patriots on both sides of the Atlantic exulted, was the greatest in the modern world, a worthy successor to Rome.

The very idea of empire evoked the growing interdependence of Britain's far-flung dominions, underwriting the claims of Anglo-Americans to equal rights and provincial autonomy in the empire that in another decade would tear the empire apart. But patriots like Franklin did not aspire to independence. To the contrary, realization of their imperial dreams depended on union with Britain and among the American provinces. Could there even be an "America" without the imperial connection? Franklin "becomes a reluctant revolutionary," according to Robert A. Ferguson's elegant summary of his subject's career, then "manages to shift at the right moment to serve as a vigorous revolutionary leader" before morphing into "a cosmopolitan diplomatic figure" and finishing, with Washington, "as one of the two leading patriotic giants of a continental republic."²⁶ Ferguson's use of the present tense is revealing, for Franklin—like all our subjects—inhabits his own historical moment as he imagines the future. More than any other contemporary figure, he was at home in the empire.

Franklin's *Autobiography*, the subject of Ferguson's essay, is a "work written for his own time, the age of Enlightenment, but carefully couched in rhetoric for the future American that he would never know." By focusing on his formative experiences as an ambitious but self-aware provincial American, conscious of the errors to which the young and ignorant are so prone, Franklin makes himself accessible to future generations. "The result," Ferguson concludes, is a "presentism that reaches beyond the historical without losing it."²⁷ The other founding fathers were obsessed with the way they would be remembered, the "fame" they earned from their great nation-making achievements.²⁸ But Franklin left a monument in an *Autobiography* that "lives on and on," bringing the author "back to life for us in the more perfect edition that he has planned for himself on the page."²⁹ Franklin moved easily, if somewhat reluctantly, from the old empire to his new national home. It was a journey on which many other Americans would embark.

John Adams was also an imperialist, Mullins persuasively argues, although his career ambitions crystallized later than Franklin's, taking on a more explicitly political form during the post-1763 period of imperial crisis and collapse. With his beloved New England under siege, Adams's imperialism focused on defending his home region by defining "the proper constitutional place of America within the British Empire." Adams and other imperial federalists sought to incorporate the Crown in the separate colonial constitutions (George III was "King of Massachusetts-Bay"), thus connecting the colonies to each other while guaranteeing their collective security. When the king withdrew his protection from his American subjects and unleashed his armies on them, Adams's empire was demolished. He called Parliament's Prohibitory Act of October 1775, authorizing a blockade of the colonies, "a compleat Dismemberment of the British Empire." By throwing the "thirteen Colonies out of the Royal Protection," he explained, the act "levels all Distinctions and makes us independent."³⁰

Over the following months, Adams impatiently waited for his congressional colleagues to acknowledge the fact that Parliament had already declared American independence. During this curious interregnum, Congress's army was effectively *defending* the empire against a wicked ministry intent on its dismemberment. Of course, Adams and his fellow patriot constitutionalists sought to mobilize their countrymen in defense of their endangered rights and liberties. But the foundation of their grievances was a widely shared conception of a customary imperial constitution that could not survive the outbreak of war.[31] By sustaining the war effort against Britain, Americans demonstrated the capacity to create a more perfect union and thereby secure their own "empire of liberty."

Union was essential. Few revolutionaries could conceive of divided state-republics living in peace with "the powers of the earth"—or with each other. The Revolution was a war for empire against the empire that betrayed American imperial patriots. But there was no "self-evident" constitutional blueprint for constructing a new American empire. Mullins coins the term "Yankee continentalism" to characterize Adams's distinctive vision of the union. Adams was both a "dedicated provincial" and an "ardent national-ist," concludes Mullins. The paradox only exists in anachronistic hindsight. What else could he be? Franklin, Adams, and their fellow founders were all shaped by their formative experiences as provincial Britons in the British Empire. British metropolis and American province were defined by their relation to each other: there could be no provincial parts without the impe-rial whole. Revolutionary imperialists were not torn apart by conflicting loyalties. "They were all provincials," Mullins neatly concludes. "They were all continentalists."[32]

Patriot continentalism took different, regionally inflected forms. The late Lance Banning aptly described James Madison, the prime author of the fed-eral Constitution, as a "Virginia continentalist."[33] George Washington was also a patriotic Virginian with a continental perspective. The young Wash-ington's career aspirations reflected his intense identification with the British Empire; as a patriotic Virginian, he answered the call to assume command of continental forces in Adams's Massachusetts. With his fellow colonists, writes Kenneth R. Bowling, Washington "resented England's attempt to stifle the rising glory of America." After the war was won and independence secured, he did not hesitate to call the new nation an "empire," modifying the term "by such adjectives as 'new,' 'great,' 'rising,' 'growing,' and 'exten-sive.'"[34] Such language was prophetic. The "father of his country" imagined a glorious future for his metaphorical sons, conjuring up an image of limit-less opportunity on a bountiful landscape. That future was deeply rooted in the history of settlement and land speculation on the imperial frontier. The abstract principles that justified revolution became intelligible as they took material form on the land. The "Spirit of 1776" was inextricably linked to what historian Michael Blaakman calls "land mania," a speculative fever that gripped enterprising Americans of all sorts, from all quarters of the union.[35] Speculators were popular prophets, promising liberty and prosperity to a people on the move.

Virginia occupied a central place in Washington's westward prospect, with the Potomac River providing "the Channel of conveyance of the extensive & valuable Trade of a rising Empire." Locating the new national capital on the Potomac (near Washington's Mount Vernon estate) "would cement the union and provide a durable foundation for its survival."[36] This was an exalted speculation, however, transcending its apparent self-interest. As a surveyor and land speculator, the younger Washington was a conventional estate-builder, a familiar figure on the agricultural frontier; as revolutionary general and statesman, his speculative impulses were sublimated in solicitude for the public good, capaciously defined. His vision of America was not simply Virginia writ large but imperial in scope. By the time he became president, Bowling writes, "Washington had grown beyond his southern roots and adopted a middle states worldview that accepted cities, economic diversity, and financial capitalism as positives."[37]

As contributors to this volume suggest, there was no necessary contradiction between continental and provincial attachments. But Bowling's Washington did press up against the increasingly conspicuous limits of post-provincial Virginian attitudes toward race and slavery. In tandem with Secretary of War Henry Knox (of Massachusetts), President Washington sought to restrain white settlement and guarantee peaceful relations with Indian nations in a "great, respectable, and flourishing empire."[38] Land-hungry Virginians preferred to think of the western wilderness as a *terra nullius*, waiting to be liberated from its "savage" denizens. Nor did the large majority of white Virginians share Washington's "abolitionist" tendencies, as the reticent president well understood. Keeping his un-Virginian views to himself during life, the dying hero went public in his will, emancipating the slaves he owned and testifying against the peculiar institution. Washington "regretted his reliance on slave labor," Bowling concludes, "but committed himself to preparing the 'rising generation for a destiny different from that in which they were born.'"[39] Washington's posthumous prophecy was respectfully received but largely ignored as the "empire of slavery" spread to the South and West. Most scions of the "rising generation" considered the old man's antiquated scruples incompatible with their imperial future. Those few who took his counsel to heart abandoned the region.

Revolutionary Americans were politicized as they were mobilized. Faced with the momentous choice of whether or not to support the Common Cause, they were confronted with immediate consequences in the intimate contexts of local communities. Some professed supporters could be described by Paine as "sunshine patriots" with no great hopes for the future beyond escaping their neighbors' wrath.[40] But many responded enthusiastically to the opportunity to defend their families and communities, exhilarated by the sense of citizen empowerment that was at the core of the revolutionary appeal. The Revolution put young men in motion, enabling them to imagine and pursue "happiness" in new ways and new places. For some committed patriots, the decision for independence was a wager on the future, a personal prophecy. Others remained attached to their home places, recoiling from disruptive changes that jeopardized liberty, property, and local community. Their temporal and spatial horizons were more compressed than those of their mobile neighbors. Wary of distant authorities, they drew on a "radical" resistance tradition in order to preserve a stable and equitable agrarian order.

From the mid-1780s to Jefferson's election in 1800, insurgencies erupted across agrarian America, including Shaysite "Regulators" in western Massachusetts, the so-called Whiskey Rebels of the Upper Ohio River, and the *Kirchenleute,* or "church people," of Pennsylvania's Lehigh Valley. For these "agrarian founders," as Paul Douglas Newman calls them, "the future was more immediate than for the likes of Hamilton or Jefferson." They were not inspired by grandiose—and highly speculative—visions of empire but focused instead on their immediate, local circumstances: "Their revolutionary legacy was the one they were living and meant to bequeath to their children."[41]

Wartime mobilization was a model for peacetime protest. Far from being "rebels," as anxious authorities dubbed them, rural insurgents saw themselves as the same sort of "legitimate and constitutional opposition" that had overthrown the king in 1776. Their conception of a constitution that the "people" authored and owned anticipated Jefferson's democratic constitutionalism. "Governments are republican," the Sage of Monticello intoned in 1816, "only in proportion as they embody the will of their people, and execute it."[42] All of these movements produced tangible results: Shaysites gained tax relief from a new state legislature; the federal government placated westerners by abandoning its whiskey excise, imposing a punitive peace on the Ohio Indians in the Treaty of Greenville, and opening the Mississippi trade in Pinckney's Treaty (both in 1795); and, according to Newman, "the Kirchenleute took local office, cheered peaceful diplomatic negotiations with France, helped turn Pennsylvania for Republicans in the 'Revolution of 1800,' and ensured the repeal of the Sedition Act." "Through these victories," Newman concludes, "these agrarians proved themselves to be the 'other founders.'"[43] To these rural democrats, the "people" was no abstraction or "fiction" invoked by the framers to authorize the consolidation of power in a new republican elite.

The prophetic language of a nation-making, neo-imperial, republican ruling class stood in contrast—and sometimes in stark opposition—to the radically conservative, democratic impulses of Newman's "agrarian founders." If rural insurgents were prophets, they were prophets of doom. Vigilant agrarians were always on the lookout for consolidationist conspiracies, knowing that what had been so hard won in the war could be easily lost. At the same time, however, they pioneered modes of popular political mobilization that could be adapted and coopted by the national political parties which emerged in the 1790s. The democratization of rule mitigated the fears of class-based factional conflict that energized the movement for a more "energetic" federal government while countering the centrifugal tendencies of a rapidly expanding federal union. This was why Jefferson's "Revolution of 1800" proved so critically important: it mobilized an overwhelmingly agricultural people, rooted in place and reflexively suspicious of change, to conquer and colonize a boundless western world, with "room enough," as Jefferson said, "for our descendants to the thousandth to the thousandth generation."[44] Ordinary Americans would make the imperial dreams of revolutionary patriots come true.

The captive nation of enslaved people and the Indian nations within and beyond America's nominal borders did not figure into Jefferson's imperial vision. Jefferson saw slavery as a state of war that could only be resolved by emancipating slaves and sending them to a country of their own. Until that happened and former slaves became a recognizable, "treaty-worthy" nation, there was no prospect of peace. Without such a peace, Jefferson darkly warned, rebellious slaves would exploit some moment of geopolitical vulnerability—such as the American Revolution itself—to break the shackles of bondage, slaughter their masters, and declare their own independence.

Revolutionary patriots also imagined an ongoing state of war with the "merciless savages" who infested frontier regions. The great difference, David Andrew Nichols persuasively argues, was that Indian nations had a long history of making war and negotiating peace with European imperial powers. Jefferson anticipated a cataclysmic race war, accentuating the violent juxtaposition of white and black, but frontier diplomats had to play a much more complicated game, recognizing the autonomy and acknowledging the territorial claims of Indian peoples in order to negotiate treaties. According to American legal codes, enslaved people were property and therefore had no "standing" and could claim no rights in American courts; in stark contrast, treaty negotiations with Indians confirmed effective American jurisdiction and made possible the proliferation of private property rights in ceded territory. Americans claimed rights *in* the bodies of enslaved Africans and African Americans, while they negotiated *with* Indians in order to secure rights to the land. Condescending white Americans could characterize Indians as uncivilized and barbarous. As a practical matter, however, they had to acknowledge Natives' political capacity and treaty-worthiness: "The primary instrument of American colonialism," Nichols writes, "was not the army but the treaty."[45] Jefferson did not have Indians in mind when he wrote the Declaration of Independence, offering friendship in peace to "the powers of the earth."[46] But Indian nations were the effective "powers" of the American earth, and Americans—however reluctantly, and however often in bad faith—had to seek their friendship.

Indian prophets mobilized resistance to white encroachments. They interpreted the long history of treaty-making as the progressive demolition of their homelands, casting their prophecies in starkly genocidal terms that still resonate with revisionist critiques of American exceptionalism and continental imperialism. Nichols offers a more nuanced perspective, reflecting the contemporary recovery and reinterpretation of Indian history. "Between 1778 and 1871," he writes, the United States "negotiated nearly four hundred ratified treaties" with Indians. These treaties helped "turn Indian nations from leagues of towns or families into bounded territorial states with national leaders and institutions." They also fostered a historical consciousness and provided a documentary record that later generations could take to court in order to vindicate their rights, turning the legal instruments of conquest against the conquerors. Treaty-making provided Indians "with the legal 'technology' that would help them retain their national identity and survive as Native Americans."[47] Nichols views Indian lawyers as the original originalists, turning to history to chart a pathway to the future true to their ancestors' original intentions.

Prophecies of "rising glory" were shadowed by prophecies of doom. The future that revolutionary republican imperialists imagined was haunted by the presence of the peoples they overlooked. The common folk who fought and died for independence would not be denied. The logic of mass military mobilization promoted popular political participation, and the "people" demanded access to land. In the South and Southwest, they also demanded access to enslaved labor to work the land. Not surprisingly, slavery did not disappear, nor did Indians vanish, despite unrelenting pressure on their homelands.

In retrospect, the Declaration of Independence offered Americans a reassuring sense of national unity that would prove increasingly elusive in years to come. Jefferson evoked the "Spirit of 1776" when he ascended to the presidency in 1801. America stood on the brink of imperial greatness, he told his fellow Americans in his inaugural address. But this would be an "empire of liberty," not of conquest, as waves of settlers swept across the continent, cultivating the land and fulfilling its—and the American people's—supposed manifest destiny. Displaced from power, Federalist critics predicted that the union they had struggled to perfect would fall apart. An ungovernable people would plunge America into anarchy, unleashing centrifugal forces that could not be contained. For a skeptical Alexander Hamilton, a "people's empire" was a contradiction in terms. The progress of democracy portended the collapse or "Dismemberment of our Empire," he warned in the last letter he wrote before his untimely death in the famous duel with archrival Aaron Burr. "DEMOCRACY" was a deadly "poison," Hamilton asserted, that would spread with the creation of new, supposedly self-governing western states, becoming all "the more concentered in each part, and consequently the more virulent."[48] Conventional diagnoses of democratic pathologies focused on upheaval from *below*, with plebeian insurgents turning the sociopolitical order on its head. But for Hamilton and fellow Federalist state-builders, the threat came from the frontiers of the overextended federal republic—as it had for British imperial authorities in the American Revolution. In America, the axis was flipped from vertical to horizontal: for better or worse, the problem—or promise—of democracy was projected across the continent's vast spaces. Hamilton feared that the new nation's imperial legacy would be squandered; Jefferson exulted in the prospect of a self-governing people creating something "new under the sun," an expanding, ever more perfect union of self-governing states. Democracy was Hamilton's problem; it was Jefferson's solution.[49]

Yet if democracy was the most profound threat to Hamilton's hopes for American empire, Todd Estes shows, Hamilton also recognized the need to adapt to democratic times. In the wake of Jefferson's election, Washington's treasury secretary "reaffirmed his faith in republican empire and tried to make sense of Jeffersonian democracy." The two great rivals would never be reconciled, but their paths converged in surprising ways. Estes underscores Hamilton's "ambivalence" about Jefferson's deployment of Hamiltonian tactics—"a strong, active presidency" and his apparent disregard of constitutional limits on executive authority—in pursuit of what Hamilton considered disastrously misguided policies. Jefferson's moves forced "Hamilton to array *his* own past self against his present self." Partisan political competition was democratizing. Federalists had to meet the Jeffersonians on their own ground, "in a 'democratic' political world of public campaigning, petitioning, electioneering, mobilizing, and mass persuasion." When Hamilton looked to the future, Estes concludes, he envisioned an "American nation that would be *both* a republic *and* a potential empire."[50] The same could be said for Jefferson.

James Madison, Jefferson's presidential successor, had been Hamilton's collaborator in drafting and promoting the ratification of a constitution that would keep the post-imperial union from falling apart. In subsequent decades, the federal Constitution became a touchstone for both national political parties as they jockeyed for comparative advantage—sometimes as a strictly construed defensive barrier against partisan foes, sometimes as a license to expand the federal government's power to serve the "public good." The paradoxical outcome was that people increasingly saw the Constitution itself as a sacred text, an object of the "veneration" that Madison called for in *The Federalist*.[51] The framers' "more perfect union" became the "most perfect" possible union, a legacy to be secured, rather than a promise to be fulfilled. As the framework was sacralized, rising generations were enjoined to heed

Washington's Farewell Address and "properly estimate the immense value of your national Union to your collective & individual happiness."[52]

Virginians played a key role in the war for American independence. But the close vote on the proposed federal Constitution at the Richmond ratifying convention anticipated profound ambivalence within the commonwealth over the future of the union that became manifest in the waning years of the "Virginia Dynasty." In retirement, Madison—the "father" of the Constitution—implored his fellow Americans to transcend increasingly conspicuous sectional differences and celebrate their glorious future as a great, united people. In office, his friend and successor James Monroe calculated the union's value for the commonwealth's slaveholding gentry. Would Virginia fare better in union with the other slave states, freed from the incubus of free states to the north that were intent on restricting slavery's expansion to the west?

"As Madison well knew," writes Drew R. McCoy, "Virginia during the 1820s and 1830s was not the most hospitable vantage point from which to contemplate the future of America's republican experiment under the Constitution." In comparison with other states, the commonwealth's fortunes and prospects had been declining for years. The population and prosperity of Ohio, a new state carved out of territory Virginia once claimed, was booming at an astonishing rate and would soon supersede the Old Dominion. Madison was a "Virginia nationalist," McCoy explains, who exulted in Ohio's rising glory, "a glowing empirical testament to the resounding success of America's republican revolution." Madison's "enlightened provincialism had always been grounded in a larger understanding of American promise that was in no way dependent on his state's dominance or even priority in the union."[53] Madison was "the last of the fathers," as McCoy has eloquently written elsewhere.[54] He was also the last of the great Virginians who could hold on to his faith in the redemptive capacity of "free Institutions" to end slavery and make Virginia more like "its sister states to the North."[55]

The synthesis of provincialism and continentalism that energized revolutionary patriots to break with Britain and declare independence lingered on in the boisterous patriotism of Monroe's "Era of Good Feelings." But good feelings did not run deep. "Over the course of the Missouri Crisis" of 1819–21, John Craig Hammond argues, "Monroe's commitment to the union became conditional, dependent on the union's ability to prop up—rather than undermine—the planter class and the institution of slavery that underwrote their power both at home and in the union."[56] Monroe had no illusions about Virginia's ability to go it alone as a sovereign state: some sort of union was essential. What changed so dramatically in the debate over the future of slavery in the new state of Missouri and across the expanding western frontier was the way Americans now imagined their "manifest destiny" as an imperial power. Could an "empire of liberty" also be an "empire of slavery"? The Missouri Compromise offered a tentative (and tenuous) affirmative answer by projecting the domains of slavery and freedom across the expanding western frontier.

Emerging national political parties, Democrats and Whigs, treated the Missouri Compromise as the epitome of high statesmanship, linking it with the original, nation-making compromises of the Constitutional Convention. A cult of the union and the founding fathers helped sustain intersectional comity, making it possible for northerners and southerners to see each other as fellow Americans. Nationalism provided cover for radically distinct, ultimately incompatible visions of the American future. But the union that patriotic Americans celebrated was a curiously thin and brittle thing, a bundle of compromises wrapped in a venerable aura, fixed in the past. American dreams could not be contained within this archaic framework.

Prophecies only make sense in a temporal framework. Visions of the future evoke and give meaning to the past; optimism and pessimism are variations on the same theme. In much different ways, revolutionary American printers Benjamin Franklin and Isaiah Thomas addressed the question of what—and how—we remember the past and what that means for sustaining the bonds of patriotic community that make prophecies possible. The more famous Franklin (Thomas's idol) made himself available to future generations in his extraordinary *Autobiography*. "Words," Robert Ferguson writes, "are the ultimate source of Franklin's power, his identity, and his awareness of the world by imposing meaning on it." Words "hold in place what otherwise will be left allusive."[57] They enable us to remember, to construct a story about our collective past. Without a past, there can be no future.

Franklin did not burden his readers with an account of his contributions to American nation-making, introducing himself instead as "B. Franklin, Printer," the modest practitioner of a useful art who, in Ferguson's words, "never loses sight of his roots or what they mean to him."[58] Printers played a crucial role in the Revolution "as they translated philosophical principles into the people's commonsense vernacular and grounded them in lived experience."[59] In his monumental *History of Printing in America,* Son of Liberty Isaiah Thomas memorialized Franklin and the many other printers who gave voice to colonists' grievances and aspirations and enabled them to become a people.[60] As founder of the American Antiquarian Society in 1812, Thomas sought to collect anything and everything that could illuminate the unfolding history of the American people, the first people in history to make their own history. "The antiquarian appeal to a 'remote and distant posterity,'" Peter S. Onuf writes, "was a kind of prayer that future generations would sustain the historical consciousness of an enlightened age and cherish the memory of those who labored to preserve the legacy of the past."[61] For Thomas and his antiquarian colleagues, collecting and preserving evidence of the people's past was a patriotic imperative. Democratic self-government was an experiment, a hopeful prophecy that could only be fulfilled if an enlightened people could find its way through its past and into a future.

Notes

1. Jefferson to Roger Weightman, June 24, 1826, Merrill D. Peterson, ed., *Thomas Jefferson: Writings* (New York, 1984), 1516–17.

2. Ibid., 1517; Andrew Burstein, *America's Jubilee* (New York, 2001).

3. Jefferson, The Declaration of Independence as Adopted by Congress, July 4, 1776, Julian P. Boyd et al., eds., *The Papers of Thomas Jefferson,* 44 vols. to date (Princeton, N.J., 1950–), 1:431 (hereafter *PTJ*); Robert Parkinson, *The Common Cause: Creating Race and Nation in the American Revolution* (Chapel Hill, N.C., 2016); Alan Taylor, *The Internal Enemy: Slavery and War in Virginia, 1772–1832* (New York, 2013).

4. Jefferson, *Notes on the State of Virginia* (London, 1787), 214–49, 270–73; Peter S. Onuf, *Jefferson's Empire: The Language of American Nationhood* (Charlottesville, Va., 2000), chap. 5; Nicholas Guyatt, *Bind Us Apart: How Enlightened Americans Invented Racial Segregation* (New York, 2016).

5. Brian Steele, "Thomas Jefferson's Gender Frontier," *Journal of American History* 95 (2008): 17–42. On women's understanding and experience of that "frontier," see the essays collected in Barbara B. Oberg, ed., *Women in the American Revolution: Gender, Politics, and the Domestic World* (Charlottesville, Va., 2019).

6. Len Travers, *Celebrating the Fourth: Independence Day and the Rites of Nationalism in the Early Republic* (Amherst, Mass., 1997).

7. Hamilton to Washington, September 15, 1790 (enclosure), Harold C. Syrett et al., eds., *The Papers of Alexander Hamilton,* 27 vols. (New York, 1961–87), 7:52–53; Thomas Paine, *Common Sense* (Philadelphia, 1776), 134.

8. James D. Drake, *The Nation's Nature: How Continental Presumptions Gave Rise to the United States of America* (Charlottesville, Va., 2011); Paine, *Common Sense*, 82.

9. George Berkeley, "Verses on the Prospect of Planting Arts and Learning in America," Alexander Campbell Fraser, ed., *The Works of George Berkeley*, 4 vols. (Oxford, 1901), 4:366.

10. Jefferson, First Inaugural Address, March 4, 1801, *PTJ*, 33:150.

11. Jefferson to Joseph Priestley, March 21, 1801, *PTJ*, 33:394.

12. Jefferson to Jean, Comte Diodati-Tronchin, March 29, 1807, Andrew A. Lipscomb and Albert Ellery Bergh, eds., *The Writings of Thomas Jefferson*, 20 vols. (Washington, D.C., 1903–4), 11:181–82.

13. Jefferson, The Declaration of Independence as Adopted by Congress, July 4, 1776, *PTJ*, 1:429.

14. T. H. Breen, "Ideology and Nationalism on the Eve of the American Revolution: Revisions Once More in Need of Revising," *Journal of American History* 84 (1997): 13–39.

15. Linda Colley, *Britons: Forging the Nation, 1707–1837* (New Haven, Conn., 1992); Liah Greenfeld, *Nationalism: Five Roads to Modernity* (Cambridge, Mass., 1992).

16. Jefferson, "Original Rough Draught" of the Declaration of Independence, June 11–July 4, 1776, *PTJ*, 1:427.

17. Michael Hattem, *Past and Prologue: Politics and Memory in the American Revolution* (New Haven, Conn., 2020).

18. Ibid.; Jefferson, Draft of Instructions to the Virginia Delegates in the Continental Congress (MS Text of *A Summary View*, &c.), [July 1774], *PTJ*, 1:122, 123.

19. T. H. Breen, *Will of the People: The Revolutionary Birth of America* (Cambridge, Mass., 2019).

20. Jefferson, Draft of Instructions to the Virginia Delegates, [July 1774], *PTJ*, 1:121–35.

21. Karin Wulf, "Lineage: Genealogy and the Politics of Connection in British America, 1680–1820" (book in progress).

22. Jefferson to James Madison, September 6, 1789, *PTJ*, 15:395, 393.

23. Jefferson to Diodati, August 3, 1789, *PTJ*, 15:326.

24. Discussed by J. Patrick Mullins, "Yankee Continentalism: The Provincial Roots of John Adams's Vision for American Union, 1755–1776," pp. 56–57 in this volume.

25. Ibid., p. 56 in this volume.

26. Robert A. Ferguson "Raconteur, Memorialist, Founder: Benjamin Franklin Meets Himself in History," p. 27 in this volume.

27. Ibid., pp. 23–24, 29 in this volume.

28. Douglass Adair, *Fame and the Founding Fathers: Essays*, ed. Trevor Colbourn (New York, 1974).

29. Ferguson, "Raconteur, Memorialist, Founder," p. 45 in this volume.

30. Mullins, "Yankee Continentalism," pp. 59, 73 in this volume.

31. Jack P. Greene, *The Constitutional Origins of the American Revolution* (New York, 2011).

32. Mullins, "Yankee Continentalism," pp. 74–78 in this volume.

33. Lance Banning, *The Sacred Fire of Liberty: James Madison and the Founding of the Federal Republic* (Ithaca, N.Y., 1995), quoted in Mullins, "Yankee Continentalism," p. 54 in this volume.

34. Kenneth R. Bowling, "George Washington's Vision for the United States," pp. 84, 85 in this volume.

35. Michael Blaakman, "Speculation Nation: Land and Mania in the Revolutionary American Republic, 1776–1803" (Ph.D. diss., Yale University, 2016).

36. Washington to Thomas Johnson, July 20, 1770, quoted in Bowling, "George Washington's Vision," p. 86 in this volume; Bowling, "George Washington's Vision," p. 86 in this volume.

37. Ibid., p. 93 in this volume.

38. Report of the Secretary of War, August 7, 1789, quoted in Bowling, "George Washington's Vision," p. 94 in this volume.

39. Bowling, "George Washington's Vision," p. 100 in this volume.

40. Thomas Paine, "The Crisis," no. 1, December 23, 1776, Moncure Daniel Conway, ed., *The Writings of Thomas Paine,* 4 vols. (New York, 1894–96), 1:170.

41. Paul Douglas Newman, "Agrarian Founders: Three 'Rebellions' as Legitimate Opposition, 1786–1799," p. 109 in this volume.

42. Jefferson to Samuel Kercheval, July 12, 1816, quoted in ibid., p. 108 in this volume.

43. Ibid., p. 129 in this volume.

44. Jefferson, First Inaugural Address, March 4, 1801, *PTJ,* 33:150.

45. David Andrew Nichols, "The Sovereign People: Indians, Treaties, and the Subversion of the Founders' Colonialist Vision," p. 136 in this volume, citing Dorothy V. Jones, *License for Empire: Colonialism by Treaty in Early America* (Chicago, 1982).

46. Jefferson, The Declaration of Independence as Adopted by Congress, July 4, 1776, *PTJ,* 1:429.

47. Nichols, "The Sovereign People," pp. 136, 147 in this volume.

48. Hamilton to Theodore Sedgwick, July 10, 1804, Syrett et al., eds. *Papers of Alexander Hamilton,* 26:309, discussed in Todd Estes, "'Arraying Him against Himself': The Jefferson Presidency and the American Future through the Eyes of Alexander Hamilton," p. 168 in this volume.

49. Jefferson to Joseph Priestley, March 21, 1801, *PTJ,* 33:394.

50. Estes, "'Arraying Him against Himself,'" pp. 162, 170 in this volume.

51. [James Madison], No. 49, Alexander Hamilton, John Jay, and James Madison, *The Federalist,* ed. George W. Carey and James McClellan (1818; Indianapolis, 2001), 262.

52. George Washington, Farewell Address, *American Daily Advertiser* (Philadelphia), September 19, 1796.

53. Drew R. McCoy, "James Madison and American Nationality: The View from Virginia," pp. 175, 176, 188 in this volume.

54. Drew R. McCoy, *The Last of the Fathers: James Madison and the Republican Legacy* (New York, 1989).

55. McCoy, "James Madison and American Nationality," pp. 185, 188 in this volume.

56. John Craig Hammond, "Mastery over Slaves, Sovereignty over Slavery: James Monroe, Virginia, and the Missouri Crisis," p. 196 in this volume.

57. Ferguson, "Raconteur, Memorialist, Founder," p. 44 in this volume.

58. Ibid.

59. Peter S. Onuf, "Antiquarian America: Isaiah Thomas and the New Nation's Future," p. 229 in this volume.

60. Isaiah Thomas, *The History of Printing in America. With a Biography of Printers, and an Account of Newspapers,* 2 vols. (Worcester, Mass., 1810).

61. Onuf, "Antiquarian America," p. 240 in this volume.

1   Raconteur, Memorialist, Founder

Benjamin Franklin Meets Himself in History

ROBERT A. FERGUSON

Benjamin Franklin belongs more profoundly than others to what the theorist of history Michael Oakeshott named "a practical past," "a present composed of objects recognized as exploits that have survived."[1] The notion applies to Franklin in many ways, not least in how his own exploits have survived. History is about the details of the past that are selected for recognition, and historians argue endlessly over "by what accident or process of attrition that minute selection of facts, out of all the myriad facts that must have once been known to somebody, had survived to become the facts of history."[2] These arguments grow when the selector of facts writes his own history and that selection prevails.

The Franklin we now know offers the most volatile personal mix of the *then* and *now* that we have from the revolutionary era. He is "the Oldest Revolutionary," born seventy years before the Declaration of Independence, and yet he is also everyone's new American on the rise.[3] His image is more immediately recognized today than any other founder except that of George Washington. Franklin's many lasting identifications outpace those of his compatriots too. He is not just a political leader, draftsman of national documents, and diplomat extraordinaire, though he is uniquely effective in those combinations. He is also an entrepreneur, businessman, scientist, inventor, philosopher, folk moralist, Enlightenment icon, and media symbol, and each of these facets of his life has held up remarkably well against the oblivion of time.

How did all of this recognition sustain itself in an ever-changing country that has always been fickle in its handling of the past? Much of the answer lies in the book that Franklin called his "Memoir," a work written for his own time, the age of Enlightenment, but carefully couched in rhetoric for the future American that he would never know. The *Autobiography*, as we now know it, epitomizes one of the many gnomic sayings of Lewis Namier about historiography. Historians, quoth Namier, "imagine the past and remember the future."[4] The past has to be written in a way that the future will want to remember it.

The *Autobiography* has two other great advantages in this regard. With few exceptions, the figures we remember most clearly from the Revolution—Franklin, John Adams, Thomas Jefferson, Alexander Hamilton, James Madison, even George Washington—hold our attention today through what they wrote.[5] The Revolution is as much a writerly event through the invention of the portable printing press as a military one at a time when "the accomplished figure demonstrated a worthiness for place and preferment by writing about the world at hand."[6] In popular reception, Franklin's book becomes the most enduring work of art that the period provides. Even so, endurance raises its own question. Does his work or any work from the period mean the same thing now as it did then?

In its second great advantage, one over other writings, the *Autobiography* stands out for a particular reason. "We see literature above all," writes the literary historian Paul Benichou, "as the crucible in which our direct experience of life and society is elaborated philosophically, but without loss of immediacy."[7] Franklin has the knack of making the past immediate without losing any of the philosophical import of his social moment, but that knack also presents several puzzles over the meaning, importance, and even sincerity of the writer's effort that will turn us back on the meaning and reception of history itself.

Many controversies about the *Autobiography* have thus to do with one of its greatest virtues. To the extent that Franklin belongs to "a practical past" available to the present, disputes over his book turn on disagreements over whether this practicality helps or hurts a later present. Critics who complain that Franklin repeatedly tells people how to go about things ignore the circumstances in which he lived.[8] Method gave form to a fairly inchoate world. A raw eighteenth-century society of uncertain dimensions needed every ordering device Franklin could provide.

One useful example of method comes early in the *Autobiography*, and it conveys as well the problematics in historical awareness. Franklin, like many other Enlightenment figures, believed that the spread of knowledge could lead to a new kind of harmonious society if there were high levels of literacy and exchange. Despite this generally shared optimism, only Franklin, among all of the accomplished holders of the revolutionary pen, tries to show future Americans how to become "a tolerable English writer." Why is it so important? "Prose Writing has been of great use to me in the Course of my Life," Franklin notes, "and was a Principal means of my Advancement."[9] You can read this claim as either one of many bland personal claims of success or as the necessary requirement in forming a successful culture.

A closer look indicates the higher purpose. Franklin personalizes his presentation about writing to help make it doubly effective for any time and place, and he is never above it all. Yes, he is the teacher posting himself in a universal classroom, but he does it through the eyes of a pupil trying to learn to write, which is to say through the person who needs help, and the device disarms pedantry by making himself that struggling pupil in a homespun presentation. The double perspective, in this case teacher and pupil, is a frequent device for plotting an immediate scene within a historical perspective, and it is just as significant that Franklin opens this discussion of writing by saying, "one does not dress for private Company as for a public Ball."[10] Not only does he understand the difference better than other writers, but the words themselves are as prophetic as they are instructive. They introduce a document that hovers *between* the public and the private in unique ways and for reasons that we need to explore. At issue is a peculiarly opportune form of instructive communication.[11]

The technique used in reaching so many readers of all ages and times cannot be overemphasized. The quiet personality Franklin presents on the page is there to help *anyone* who is willing to listen, and that listener is engaged by the practical effort involved as much as by its eventual success. The lesson in writing proceeds through admissions of personal failings. From his father, Franklin realizes, "I fell far short in elegance of Expression, in Method and Perspicuity, of which he convinced me by several Instances . . . and thence grew more attentive to the *Manner* in Writing."[12] The rhetorical boost given to all frustrated future students is a palpable one: don't worry; as I improved, so can you improve.

Consider how Franklin's four strategies in writing work. Again they are based on method, the primary source of order. First, you jot down the ideas of a text and duplicate its merits in your own essay. Second, you compare the original to your effort while turning to a related text in another genre (in Franklin's case poetry) to extend vocabulary, master form, and develop an ear for tone. Third, you rewrite ideas back and forth between poetry and prose to study concision, generic priorities, and style. Fourth, you jumble the ideas of a popular text into "Confusion" and rewrite the essay. This fourth stipulation provides the final "Method in the Arrangement of Thoughts."[13] Notice how Franklin holds onto the *pleasure* in writing against the dull drill in most expository writing exercises. Even today you will find no better guide to an effective and graceful style anywhere.

The determined presentism in this writing lesson notwithstanding, it contains a boon for historians. Franklin reveals his sources in developing a style, and they figure in the themes of the *Autobiography.* John Bunyan's *Pilgrim's Progress,* Plutarch's *Lives,* Daniel Defoe's *Essays on Projects,* and Cotton Mather's *Essays to Do Good* were all favorites. Thomas Hobbes, in arguably the best advice he ever gave to historians, explains another use: "There being nothing in the world Universall but Names; for the things named, are every one of them Individuall and Singular."[14] Words change their meanings. They migrate across time and mean different things to different people. Critics of the *Autobiography* make a mistake when they read Franklin without allowing for the variation in words, forms, concepts, and audience from the eighteenth century to the twenty-first. Franklin's sources help us to track down accuracies in meaning, though more needs to be done on this level of interpretation to recover the historical document from its later influence. For if the *Autobiography* is obviously written to help others, as the writing lesson portends, it is regularly criticized for trying to be helpful even though interpreters concede that it is the second most influential autobiography in Western literature after Jean-Jacques Rousseau's *Les Confessions,* written a few years before Franklin's effort.[15]

Is Franklin's self-styled "Memoir" really an autobiography? Is Franklin sincere or an artificer in what he writes despite his seemingly candid admissions of error? Does he really tell us who he is? Is he mainly a prophet of the pernicious aspects of capitalism? Has the writer used a mask to hide his real person? Why do most people only remember the first two sections of a book that is written in disparate moments across nineteen years in four sections, starting in 1771 and ending in 1790?[16] Most frustrating of all, why does this most facile, gifted, and prolific of rapid writers fail to get to the thrilling revolutionary years? The *Autobiography* stops abruptly in 1757.

All of these questions are frequently asked in ahistorical ways. We forget, against the timeless quality in so much of the *Autobiography*, that Franklin is an eighteenth-century man, and an early eighteenth-century man at that. He is a contemporary of Jonathan Edwards, the architect of the First Great Awakening in the 1730s, and knew Cotton Mather, the greatest divine of the previous Puritan generation. Critics go after Franklin in part because he seems fully available to them when he is only partially accessible on current terms.

We must recover a book written well over two hundred years ago but also meant for future generations of Americans. Franklin understood the possibility in those future generations but could only guess at the evolution of the country. How startling, even unsettling, was that evolution to a writer who, whatever his misgivings, always seems calmly afloat in his milieu and who wants to be seen that way? Certainly that equanimity was hard won in a world that changed so constantly under him and forced him to change.

Mark just how much change there was. Franklin begins as a loyal colonial subject with thoughts of staying in England. He becomes a reluctant revolutionary, manages to shift at the right moment to serve as a vigorous revolutionary leader, then morphs into a cosmopolitan diplomatic figure who looks on France as "the country he loves most in all of the world," and finishes as one of the two leading patriotic giants of a continental republic, alongside only George Washington, with service as a framer of the federal Constitution and president of Pennsylvania.[17] The beginning of this life could not have imagined its end or what would follow, problems for any autobiographer.

A fourfold response to these puzzles guides the rest of this essay. First, we must establish the generic nature of the text as it was understood in its own time and later in order to come to grips with the sensibilities of Franklin's own time. Second, we need to evaluate the question of sincerity in the speaker of the text and the degree to which that quality conveys or obfuscates the authenticity of the historical persona presented there. Third, there is the tangled narrative trajectory of a work written not only in four parts at separate times and circumstances but with very different purposes in mind.[18] Fourth, and with these elements in place, how can we interpret the fragmented nature of the text as a holistic enterprise and work of art today?

Academic debates over whether the memoir qualifies as an autobiography are pointless except insofar as they point to the contextual dimension in which Franklin wrote. The word "autobiography" does not appear until 1786. Franklin did not know the word, which entered general usage only in the middle of the nineteenth century. Is it better, then, to denote Franklin's effort as "a self-biography"? The awkwardness of the phrase in light of current connotations speaks for itself. The word "autobiography" technically conjoins three meanings in one word: "self-life-writing." Whether you call Franklin's book a memoir, the term of choice then, or an autobiography, the designation the world uses now, it is important to hold onto the concept of self-life-writing for what it meant to the actual writer at the time.[19]

Every historian has to account for the shifting nature of "the *explanatory schemes* on which we humans rely to make sense of our experience."[20] What do the details in what one selects to record of one's history tell us about the sensibilities and the direction of a writer? Today we think of an autobiography as having a beginning, middle, and end. There is evidence that Franklin might not have thought that way at all, even though he proceeds through his life. He seems to have been much more interested in explaining the world around him and holding it in place.

In "The History of Civilizations," Fernand Braudel helps us to see the difference when he says "let us no longer say that it is born, develops, and dies, which comes to the same thing as lending it a simple, linear, human destiny."[21] Franklin as an Enlightenment figure does believe in progress, but another side of him is filled with the contingencies in history, and beyond the utilitarian goal of writing to create a better society, his book reveals that side of history in understated but apparent ways. Less than the trajectory of the career is the driving need to convey the difficult ways of the world and how to handle them.

Franklin himself spoke late in life of being "diligently employed in writing the History of my Life."[22] The more appropriate issue turns therefore on the meaning of a life to the writer, and we can logically privilege the mentality of an eighteenth-century man steeped in Enlightenment thought and practice. In one of the most perceptive accounts of that context and period, we learn, "The eighteenth-century philosopher is not an isolated hero giving shape to what would otherwise be unintelligible, but a cultural spokesman who explores the way in which everybody *already does* make sense of the world." Franklin was just such a philosopher with a need "to dispel illusions and identify a bedrock of experience."[23]

To these thoughts we can add another. As a cultural signifier, a writer of the period presents life through evolving concentric involvements. Proper development progresses from the domestic to the local and then on to the public sphere. The well-spent life moves toward greater obligation, duty, and commitment in the world, and it is a movement that the *Autobiography* honors. Franklin accepts concentric circles of wider involvement as an essential duty of identification. When read in this way, the *Autobiography* becomes all of a piece despite its disjointed creation at different times with different purposes in mind.

It does not follow from this description, as some modern critics construe, that happiness for Franklin meant "public recognition rather than domestic pleasure."[24] The proper neoclassical life builds from the domestic sphere toward the public but never forgets the former. Franklin makes the point repeatedly by returning over and over again to the personal foibles in human nature that amuse us, even as he points toward the need for correction, further education, and some kind of subsequent advance. A simple record of public achievements could never have held a reader then or now. Nor does Franklin hesitate to tell us about the pleasures he takes from life. His curiosity about the world is as personal as it is civic in implication, and the personal aspects are the parts that most readers remember and value.

The combination—the successful life and the separate pleasure that the episodic nature of existence can give—furnishes much of the timeless quality that the *Autobiography* attains. This quality is essential for the writer reaching for future America. As achievement gives order, so the pleasure in life beguiles. The result is a presentism that reaches beyond the historical without losing it. When Franklin tells of an error he has made through "that hard-to-be-govern'd Passion of Youth," a reader has to believe it happened and that it will happen again anywhere in the world.[25]

What other founder, this side of Aaron Burr's scandalous private journal of visits to prostitutes, would have admitted to "Intrigues with low Women that fell in my Way"?[26] We have never learned the mother of Franklin's illegitimate son, William Franklin, to whom the first part of the *Autobiography* is officially directed. Franklin never hesitated to recognize this son, but

William was the forty-year-old governor of New Jersey in 1771 as Franklin begins his memoir. William needs no parental advice, and the two grown men were not close. The introductory address to "Dear Son" is a conceit, a sign of Franklin's care for the generic conventions of the time.[27]

The personal as public is everywhere in the *Autobiography* and at levels where others fear to tread. How many revolutionary heroes can you name who would have revealed the problems in what was a customary but largely secret eighteenth-century matrimonial minuet over how much money would be brought to an arranged marriage by each side, especially a minuet that fails? Yet Franklin reveals in great detail the mildly sordid details in his troubled courtship with his eventual wife, Deborah Read.[28]

This account and Franklin's other early experiences in public exchange expose errors in understanding the world. They try to explain the world as much as Franklin. The errata that Franklin admits to and then corrects—in the way that a printer would correct an error in a font of type by removing it and replacing it with another so as to erase the fault—are instructive in this regard, but they form only a partial record of incidents that demonstrate Franklin's awkward management of personal behavior and acknowledged mistakes in the public realm, both major concerns in the first part of the *Autobiography.* They all point to the fact that the world is not easily mastered, nor a place where benevolence reigns.[29]

We always see the persona on the page clearly in these moments. One example may stand for the rest in a regular pattern. Franklin, in his first declared erratum, uses a technicality to dissolve his apprenticeship as a printer's helper under the control of his abusive brother James in Boston, and this allows him to escape to Philadelphia. Thus far, one might characterize the event through Franklin's justification for breaking with his brother: "I fancy his harsh and tyrannical Treatment of me, might be a means of impressing me with that Aversion to arbitrary Power that has struck me thro' my whole life."[30] The story typically serves dual purposes. It explains the difficulties in indenture and apprentice arrangements in eighteenth-century commerce, but the comment, added much later, hints at Franklin's future revolutionary stands against British authority. Two notions of time, then and now, are always somewhere on the page.

We can believe both the situation and the comment by the writer about the persona it describes, but when Franklin returns from Philadelphia and shows up James in his brother's own printing-house by appearing ostentatiously in fine clothes, displaying his new watch, and distributing money to James's employees in "a kind of Raree-Show" or staged performance, it is Franklin's mother, not the oblivious writer, who reveals the visit "had insulted [James] in such a Manner before his People that he could never forget or forgive it." All Franklin can say for himself after this scene is that James "was mistaken."[31] This time, we realize the persona still does not quite know itself. Franklin has not yet learned how to disguise his success through humble inquiry or decided, as he later does, to deflect achievement to others.

The *Autobiography* has often been dubbed an anti-conversion narrative, even though John Bunyan's *Pilgrim's Progress* is one of Franklin's models.[32] There is no one epiphany in the life that leads to a conversion. Instead, a series of minor realizations alter behavior through experience of the world. "Human Felicity," Franklin explains, "is produc'd not so much by great Pieces of good Fortune that seldom happen, as by little Advantages that occur every Day."[33] Of course, in order to create interest, these little advantages are accompanied by occasional disadvantages and problems that the young Franklin must master.

The result, at least through the early part of the *Autobiography*, is the story of a youth of eighteen to twenty who is portrayed as uncertain of how to behave in given situations. He is essentially a comic figure. Lost in understanding of this aspect of the writer's presentation is an artful mask of disarming humor and wit. Franklin is never slow to turn these devices on himself. The oft-repeated story of his "most awkward ridiculous Appearance" on first entering the city of Philadelphia, based in part on ignorance of local practices, supplies an obvious case in point, even if it is done to show what a considerable figure he later becomes.[34]

No other founder possesses these qualities of wit and humor in narrative form to the degree that Franklin has mastered or, for that matter, the self-deprecating form they often take when he is his own subject, and we need to define how the devices worked in the eighteenth century. As one dictionary notes, "*Wit* especially implies mental keenness, ability to discern those elements of a situation or condition that relate to what is comic." "*Humor,* closely related, suggests the ability to recognize the incongruity and absurdity inherent in life."[35]

The overall idea of fun is a movable feast in history. It changes dramatically with the times. Eighteenth-century experience emphasized "the tempering of wit with good nature." Used together, they sought to produce a smile rather than a laugh, and these are the frequently misunderstood qualities we find in Franklin. Readers today mistake a moment of wit for insincerity or superficiality. By the nineteenth century, "an increasing confidence in the goodness and free play of natural emotion and spirits made frank laughter a sign of an open and universal humanity." Laughter becomes amiable and wit devolves into a trivial resort.[36] This is why Franklin's brand of humor can appear shallow to a modern reader.

A better appreciation is crucial because comedy always serves a larger point in Franklin. Again one example can stand for all. The young Franklin, a declared vegetarian, self-righteously feels "the taking of every Fish as a kind of unprovok'd Murder, since none of them had or ever could do us any Injury," but when he finds himself "becalm'd off Block Island" aboard ship on his way to Philadelphia and sees other passengers fry and eat the cod they have caught, he gets hungry and soon manages to balance "Principle and Inclination." He notices that the fish being fried have smaller fish in their bellies. "Then, thought I, if you eat one another, I don't see why we mayn't eat you. So I dined upon Cod very heartily" along with the other passengers. "So convenient a thing it is to be a *reasonable Creature*," Franklin concludes, "since it enables one to find or make a Reason for everything one has a mind to do."[37]

Franklin actually retraces previous steps in the narrative to tell this story on himself in the knowledge that wit, through indirection, can make a dangerous point safely. Why the point can be dangerous is a matter of historical context. Think about Franklin's underlying purpose here: The man who personifies the age of reason has just declared that reason can justify just about anything we want to do. A supposedly objective Enlightenment barometer for measuring the pressures and supplying a guide in human behavior is suddenly a completely subjective one, and we are once again left with questionable standards for making our way in an uncertain world of assumed forms where many of the assumptions are up for grabs.

The story is revelatory of self and the larger problem it faces but in a light vein. The fact that the conflicts and uncertainties under Franklin's gaze are spun out in amiable tones should not prevent them from being taken as authentic historical material of importance. A postmodern age likes its life stories told through crises and with angst. Franklin, the good eighteenth-century man, knows to display a calm demeanor that he does not always feel.

What if reason, after all, is not in control of human behavior or a means of resolving argument as so many hoped at the time? At stake in Franklin's funny story is a major debate of the age. The Enlightenment's focus on individual capacity gives aspirational heft to human nature and turns attention to new possibilities as a gauge of historical development, but it simultaneously raises a troubling question: is human nature an exalted vehicle that will improve existence or is it forever mired within the mediocrity of its own imperfections? The older writer who looks at this eighteen-year-old boy eating cod—Franklin is sixty-five as he writes—has seen a world full of contention, and he knows the question is a close one.

Franklin's strategy of raising serious philosophical problems indirectly, even comically, and his arch stance somewhere above the persona on the page leads many to question the sincerity and accuracy of the *Autobiography*.[38] Ahistoricism lies behind these and other dismissals, and most of them are grounded in fear of the influence the *Autobiography* is thought to have. Even the severest critics do not deny the power of this influence. No interpreter questions the effect of Franklin's words. Left unexplored is the way those words actually work: their affect. To grasp what Franklin manages to do, we must turn to deeper understandings of language and narrative.

A literary historian must know the way of words to gain their full meaning, and with that in mind, we should distinguish between the technical concepts of sincerity and authenticity in the *Autobiography*. The word "sincerity" "refers primarily to a congruence between avowal and actual feeling." Authenticity invokes, in the words of Lionel Trilling, "a more strenuous moral experience than 'sincerity' does"; it contains "a more exigent conception of the self and of what being true to it consists in, a wider reference to the universe and man's place in it." Sincerity can thus be seen and accepted as a constant if we can connect avowal to feeling. "Authenticity," the higher artistic standard, changes across time and culture. "At the behest of the criterion of authenticity, much that was once thought to make up the very fabric of culture has come to seem of little account, mere fantasy or ritual, or downright falsification."[39]

By these standards, Franklin, writing in his eighteenth-century mode, may be insincere at times without questioning his authenticity as a historical figure. His power and truth lie in precisely that "wider reference to the universe." When, for example, Franklin thinks he is mortally ill from pleurisy and at the same time suddenly loses the one older mentor who has proven worthy in a devious world (the Philadelphia merchant Thomas Denham, whom Franklin in rare praise says, "I respected and lov'd him"), the later writer speaks all too casually of his youthful persona's close recovery: "I suffered a good deal, gave up the Point in my own mind, and was rather disappointed when I found myself recovering; regretting in some degree that I must now sometime or other have all that disagreeable Work to do over again."[40]

Surely Franklin felt relief on avoiding death. The description of his recovery cannot be taken at face value. Nor can we countenance his regret that in living he has "all that disagreeable Work to do over again." The same writer celebrates the value of industry throughout the *Autobiography*. But if he is insincere, Franklin's words serve an authentic historical purpose. A Senecan strain of stoicism percolates throughout eighteenth-century thought in a culture where people died early and late and sometimes in droves.[41] Disease, accident, and bad medical practices carried off the sick and wounded with little notice; whole towns and even cities were decimated by smallpox, diphtheria, and fever epidemics. People, especially the young, were expected to face eternity with equanimity. Franklin's near-death scene proves that he endured the maladies of his time and that he did so with appropriate poise, resignation, and composure.[42]

Nothing is simple here. One mere episode again makes a general philosophical point. One mere episode is always more than that. To the extent that Franklin is giving a history of himself, we have to pay attention to what he chooses to tell us out of the myriad possibilities available to him in a long life. Moreover, we can only recognize this extraordinary dynamo of energy and talent if we also know the cultural milieu, or rather the vacuums in it, that he works so hard to fill and answer and explain to us in his own way.

This is no easy matter, but it has its rewards if we tie Franklin's purposes to a closer historical context. Of his age, Franklin extends it through his differences from it. Great religious enthusiasm and wave after wave of revivalism swept America in Franklin's lifetime, and yet the writer of the *Autobiography* quietly admits, "Revelation had indeed no weight with me as such." The admission means that his rise in the world retains a certain mystery that his peers in such an intense Bible culture took for granted in themselves as part of the guiding hand of Providence.[43] The difference makes the *Autobiography* part of the history of ideas.

Franklin sees that all of his success has been a near thing in the light of "Inexperience and the Knavery of others." He also realizes that he could just as easily have died as lived from his bout of pleurisy with no larger purpose, destiny, or concern in the difference. He tells us so in amiable tones that quietly disturb the verities of his day when he pauses to wonder whether or not "the kind hand of Providence, or some guardian Angel, or accidental favorable Circumstances and Situations, or all together preserved me."[44]

The cosmic and secular alternatives are spelled out here but Franklin does not choose between them. Left that way, they hint at what historian Bernard Bailyn once designated "soft ambiguous moments . . . of true origination" in thought.[45] A later generation would be undone by some of the implications. Franklin gives us only a glimpse, but it is there. Are we the "uncaused cause" that independently determines our own fate, or are we "terminations foreordained by antecedent events"? Franklin is not stopped by the modern conundrum of freedom against fate as John Stuart Mill temporarily would be, or puzzled by it as Ralph Waldo Emerson would announce, but he sees far enough to ask the question.[46] Even the question shakes things. To the extent that history is all about theories of causation, the question makes Franklin a writer grappling with the idea of history.

Religion could not supply historical context for Franklin. He saw far too much disputation among the sects around him and joined none of them. The deism in him does not deny a godhead, but he implies a conceivable indifference in that potentially very distant figure, and it separates him off from the conventional wisdom of his day.[47] He finds no evidence that Providence keeps a close watch over daily machinations in the human world. We have not entered Herman Melville's "wicked world in all meridians," but we do have a writer exhibiting serious concern while searching for meaning in a universe that might not care about him.[48] In Isaiah Berlin's words, Franklin penetrates a "widespread attitude, and isolating that and questioning it," he pauses to wonder "how it might be if it were otherwise."[49]

The authenticity of Franklin's presentation, an exigent self in search of its reference to the universe, is accordingly clear enough, but to explain how it works and how it could be so misunderstood, we must wrestle with the interpretation of words at a deeper level. The critic Frank Kermode can help us here. He identified a confusion in the evaluation of a text by readers who fail to distinguish between the carnal and spiritual senses in narrative.

The carnal or literal meaning of a story is available to all readers; they are "the outsiders" who read for plot and the surfaces of meaning. Franklin, the newspaperman, is a master at this level of narrative. The spiritual in narrative enlists another level of interpretation from readers who feel "inside" the purposes behind the story, and this level involves Franklin, the practical philosopher. Kermode wrote, "Carnal readings are much the same. Spiritual readings are very different," and among initiates there is "a preference for spiritual over carnal readings." Not surprisingly, "texts upon which a high value has been placed become especially susceptible to the transformations wrought by those who seek spiritual senses behind the carnal."[50]

Franklin's *Autobiography* lends itself to these confusions and transformations. On the surface it is a carnal guide on how the young might succeed in material life, but it registers on other levels for those who fear the tenuous aspects of a still-forming American society. This second level of the *Autobiography* is aimed at an anxious elite that worries about such things, and the book becomes a very different kind of guide to both communal and personal intellectual well-being as a result.

Franklin shows his canniness as a writer and thinker by tying this higher issue in the history of his life to external sources from his own time. Always the *Autobiography* has two audiences in mind: the present and the future, in a style that forces the true reader to interpret his book through now and then, and in that spirit, the writer's insertion of two letters from his acquaintances conveys what we can see as the dual nature of carnal and spiritual levels of narrative concern.

These externalities also signal a shift, coming as they do at the outset of part 2 of the memoir. In the first letter, Abel James hopes Franklin will lead "Youth into the Resolution of endeavoring to become as good and as eminent as the Journalist," but he expects much more: nothing less than permanent inspiration for "millions" to come in securing "Merit and Use in the World," both of which are apparently in need of reinforcement. Benjamin Vaughn is even more explicit about the problems involved. "When we see our race has been blundering on in the dark, almost without a guide," Vaughn writes, Franklin's book can be "a sort of key to life." Franklin must "think of bettering the whole race of men." At risk are "the manners and situation of a *rising* people." "I do not think," said Vaughn of the book's universal appeal, "that the writings of Caesar and Tacitus can be more interesting to a true judge of human nature and society."[51]

The Enlightenment impulses behind these claims become apparent when Franklin plays the *philosophe* in part 2 of the *Autobiography* while serving as a diplomat in Paris. Written thirteen years later in 1784, this is where Franklin offers his "bold and arduous Project of arriving at moral Perfection." The plan is frequently dismissed as a callow exercise, particularly when we get to the writer's final desire to "imitate Jesus and Socrates," neither of whom Franklin is even remotely ready to follow to their deaths at the hands of their cultures. Be that as it may, the crux of thought in Franklin's list of thirteen virtues and his attempt to comply with them come through his inability to maintain what many would consider the easiest to maintain. Third on this long list with such virtues as "temperance, resolution, frugality, industry, and cleanliness" is "order," and it is the one virtue that Franklin cannot sustain in six days out of the seven listed by him in daily practice.[52]

The *Autobiography* is at times a troubled and unfinished work by a man who succeeds but also fails frequently enough, and, as we turn to an increasingly fragmented narrative, it is important to indicate what Franklin resists in the culture around him. To the extent that he writes for the future of America, what worries him the most? What is Franklin *against?* He dislikes needless argumentation, religious dogmatism, false premises in education, and military zeal.[53] Are these not major problems in our own day, and are there answers to them?

There are good reasons why readers remember certain parts of Franklin's work and not others. The *Autobiography* has an overall theme that reaches from Franklin's present to the future of America: method can supply order in a world that lacks it if people can be made to understand what is required. A worry follows: can method impose itself on a grander extent in a country that is developing on a previously unimagined scale? As long as Franklin is arranging for libraries, better town lighting, a more professional constable system, a fire company, municipal defense, and paved and cleaner streets in Philadelphia, he presents an image and pattern of success where it becomes generally known "there was no such thing as carrying a public-spirited Project through, without my being concern'd in it."[54]

But Franklin's method works less well when he moves toward more continental projects in the Seven Years' War (1756–63). The idea of concentric civic involvements works best on a local level. Yes, gratifying universal honors and attention begin to flow Franklin's way as he becomes a colonial personage and deputy postmaster general of North America in 1753, but his larger political concerns bring mostly frustration.[55] His "Plan for the Union of all of the Colonies" for better defense and general purposes (the Albany Plan) fails to receive either colonial or British approval after acrimonious debate and much time wasted on it. The material provisions that Franklin provides out of his own pocket during the Seven Years' War are never fully recompensed. Instead, he is cavalierly dismissed for being naive in not taking advantage of the situation on his own by becoming a war profiteer.[56]

The lessons that Franklin learns from continental involvement belie the claims of method and order. "The best public Measures are therefore seldom *adopted from previous Wisdom,* but *forc'd by the Occasion,*" he complains, and he finds it much harder to overcome "public Quarrels" and "the continual Wrangle" in governmental matters than he did in fostering communal improvements in Philadelphia. Even his seemingly safer and objective experiments in electricity lead to international dispute over prior claims of originality. The *Autobiography* ends in 1757 with tangled negotiations in England between Franklin and others over relevant taxing powers. Franklin's good offices are met here with "Enmity" and the anger of others who raise questions about Franklin's "candor" and reliability.[57]

The *Autobiography,* like most memoirs, distorts history in a particular way. It gets back at those opponents who have made life more difficult. But Franklin's dismissal of his later political enemies never matches in interest or artistry his amusing jabs at the personal foibles of earlier, more intimate opponents. Take, for instance, his hilarious account of Samuel Keimer, a devious rival printer whom Franklin persuades to try a vegetarian diet: "He was usually a great Glutton, and I promis'd myself some Diversion in half-starving him." The denouement is pure Franklin: "I went on pleasantly, but Poor Keimer suffer'd grievously, tir'd of the Project, long'd for the Flesh Pots of Egypt, and order'd a roast Pig; He invited me and two Women Friends to dine with him, but in being brought too soon upon table, he could not resist the Temptation, and ate it all up before we came."[58]

Failures naturally rankle in a book about success, but something else changes as we move along in the pages of the *Autobiography.* As often as not, the writer traces early problems to his own mistakes. Thus, as "the 'water American,'" Franklin finds that his materials are tampered with in an English print shop after he refuses to contribute to an initiation fee he had previously paid in another part of the shop, and he learns that he has to pay up anyway, "convinc'd of the Folly of being on ill Terms with those one is to live with continually."[59] Here, too, we are learning about the ways of the world in a fashion that will help others to come.

Later on Franklin reverses this tendency and blames others. The British government, he points out, stupidly wastes money when, for his political views, it dismisses him and loses his efficient management as deputy post-master general of North America. Those who foolishly block his Albany Plan of colonial union are made responsible for the revolutionary war. Incessant colonial quarrels are invariably the fault of the royal governors.[60] Whatever the accuracy in such claims, they interest us less. When Franklin is wrong, we are amused and appreciate what we learn from him. When he is always right, we record the occurrence and pass on, though often enough we want to hear the other side of the story.

Curiously, the trajectory of Franklin's narrative is toward the mundane even as it shows the persona's increased power and influence. It may be that the fact of success is less interesting than the earlier struggle to be successful, particularly when that success begins to depend on inherent skill rather than a proposed method that anyone might adopt. Perhaps, as well, the writer begins to lose energy and drive when turning to the last part of the *Autobiography* in 1790, his eighty-fifth and last year of life. The memoir reaches only to 1757 in ways that tantalize a current reader. We see the beginning of serious tensions with the mother country but none of the events that would cap Franklin's fame as a revolutionary leader.

Do we ask too much of Franklin in this regard? Quite possibly. But why does the writer not reach for the later years with pages that would have held every reader? Franklin is not only a signer but an actual writer of the Declaration of Independence on the drafting committee established by the Continental Congress. In 1778, after the stunning American victory at Saratoga, he orchestrates the treaty of alliance with France that proves decisive three years later when the arrival of the French fleet insures the British surrender at Yorktown. The list is long. He orchestrates and signs the delicately arranged Treaty of Paris that ends the Revolutionary War, he is a framer of the federal Constitution, and he meets everyone of importance.

None of these events make the *Autobiography.* The question over why not is an interesting one because there is no more skilled or rapid writer than Franklin even at a late age. What really lies behind his decisions? Recall the three issues already identified in the creation of history: the explanatory

scheme on which historians have to rely to make sense of previous experience, the acknowledgment of changing sensibilities, and the choices that
are made in deciding what will survive as the facts of history. Franklin may
have been at his most perceptive in deciding these three issues because they
are the keys that allowed him to produce a timeless work which is at once
valuable history and absorbing literature.

Could it be that Franklin knew that the initial portrait of himself would
prove to be the vital message to later generations as indeed it becomes? He
may have been the first in a long line of New World writers to realize that a
story of developing youth, of young America, would cover a host of difficulties in a country full of growing pains. Think as well of how Franklin holds
changing sensibilities in place to form a timeless story. In all ages, whatever
mistakes the young make, they are more easily forgiven in their relative
innocence and prospect of reform. Early Franklin is always getting better
at what he does even when he does not succeed. In the scheme of things,
Franklin sees that the struggle to develop holds an American audience better and longer than a record of accomplishment, even if that record has to
appear as the proof of the success he achieves.[61]

The episodes that we most remember involve that struggle toward success
and are carefully chosen with that in mind. Take an obvious but seemingly
trivial example that again serves larger purposes. The famous plan for moral
perfection ends in the story of a man who wants all of his axe to be as shiny
as the edge but soon grows tired of turning the grinding wheel while the
blacksmith, a neighbor of Franklin's, holds the axe broadly against the wheel
making it hard to turn. Pretty soon, the owner of the axe decides, "I think
I like a speckled Axe best."[62] Effort must not only be serious but worth it.
In the larger struggle of existence, when is it enough that only the edge is
sharp? How often do we fool ourselves in the process of making the choices
that have to be made?

Franklin's obvious struggles against the forces of his world come early.
Still, he sends us a late message to indicate that the struggle is never over,
that it always must encounter the unforeseen, that life itself, no matter how
much success comes to it, is full of precarious moments. On his way to
England in 1757 as the Pennsylvania Assembly's agent in London, he makes
much of a narrowly "escap'd Shipwreck" when an inattentive watchman
nearly brings the arriving ship "running right upon the rocks."[63]

Franklin's response to the incident provides a typical conflation of technical ingenuity and philosophical awareness. "This Deliverance impress'd me strongly with the Utility of Lighthouses, and made me resolve to encourage the building of them in America, if I should live to return there." He has been "delivered" from a terrible fate. Will that continue to happen? "If I should live" raises the question. At the time, in correspondence, Franklin maintained a more jocular stance. "Were I a Roman Catholic, perhaps I should on this occasion vow to build a chapel to some saint," he wrote, "but as I am not, if I were to vow at all, it should be to build a *lighthouse*." Left unsaid in this earlier letter but emphasized in the *Autobiography* is the irony that Franklin's ship nearly runs aground *on* a lighthouse, "we bearing so very near it," "the light appearing to me as big as a Cart Wheel."[64]

So easily does simple human error by a common sailor defy all ingenuity and method. Contingencies out of one's control threaten everything. There is no more complicated and varied observer of the world in his time than this man, Benjamin Franklin. Leave it to him to use the constitutive metaphor of the Enlightenment against itself, the near catastrophe of being destroyed by illumination, without ever deserting its central meaning, the called for spread of light. That ambiguity may be one reason for including the incident, but still we are left with the question: Why this incident rather than others? Why not take on the great events of the Revolution? The oldest revolutionary knows that his fame is secure long before the events of national formation. Proof can be seen in the fact that he has no need—unlike his younger compatriots who made their reputations through those events—to defend in writing his own distinct role against others. Franklin lives out his life comfortable with the official record of his presence in the salient events of the Revolution, but there is even more to say about this decision in the man who writes the history of his times through the account of his own life.

As Franklin pens the last sections of the *Autobiography* between 1788 and 1790, he is more than just an international figure through a variety of identifications. He is the cosmopolitan icon of the spread of Enlightenment. As such, he clearly sees both sides of the Atlantic Ocean as his audience. Why not concentrate on what *everyone* needs, in this case lighthouses, and by doing so, become the symbol of them? For if men remain bound in their petty controversies, a frequent theme in the *Autobiography*, rapid mechanical advance in the eighteenth century was a different matter and a source of general curiosity and optimism. Franklin not only lived in an age of great invention; he could claim to be the avatar of it, and thereby the representative of a universal movement in history.

The tension between what men are and what they might accomplish if properly directed through method and industry is the lodestone in Franklin's sense of historical trajectory—a trajectory compounded by dangers in the American psyche that need to be countered to maintain well-being.

Most leading American intellectuals with a philosophical bent turn into historical pessimists as the country changes out from under them. The continuing optimists among serious leading thinkers can be numbered on one hand, and Franklin is one of them along with such figures as Jefferson, William James, John Dewey, and possibly, in our own age, John Rawls, but Franklin's optimism, at least as it appears in the *Autobiography*, is particularly hard won, given his jaundiced view of the relentless selfishness he attaches to human nature. "Few in Public Affairs," he writes, "act from a mere View of the Good of their Country, whatever they may pretend. . . . Fewer still in public Affairs act with a View to the Good of Mankind." Over and over again Franklin believes people have to be tricked into good works.[65]

The first source of intransigence are the many naysayers in a world full of change. They are represented by the prosperous Philadelphia merchant Samuel Mickle, "a Person of Note, an elderly Man with a wise Look and very grave Manner of Speaking." In Franklin's treatment of him, Mickle will be known ever after simply as "the croaker." "There are croakers," Franklin explains, "in every Country always boding its Ruin." Mickle is one of them and goes out of his way to discourage the uncertain, new, and very young printer in town. "He gave me such a Detail of Misfortunes now existing or that were soon to exist, that he left me half-melancholy." Franklin perseveres, but he lets us know it was a near thing: "Had I known him before I engaged in this Business, probably I never should have done it."[66]

Why do things happen or not happen in history? The world divides between the risk in action and the caution of quiescence. Slow to join the revolutionary movement out of an intrinsic prudence, Franklin never finds this division an easy one to negotiate. Many of his proverbs and maxims as "Poor Richard" say as much, but he is against a conformity that stays in place when improvement is possible. Optimism is the necessary virtue against adversity. It allows the taking of meaningful risks in the adventure that life should be. Mickle has *looked* wise without being so, but perhaps that judgment merely states the obvious, the difference between success and failure, the hallmarks of validation in history.[67]

Franklin is clear about the cost that optimism requires: "I have always thought that one Man of tolerable Abilities may work great Changes, and accomplish great Affairs among Mankind, if he first forms a good Plan, and cutting off all Amusements or other Employments that would divert his Attention, makes the Execution of that same Plan his sole Study and Business."[68] The comment obliquely cues the determination and skill required to accomplish anything of importance against the habit, laziness, self-interest, and ignorance of the world.

Still, the optimism remains. Franklin's sense of history, that knowledge leads to general progress, belies the notion that his main goal is a narrow prosperity. He could have become fabulously wealthy off of his many inventions—the Franklin stove, bifocals, a new urinary catheter, the design of bulkheads to make safer ships, the lightning rod, an odometer, a better chimney damper, and others. But Franklin refused to benefit from his creations. He observes, "That as we enjoy great Advantages from the Inventions of Others, we should be glad of an Opportunity to serve others by any Invention of ours, and this we should do freely and generously."[69] Compare these words to the legal battles of today over who will be allowed to own genetic aspects of the human body.

Here and elsewhere the concentric civic-mindedness of the neoclassical tradition is alive in Franklin. He does not imbibe the religious aspects of Cotton Mather's *Essays to Do Good,* but he believes the good life will spread if all attend to it together. We forget that at age forty-two, he leaves private business to dedicate himself to study and public life. This decision and its explanation are ones that "the better off" in American society rarely heed today. "When I disengag'd myself as above-mentioned from private Business," he comments, "I flatter'd myself that, by the sufficient tho' moderate Fortune I had acquir'd, I had secur'd Leisure during the rest of my Life, for Philosophical Studies and Amusements. . . . And I conceiv'd my becoming a Member [of the City Council] would enlarge my Power of doing Good."[70] The second half of this long life is given over to public service and the education of others.

Franklin does a great deal of "good" in that life, and yet the range of his accomplishments, while unprecedented in his time, is worn lightly in print and with a characteristic self-restraint, even self-effacement. Admittedly, the *Autobiography* is about taking back credit where credit is due, but even here Franklin never loses his balance or his sense of humor in dealing with the world. What comes through more than any other single feature in this memoir is the man's clear and unvarnished knowledge of himself.

That is why he can create such a believable self on the page and assume such a knowing place in history. The person who liked to refer to himself as "B. Franklin, Printer" never loses sight of his roots or what they mean to him. Always the printer, really always the writer, he is held in place by his own disciplined and incisive knowledge of that craft and what it can mean. We see it most trenchantly in what he has to say about the writing process, which contains its own implicit theory of history.

In one of the most luminous comments on the plain style that one can find anywhere in English literature, Franklin argues that good writing "should proceed regularly from things known to things unknown distinctly and clearly without confusion. Nothing should be expressed in two words that can be as well expressed in one; that is, no synonyms should be used, or very rarely, but the whole should be as short as possible, consistent with clearness; the words should be so placed as to be agreeable to the ear in reading; summarily it should be smooth, clear, short, for the contrary qualities are displeasing."[71]

The life is grounded and balanced in the sound and the formation of words. The simplicity and clarity of the proper words reflect the concreteness of experience as history. They supply the ultimate "Method" in Franklin's constant insistence on that term.[72] Method is how things happen if anything is to advance out of disruption and self-interest. For the eighteenth-century man, the nature in things remains the same unless you understand the change in it by moving from "things known to things unknown" and do it "clearly without confusion."

Words are the ultimate source of Franklin's power, his identity, and his awareness of the world by imposing meaning on it. The management of words is everything because they hold in place what otherwise will be left allusive. You can, in consequence, read the *Autobiography* as either a settling of unresolved debts in a life full of conflict or you can find in it the rounding out of a life and its purposes—a life that Franklin knows will be poured over endlessly. The writer, in keeping with other endeavors, does not want to leave that life to others to control.

The integrity and identifying consistency that this process brings to the *Autobiography* can be seen in the way that Franklin turns himself into a veritable book of printed matter by using the printer's conceit of correcting error, the errata, to define the shape of his life. The image, along with the humble nature of the vocation behind it, stays with him to the very end. The famous epigraph on his tombstone reads, "The Body of B. Franklin, Printer . . . Lies here, Food for Worms. But the Work shall not be wholly lost: For it will, as he believ'd, appear once more, In a new *& more perfect* Edition, Corrected and amended By the Author."[73]

To the last Franklin means to amuse us with the double meanings that his complicated philosophy requires. Books, like bodies, turn into food for worms—the unembellished meaning of bookworm—but the book itself, in this case the *Autobiography,* however worn, has an afterlife under the control of its author. It lives on and on, never ending, in the new editions that bring Franklin back to life for us in the more perfect edition that he has planned for himself on the page. That way he cannot be "wholly lost."

Does this writer hope for more? On eternal life Franklin remains coy. One senses instead an echo of Shakespeare's "fearful meditation" in sonnet 65. Recounting time's "wrackfull siege of battring days," the poet wonders, "what strong hand can hold his swift foote back?" And he answers, "O none, unless this miracle have might, / That in black ink my love may still shine bright."[74] Franklin gives us a life and its meaning set and saved in that ink.

Notes

1. Michael Oakeshott, *On History and Other Essays,* ed. Timothy Fuller (1983; rpt. Indianapolis, 1999), 48, 50, 56.

2. E. H. Carr, *What Is History?* (New York, 1961), 11.

3. J. A. Leo Lemay, *The Oldest Revolutionary: Essays on Benjamin Franklin* (Philadelphia, 1976).

4. Lewis Namier, *Conflicts* (London, 1942), 70.

5. Adrienne Koch's groundbreaking collection of the founders' writings includes the first five, but not Washington, in Koch, ed., *The American Enlightenment: The Shaping of the American Experience and a Free Society* (New York, 1965). If Washington

seems strange in this company of writers, he is, in fact, remembered most for his two farewells, the first on resigning from the Continental Army in 1783 and the second as he prepared to leave the presidency in 1796.

6. Robert A. Ferguson, *The American Enlightenment: 1750–1820* (Cambridge, Mass., 1994), 4, and more generally pp. 1–8 on "the Revolution as a literary phenomenon."

7. Paul Benichou, *Man and Ethics: Studies in French Classicism,* trans. Elizabeth Hughes (Garden City, N.Y., 1971), x.

8. To take only the most famous criticisms: D. H. Lawrence accused "Old Daddy Franklin" of holding future generations into "materialistic instruments" like himself and of fabricating "this dummy of a perfect citizen as a pattern to America." Lawrence, "Benjamin Franklin," in *Studies in Classic American Literature* (1921; Garden City, N.Y., 1951), 19, 21, 24, 30. Mark Twain wrote, "The subject of this memoir was of a vicious disposition, and prostituted his talents to the invention of maxims and aphorisms calculated to inflict suffering upon the rising generation of all subsequent ages." He was especially "full of animosity toward boys." Twain, "The Late Benjamin Franklin," *The Galaxy,* July 1870, 138–39.

9. Benjamin Franklin, *Benjamin Franklin's Autobiography,* ed. Joyce E. Chaplin (New York, 2012), 19 (hereafter Chaplin, ed., *Autobiography*).

10. Ibid., 17.

11. No other memoir of the period moves back and forth between the intimately private and public spheres in this way. Compare, for example, Jefferson's memoir where early on he says, "I am already tired of talking about myself," and in fact he never does. "Autobiography of Thomas Jefferson," Adrienne Koch and William Peden, eds., *The Life and Writings of Thomas Jefferson,* 51.

12. Chaplin, ed., *Autobiography,* 19.

13. Ibid., 20.

14. Thomas Hobbes, "Part I: Of Man, Chapter IV: *Of* Speech," in *Leviathan,* ed. Richard Tuck (Cambridge, U.K., 1996), 26.

15. The confessions were written in 1770 and published posthumously in 1782.

16. Franklin writes his memoir in four sections across nineteen years, starting in 1771, and adding material in 1784, 1788, and 1790. Each section may be said to have different purposes and even a different audience.

17. Said to Madame Helvétius shortly before leaving the country. See Edmund S. Morgan, *Benjamin Franklin* (New Haven, Conn., 2002), 298.

18. Part 1 of Franklin's *Memoir* was written in just two weeks of leisure in 1771 while he served as agent for Massachusetts in England amid growing acrimony between England and America and while a guest at Twyford House, the large manor of Bishop Jonathan Shipley in Winchester, England. Part 2 was written in Paris in 1784 shortly after formal ratification of the Treaty of Paris ended the Revolutionary War with Franklin as commissioner to France, minister plenipotentiary, and one of the five peace commissioners who negotiated the treaty. Part 3 was written in 1788 shortly after Franklin wrote his last will and testament. He was then eighty-two and ailing but still president of the Supreme Executive Council of Pennsylvania. Part 4

was written in 1790, the year of his death. No part of the life is covered after 1757 in the *Memoir.*

19. I am indebted for the information in this paragraph but not the conclusions to Stephen Carl Arch, *After Franklin: The Emergence of Autobiography in Post-Revolutionary America, 1780–1830* (Hanover, N.H., 2001), 3–11. Arch wants a sharp distinction between memoir and autobiography. For an account that uses the terms interchangeably, see Ben Yagoda, *Memoir: A History* (New York, 2009), 1–3.

20. Thomas Haskell, *Objectivity Is Not Neutrality: Explanatory Schemes in History* (Baltimore, 1998), 2.

21. Fernand Braudel, "The History of Civilizations," in *On History,* trans. Sarah Matthews (Chicago, 1980), 200.

22. Benjamin Franklin to Benjamin Vaughan, October 24, 1788, Chaplin, ed., *Autobiography,* 230.

23. Leo Damrosch, *Fictions of Reality in the Age of Hume and Johnson* (Madison, Wis., 1989), 22–23.

24. Jill Ker Conway, *When Memory Speaks: Exploring the Art of Autobiography* (New York, 1998), 22.

25. Chaplin, ed., *Autobiography,* 66.

26. For Aaron Burr's singular descriptions of his encounters with prostitutes while in exile in Paris, see *The Private Journal of Aaron Burr, during His Residence of Four Years in Europe with Selections from His Correspondence,* ed. Matthew L. Davis, 2 vols. (New York, 1838). For Franklin's comment, see Chaplin, ed., *Autobiography,* 66.

27. Chaplin, ed., *Autobiography,* 9. The convention of paternal advice to a son about to venture in the world is at least as old as Shakespeare, with Polonius adding "these few precepts in thy memory" to the departing Laertes in act 1, scene 3, of *Hamlet.* The model in Franklin's own time would have been Lord Chesterfield's *Letters to His Son on the Art of Becoming a Man of the World and a Gentleman,* published posthumously in 1774, but many of Chesterfield's four hundred letters written between 1737 and 1768 would have been well known earlier.

28. Chaplin, ed., *Autobiography,* 55, 65–66.

29. The five errata that Franklin lists are, in order, breaking his indenture in the printing shop of his brother James; using the money held in trust for Samuel Vernon, who had entrusted Franklin to collect a debt; not writing to Deborah Read, his future wife, while in England; writing the religiously radical tract *A Dissertation on Freedom and Necessity, Pleasure and Pain;* and attempting familiarities with his friend James Ralph's mistress. See Chaplin, ed., *Autobiography,* 25, 34–36, 43, 45, 66. Franklin added the concept of erratum after his original writing of this section, and there are more instances where the concept of "error" might be said to apply. The whole first section might well be termed the overcoming of errors or avoidable adversity. The errata are highlights rather than exceptions to the rule.

30. Chaplin, ed., *Autobiography,* 24.

31. Ibid., 33.

32. Franklin calls *Pilgrim's Progress* "my old favorite" and "more generally read than any other Book except the Bible. Honest John was the first I know of who mix'd Narrative and Dialogue." That is Franklin's method in the telling of his life. See Chaplin, ed., *Autobiography,* 26.

33. Chaplin, ed., *Autobiography,* 121. The context for these remarks is a discussion of smaller triumphs mixed with "Doubts of the Practicability" of some of them.

34. Ibid., 28–29.

35. William Morris, ed., *The American Heritage Dictionary of the English Language* (Boston, 1981), 1470.

36. See Stuart M. Tave, *The Amiable Humorist: A Study in the Comic Theory and Criticism of the Eighteenth and Early Nineteenth Centuries* (Chicago, 1960), 13, 43–44. See, more generally, chap. 2, "Wit and Good Nature," and chap. 3, "Laughter and Wit," 16–42, 43–67.

37. Chaplin, ed., *Autobiography,* 37.

38. Even quite recent explications of the *Autobiography* have dismissed "Franklin's self-presentation" as little more than "the archetypal figure of the capitalist hero," one "content to accumulate wealth," or find him to be a superficial figure bothered only by "momentary discomfort or inconvenience, not soul torment or even self-doubt." See Conway, *When Memory Speaks,* 19, and Yagoda, *Memoir,* 72.

39. I paraphrase and quote from Lionel Trilling, *Sincerity and Authenticity* (Cambridge, Mass., 1971), 2–11, 35.

40. Chaplin, ed., *Autobiography,* 50–51.

41. Colonial Americans read Seneca generally through "one of the most popular books of the eighteenth century" in Sir Roger L'Estrange, *Seneca's Morals by Way of Abstract,* first published in 1678 but frequently republished throughout the eighteenth century. See Meyer Reinhold, *Classical Reading of Eighteenth-Century Americans* (Philadelphia, 1975), 73–76. Deists like Jefferson and Franklin were particularly attracted to the stoicism of Seneca, Epictetus, and Marcus Aurelius. See Reinhold, *Classica Americana: The Greek and Roman Heritage in the United States* (Detroit, 1984), 151–52.

42. Poise in the face of adversity was thought to be not only a virtue but a counter to fever and disease. See Mathew Carey, *A Short Account of the Malignant Fever, Lately Prevalent in Philadelphia,* 4th ed. (Philadelphia, 1794); J. H. Powell, *Bring Out Your Dead: The Great Plague of Yellow Fever in Philadelphia in 1793* (1949; rpt. New York, 1965); and Robert A. Ferguson, "'The Nameless Charm' of Yellow Fever," in *Law and Letters in American Culture* (Cambridge, Mass., 1984), 142–47. Franklin writes before these events but with the same assumptions.

43. Chaplin, ed., *Autobiography,* 56.

44. Ibid., 56.

45. Bernard Bailyn, *Education in the Forming of American Society* (Chapel Hill, N.C., 1960), 14.

46. Haskell, *Objectivity Is Not Neutrality,* 318–21.

47. Chaplin, ed., *Autobiography,* 55.

48. Herman Melville, *Moby-Dick* (1851; rpt. New York, 1964), 89.

49. Isaiah Berlin, *The Sense of Reality: Studies in Ideas and Their History* (New York, 1996), 16.

50. Frank Kermode, "I: Carnal and Spiritual Senses," in *The Genesis of Secrecy: On the Interpretation of Narrative* (Cambridge, Mass., 1979), 9, 18–20.

51. Chaplin, ed., *Autobiography,* 69, 70–71, 74.

52. Ibid., 78–82.

53. Ibid., 22–23, 88 (on argumentation), 78, 93–95, 104, 110 (on unnecessary religious controversy and poor educational policies), 141–43 (on the problems with military zeal).

54. Ibid., 115.

55. Franklin in 1753 received honorary degrees from Harvard and Yale as well as the Copley Medal from the Royal Society of London for his writings.

56. Chaplin, ed., *Autobiography,* 122–23, 132–34, 153–54.

57. Ibid., 123, 125, 143, 145–47, 158–60.

58. Ibid., 38.

59. Ibid., 45–46.

60. Ibid., 121, 123, 125.

61. For an account on how the American psyche dwells on youth and steers literary endeavor in that direction, see Robert A. Ferguson, "Louisa May Alcott Meets Mark Twain over the Young Face of Change," in *Alone in America: The Stories That Matter* (Cambridge, Mass., 2013), 61–89.

62. Chaplin, ed., *Autobiography,* 84.

63. Ibid., 156.

64. Ibid.; Benjamin Franklin to Deborah Franklin, July 17, 1757, Leonard W. Labaree et al., eds., *The Papers of Benjamin Franklin,* 43 vols. to date (New Haven, Conn., 1959–), 7:243.

65. Chaplin, ed., *Autobiography,* 89. Franklin takes credit in his memoir, but in life he learned to give credit to others in order to get things done, "avoiding as much as I could, according to my usual Rule, the presenting myself to the Public as the Author of any Scheme for their Benefit" (111). See also pp. 76 ("the Impropriety of presenting myself as the Proposer of any useful Project," here over a subscription library), 96 (the secret activities of the Junto in persuading good works), and 97 (Franklin turning an enemy into a friend through amiable if devious means).

66. Ibid., 56–57.

67. Franklin being Franklin glosses the importance of this story by gloating over the way Mickle's pessimism later cost him money.

68. Ibid., 91.

69. Ibid., 110–11.

70. Ibid., 113–14.

71. Franklin, "Query," Albert Henry Smyth, ed., *The Writings of Benjamin Franklin,* 10 vols. (New York, 1905–7), 1:37. The same words appear as "Supplement" after "Proposals and Queries for Consideration of the Junto," Jared Sparks, ed., *The Works of Benjamin Franklin,* 10 vols. (Milwaukee, 1856), 2:553. For parallel and more public

commentary on the same virtues in writing, see Franklin "On Literary Style," Labaree et al., eds., *The Papers of Benjamin Franklin*, 1:328–31 (first published in the *Pennsylvania Gazette*, August 2, 1733).

72. Franklin, "On Literary Style," 1:327: "But supposing the most proper Words and Expressions chosen, the Performance may yet be weak and obscure, if it has not *Method*."

73. Franklin's Epitaph, n.d., *The Papers of Benjamin Franklin, Digital Edition* (Packard Humanities Institute), https://franklinpapers.org/framedVolumes.jsp.

74. See Shakespeare, "Sonnet 65," *Shakespeare's Sonnets: Being a Reproduction in Facsimile of the First Edition, 1609,* ed. Sidney Lee (Oxford, 1905), 108.

2   Yankee Continentalism

The Provincial Roots of John Adams's
Vision for American Union, 1755–1776

J. Patrick Mullins

On July 3, 1776, John Adams took a moment to reflect on Congress's adoption of a resolution declaring the thirteen colonies to be thirteen states, independent of the British Crown. The delegate from Massachusetts wrote his wife, Abigail, a letter often quoted in future centuries for its powers of prophecy. "Yesterday the greatest Question was decided, which ever was debated in America," he scrawled breathlessly, "and a greater perhaps, never was or will be decided among Men." He predicted that the "Second Day of July 1776, will be the most memorable Epocha, in the History of America." It "will be celebrated, by succeeding Generations, as the great anniversary Festival" and "solemnized with Pomp and Parade, with Shews, Games, Sports, Guns, Bells, Bonfires and Illuminations from one End of this Continent to the other from this Time forward forever more." Today's casual readers of the letter may delight in Adams's forecast of our summertime parades and fireworks displays, chuckling wryly at his error in thinking that July 2 would be celebrated as our nation's birthday. Taking the outcome of the war and the survival of the union for granted, they may overlook the truly astonishing prophecy this letter contains. Adams predicted confidently that the Revolutionary War against the British Empire would succeed in securing American independence, that America would extend "from one End of this Continent to the other," and that this independent, continental, and united America would persist "forever more."[1]

There seemed to be little basis for such optimism on July 3, 1776. On the same day that John Adams composed his letter, British regulars landed on Staten Island, the vanguard for an invasion of New York by the largest expeditionary force Britain had ever deployed. As John wrote Abigail from Philadelphia, there were many sound reasons to question America's prospects in its bid for independence from the mightiest empire in Europe. John Adams knew his exuberant prediction that Americans would celebrate their national independence "from this Time forward forever more" might come across to his wife as no better grounded in reason and evidence than the millenarian prophecies of New Light evangelists touched with religious "Enthusiasm." Adams immediately added,

> You will think me transported with Enthusiasm but I am not—I am
> well aware of the Toil and Blood and Treasure, that it will cost Us to
> maintain this Declaration, and support and defend these States.—
> Yet through all the Gloom I can see the Rays of ravishing Light and
> Glory. I can see that the End is more than worth all the Means.
> And that Posterity will tryumph in that Days Transaction, even
> altho We should rue it, which I trust in God We shall not.[2]

Why, indeed, in the absence of wishful thinking or ignorance of the "Toil and Blood and Treasure" required for victory, could Adams be so confident that the Revolutionary War would end in American independence? Why was Adams committed so firmly to a vision of America as a successful continental union? Why did he believe the American people capable of responsible self-government through the mechanism of a representative, constitutional republic, independent of direction from a hereditary king or aristocracy?

John Adams was no more a foolish dreamer than he was a cynical curmudgeon. He was a practical idealist whose prophecies of America as a successful continental republic followed from his Harvard education and Protestant upbringing, careful observation of human behavior, critical reflection on New England's history, and personal experience with law and politics in Massachusetts and the Continental Congress. In a 1755 letter to his friend Nathan Webb at the start of the Seven Years' War, the recent Harvard graduate offered a forecast of British America's future as a continental power, but it remained abstract and derivative. From his work as a Yankee attorney and his firsthand observation of growing political conflict between Massachusetts and the British Crown, Adams had developed by 1765 a vision of America as a stronghold of civil and religious liberty, blessed with a balanced constitution, a pious and well-educated population, and over a century of experience with self-government on the township and provincial levels. Lacking direct knowledge of the colonies outside of New England, young Adams initially imagined "America" in his *Dissertation on the Canon and the Feudal Law* as if it were New England writ large, applying to all thirteen colonies the generalizations he had formed about New England's fitness for liberty. Perhaps greater understanding of the more aristocratic cast of politics in the middle and southern colonies would have given him pause. Ironically, Adams's very provincialism insulated him from early doubts about the American people's ability to govern themselves through consensual political institutions on a continental scale.

As service in the First and Second Continental Congresses brought Adams into contact with the mercantile and planter gentry who largely prevailed as the ruling class of the middle and southern colonies, he became better informed of the differences in social structure, economic interest, political culture, and diplomatic objectives among British America's regions. With experience in Congress, Adams adjusted his vision of union to accommodate such regional distinctions, as he acknowledged that only union with the other colonies could secure the rights and interests of New England against Britain's military onslaught in 1775. Adams came to worry about the republican *bona fides* of non-Yankees and the future outlook for New England in a union with slaveholding aristocrats and gentlemen of substantial fortune. Yet he distinguished himself in Congress as a strenuous advocate for continental union and ultimately the foremost champion of American independence. His wartime unionism was more realistic in its acknowledgment of regional differences among the colonies, but it was no less ardent. And it remained grounded in an unwavering identification with New England. In the spring of 1776, Adams worked for the formation of republican governments by the states. His *Thoughts on Government* provided the outline for a completely republican state constitution, based largely on the Massachusetts provincial charter. With this constitutional model, New England would offer guidance in popular self-government and constitutionalism to the other states. By the moral and intellectual example of its people, New England would serve as the bulwark of civic virtue and civil liberty in America's experiment with continental republicanism.

From its first stirrings in September 1755 to its full development by July 1776, Adams's distinctive vision of American union was paradoxically provincial in its roots. "No American leader," notes historian Richard Alan Ryerson, "was a more dedicated provincial—in 1765, in 1776, or in 1789—than the ardent nationalist John Adams, of Braintree, Massachusetts." Adams was not alone among the statesmen of the revolutionary era in being provincial and "nationalist" at the same time. Rejecting the interpretation that James Madison had been a centralizing nationalist in the 1780s, historian Lance Banning describes Madison as a "Virginia continentalist" whose "special kind of continentalism was a distinctive product of his experiences and perspectives as a statesman of the Old Dominion." Banning notes that Madison's vision of continental union aimed to accommodate "sectional differences," and he pursued the strengthening of the union through a new federal constitution as the best security for the long-term interests of Virginia. Adams believed that the same was true for his native Massachusetts in particular and New England in general. Like Madison's "Virginia continentalism," Adams's vision of American union can best be understood not as some anticipation of a nineteenth-century-style American nationalism but as "Yankee continentalism," a vision of continental union following and inseparable from Adams's formative experience with eighteenth-century Massachusetts politics.[3]

Adams's devotion to both America and New England remained constant throughout his adult life, but his understanding of America and how New England related to it developed over time. In tracking the emergence and evolution of his Yankee continentalism, I focus on key indicators of his political thinking from 1755 to the publication of his *Thoughts on Government* in 1776. Over these two decades, Adams's vision for America took three major forms: America as New England in macrocosm, the union as the best security for New England's interests, and an American republic as reformed in accord with the New England model. As "Virginia continentalism" helped Lance Banning answer the "James Madison problem," so the interpretive concept of Yankee continentalism enables us to reconcile Adams's lifelong attachment to New England with his lifelong commitment to continental union, thereby resolving the paradox of Adams as both a "dedicated provincial" and an "ardent nationalist."

John Adams had formed the concept of America as a continental union of self-governing colonies at least by the week preceding his twentieth birthday, during the second year of the Seven Years' War. In the wake of General William Johnson's strategic victory in the Battle of Lake George on September 8, 1755, Yankee hopes rebounded that British forces might achieve their objective of expelling the French from Canada, thereby securing New England from frontier raids by Indians and long dreaded invasion by French Catholic troops. Young Adams imbibed the renewed morale and participated in political debate on the progress of the war. A recent graduate of Harvard College, he was teaching school in Worcester, Massachusetts, when he wrote his friend Nathan Webb a letter on October 12, 1755. "If we look into History," he observed, "we shall find some nations rising from contemptible beginnings, and spreading their influence, 'till the whole Globe is subjected to their sway. When they have reach'd the summit of Grandeur, some minute and unsuspected Cause commonly effects their Ruin, and the Empire of the world is transferr'd to some other place." He cited the rise of ancient Rome and modern England from rural poverty and peripheral insignificance to commercial wealth and geopolitical hegemony as examples of the rise and fall of empires. This cyclical view of history and the recent circumstances of war led him to exuberant thoughts about the destiny of British America.[4]

True to his upbringing in New England Congregationalism, Adams saw the Protestant Reformation as the primary force that set in motion British settlement of eastern North America. "Soon after the Reformation," he wrote Webb, "a few people came over into this new world for Conscience sake. Perhaps this (apparently) trivial incident, may transfer the great seat of Empire into America. It looks likely to me. For if we can remove the turbulent Gallicks, our People according to the exactest Computations, will in another Century, become more numerous than England itself." Another factor contributing to the shift of world power from England to America, Adams believed, was New England's production of naval stores, for the manufacture and outfitting of a fleet would enable British America to "gain the mastery of the seas, and then the united force of all Europe, will not be able to subdue us." He noted that the principal factor obstructing this destiny was the division of British America into thirteen colonies. "The only way to keep us from setting up for ourselves, is to disunite us," he concluded. "Divide et impera." He saw this disunity as the result not of plotting London officials but of machinations by politicians in each colony, ambitious to dominate the others. He likely had in mind the failure of the Albany Plan of Union to gain support within provincial assemblies the preceding year.[5]

Adams's 1755 letter to Nathan Webb is certainly the stuff of prophecy. It conflates his idea of "America" with New England, as he considered the religious convictions of Protestant dissenters from the Church of England to be the primary motive for settlement of the thirteen colonies, a claim than can reasonably be made only of New England. But he predicted correctly the exponential growth of the British American population until it surpassed the population of England, the continental unification of the colonies, the political independence of America from Britain, America's naval and maritime power as the key to national security, America's replacement of Britain as the world's hegemonic power, and the threat posed to continental union by provincial factionalism. This vision of America's future as a continental power seems extraordinary in a twenty-year-old schoolteacher in 1755. But such heady dreams were in the cultural air at the time, stimulated by the bold objectives of the British war effort to seize control of Canada from France. Adams remarked to Webb in the same letter, "Be not surprised that I am turn'd Politician. This whole town is immers'd in Politics. The interests of Nations, and all the dira of War, make the subject of every Conversation."[6]

Adams's claim in his letter that "our People according to the exactest Computations, will in another Century, become more numerous than England itself" suggests the influence of Benjamin Franklin's pamphlet *Observations Concerning the Increase of Mankind.* Aggravated by Britain's restraint of colonial manufacturing with the Iron Act of 1750, Franklin wrote his essay in 1751, but it was not published until 1755. He provided his own prophecy of America's future as a great power, derived from statistical analysis. Positing that population growth follows from the number of marriages, and the number of marriages increases with "the Ease and Convenience of supporting a Family," Franklin contended, "When Families can be easily supported, more Persons marry, and earlier in Life." With a greater number of marriages beginning earlier in life, America could expect to see its population double in size roughly every twenty years. "This Million doubling, suppose but once in 25 Years, will in another Century be more than the People of England," Franklin concluded, "and the greatest Number of Englishmen will be on this Side the Water."[7]

While Franklin saw demographic growth through natural reproduction, facilitated by the abundance of cheap land, as the inexorable engine of American power, Adams came to see America's destiny as conditional on the rationality and virtue of the American people. During his education at Harvard, Adams was immersed in a worldview that historians have styled enlightened dissent or rational dissent, a synthesis of British Enlightenment rationalism with Protestant dissent against the Church of England. This intellectual persuasion affirmed the value of reason for comprehension of scripture as well as the natural world, and the value of liberty in governance of church as well as state. Throughout his life, Adams extolled the human capacity to understand and command the natural world through reason. In his diary entry of May 17, 1756, he wrote that man, "by the Exercise of his Reason can invent Engines and Instruments, to take advantage of the Powers in Nature, and accomplish the most astonishing Designs," such as turning a valley into a mountain and a mountain into a valley. Man can cultivate the land and make it more fruitful, communicate over vast distances, and explore both the heavens and the microscopic world with scientific instruments. In the entry of June 15, 1756, he similarly remarked on the transformation of the American landscape over less than two centuries, from "one continued dismall Wilderness, the haunt of Wolves and Bears and more savage men," to abundant crops and orchards and "the magnificent Habitations of rational and civilized People." The settlement and cultivation of North America's Atlantic Coast provided ample empirical evidence of the human rational faculty and its exercise by average people to improve their condition of life and pursue earthly happiness.[8]

Young Adams believed that human goodness and happiness depend on the active direction of action by reason, the rigorous cultivation of moral character, and the systematic education of intellect and refinement of appetite. On June 21, 1756, he expressed his "fixt Determination" to improve his knowledge. "May I blush whenever I suffer one hour to pass unimproved," he wrote. "I will rouse up my mind, and fix my Attention. I will stand collected within my self and think upon what I read and what I see. I will strive with all my soul to be something more than Persons who have less Advantages than myself." With an intellectual debt to both John Locke and Adams's soul-searching Puritan forbears, the diary demonstrates Adams's internal struggle to exercise reason, practice virtue, and wrestle with his own vices, such as vanity and sloth. From his literary research, observation of human behavior, introspection, and projection of his own mental states onto his fellow humans, Adams concluded that human nature includes both a rational faculty and passions that can lead it astray. He scribbled in his diary on May 11, 1756, that truth and right are universal, and "pure unbiassed Reason" can grasp universal truth and right, but humans can "suffer our Understandings to be blinded or perverted" by "Passion, Prejudice, Interest, Custom, and Fancy." The odds are "millions to one, that we shall embrace error. And hence arises that endless Variety of Opinions entertained by Mankind." While Adams's interpretation of human behavior and of America's historical development shifted in emphasis over time according to private and public circumstances, these shifts occurred within the parameters set by a conception of human nature that drew on and sought to reconcile Enlightenment rationalism and New England Congregationalism.[9]

At the height of his political career as vice president and president in the 1790s, Adams acquired the reputation of an admirer of hereditary monarchy and aristocracy, skeptical about the capacity of common people for self-government. As early as the 1760s, however, he demonstrated a respect for the mind of the common person, which followed from his belief in the natural capacity of men and women for reason and virtue, and each individual's natural duty to think independently. In a 1761 letter to fellow Boston lawyer Samuel Quincy, Adams rejected the characterization of "Genius" as "a rare Phenomenon" by such modern English authors as Lord Bolingbroke or Alexander Pope, comparing this elitist view unfavorably with the Calvinist doctrine of unconditional election. "We have much higher Notions of the efficacy of human endeavours in all Cases," he intoned. All humans are born with the natural capacity for genius, just as they possess height, beauty, strength, and sensibility, albeit in differing, unequal degrees. Old World elitists acknowledged genius only in "those few, who have been directed, by their birth, education and lucky accidents, to distinguish themselves in arts and sciences, or in the execution of what the World calls great Affairs, instead of planting Corn, freighting Oysters, and killing Deer, the worthy employments in which most real Geniuses are engaged—for in truth according to that definition the world swarms with Them." Possessing that degree of genius known as "Common Sense," common people display their creative thinking in their daily labor.[10] Adams waxed poetic:

> Go on board an Oyster-boat, and converse with the Skipper, he
> will relate as many instances of invention, and intrepidity too, as
> you will find in the lives of many British Admirals, who shine in
> history as the ornaments of their Country. Enquire of a Gunner in
> Braintree-bay, or of a Hunter upon the Frontiers of their Province,
> and you will hear of as many artful devices to take their Game, as
> you will read in the lives of Caesar, or Charles or Frederick. And
> as genius is more common, it seems to me it is much more powerful

than is generally thought. . . . The gods sell all Things to Industry, and Invention among the Rest.[11]

Persuaded that all people possess the natural right, duty, and ability to think for themselves, Adams believed that the average working person was capable of independent reasoning, moral self-direction, and economic self-support. This conviction was affirmed empirically in part from Adams's observation of his fellow New Englanders: the farmer, hunter, oysterman, and "Gunner in Braintree-bay." His experience with the Yankee middling sort and laboring folk fed Adams's confidence in the common people's capacity to improve their own condition, behave virtuously, and govern themselves responsibly.

A crisis in constitutional relations between the British government and the American colonies gathered momentum over the course of the 1760s, drawing the Braintree lawyer into public commentary on the nature of government and the proper constitutional place of America within the British Empire. In the summer of 1763, Adams wrote a series of anonymous articles about local political controversies for the *Boston Gazette*. In one essay that he did not submit for publication, Adams expounded on the human appetite for power. While he believed that all humans have a natural capacity for virtue and reason, he did not think that virtuous and rational behavior would come automatically, for there are countervailing passions that require firm restraint. Adams claimed provocatively that "all Men would be Tyrants if they could." He insisted that he did not mean, by this maxim, that human nature had been depraved totally by original sin. Rather, it followed from the observation that any person's capacity for "self-love" will always prevail over his capacity for sociability if he is "left to the natural Emotions of his own Mind, unrestrained and uncheckd by other Power extrinsic to himself." Even the wisest man, once endowed with power over other men, will abuse it for his own advantage. "Power is a Thing of infinite Danger and Delicacy, and was never yet confided to any Man or any Body of Men without turning their heads," he warned. Adams's understanding of the "usurping and encroaching Nature of Power" as woven into the nature of man led him to his core principle on the question of the proper form of government: "No simple Form of Government, can possibly secure Men against the Violences of Power." Monarchy metastasizes into despotism, aristocracy degenerates into oligarchy, and democracy slides headlong into anarchy. Only by placing checks on the exercise of power by humans over other humans—whether the one, the few, or the many—can there be security for "Mans life or Property or Reputation or Liberty," which is the proper object of government. Developed by Adams early in the imperial crisis, these basic principles about the proper form of government guided him throughout his life and informed both his hopes and fears for the future of America.[12]

Adams published his first formal political pamphlet at the height of the Stamp Act Crisis. Printed in the *Boston Gazette* as a series of installments in August, September, and October 1765, it was subsequently published in November and December 1765 in the *London Chronicle,* under the auspices of English philanthropist Thomas Hollis, with Hollis's title, *A Dissertation on the Canon and the Feudal Law.* In the *Dissertation,* Adams offered an account of the sources of liberty in British America—and the growing threats to it. The central premise of the *Dissertation,* presented early in the first of four installments, is that "whenever a general knowledge and sensibility have prevail'd among the *people,* arbitrary government, and every kind of oppression, have lessened and disappeared in proportion."[13] Far from a Calvinist advocate of the total depravity of man, Adams intoned that "Man has certainly an exalted soul!" But that soul is capable of descending to great depths as well as reaching great heights. He claimed that the "love of power" is rooted in the human soul. The love of power—when its object is control of other men—"has always prompted the princes and nobles of the earth, by every species of fraud and violence, to shake off, all the *limitations* of their power." That same love of power, however, fuels the people's yearning for self-government, having "always stimulated the common people to aspire at independency, and to endeavor at confining the power of the great within the limits of *equity* and *reason.*" The universal love of power—springing from the self-love that Adams described in an unpublished 1763 essay—can therefore be enlisted in "the cause of *slavery*" as well as in "the cause of *freedom.*" Lacking "leisure or opportunity" to acquire the knowledge of "arts and letters" required to "form an union and exert their strength," the "poor people" have more often failed in their struggle for freedom than they have succeeded. Despite their small numbers, Adams explained, kings and nobles rule with impunity by keeping the masses ignorant of "the knowledge of their rights and wrongs, and the power to assert the former or redress the latter." The people can only prevail against their oppressors when the love of freedom is guided by a rational understanding of their rights and the best way to secure those rights. Adams took a moment to make clear that these rights are not mere privileges granted by kings in charters. They are rights "antecedent to all earthly government—*Rights* that cannot be repealed or restrained by human laws—*Rights* derived from the great legislator of the universe."[14]

From the dawn of the Christian era, Adams contended in the *Dissertation,* the natural rights of the people have been systematically suppressed by "the two greatest systems of tyranny," namely the canon law, which gave the Roman Catholic Church jurisdiction over the minds of people, and the feudal law, which gave princes and nobles jurisdiction over their bodies. The Catholic Church and Europe's feudal monarchies struck up "a wicked confederacy" to support one another in their coordinated conspiracy against the commoners. In the Middle Ages, "Liberty, and with her, Knowledge and Virtue too, seem to have deserted the earth." Adams credited the Protestant Reformation, "especially in *England,*" with beginning the process of reopening the minds of the common people. With the spread of knowledge, "*ecclesiastical* and *civil* tyranny" declined. True to his Yankee identification with British Protestant nonconformity, Adams viewed the episcopal polity of the Church of England as a species of ecclesiastical tyranny, violating a congregation's right to govern itself. In seventeenth-century England, the Stuart dynasty tried to roll back the advancement of religious and political knowledge and civil and religious liberty in England, resulting in bloody civil war. "It was this great struggle, that peopled America," Adams contended. "It was not religion *alone,* as is commonly supposed; but it was a love of *universal Liberty,* and an hatred, a dread, an horror of the infernal confederacy, before described, that projected, conducted, and accomplished the settlement of America."[15] Under the rising menace of British despotism, Adams's vision had expanded. In his 1765 account of the peopling of America, his ancestors, the English Puritans, still played the central role, but he characterized them in terms of the worldview of rational dissent. They were distinguished from England's Episcopalian majority not just by tender consciences on the fine points of theology and forms of worship but by a principled commitment to civil and religious liberty. Reinterpreting New England history in light of the Stamp Act Crisis, Adams came to see opposition to all arbitrary power—oppressive kings along with oppressive bishops—as the fundamental motive spurring Protestant nonconformists to leave Britain for North America's Atlantic seaboard.

The seventeenth-century Puritans of Adams's *Dissertation* were both proto-Enlightenment rationalists (though not freethinkers) and proto-Whig libertarians (though not republicans). While acknowledging their "imperfections," he denied that the Puritans were "enthusiastical, superstitious and republican." He styled New England's Puritan settlers as "a sensible people" who had "become intelligent in general, and many of them learned." They were religious enthusiasts in an enthusiastic era, but their religion demonstrated "wise, humane and benevolent principles," "founded in revelation, and in reason too." Adams explained that the Puritans had been persecuted by civil and ecclesiastical authorities in England "for no other crime than their knowledge, and their freedom of enquiry and examination." The Puritans fled to the New England wilderness and secured both civil and religious liberty by framing the constitution of their church and state "in *direct opposition* to the *cannon* and the *feudal* systems." Finding the Puritans admirable by Enlightenment standards, he extolled them for a hatred of "Tyranny in every form, shape, and appearance." Adams insisted that the Puritans were not regicidal republicans, but they saw the need for "popular powers" to serve as "a guard, a controul, a balance, to the powers of the monarch, and the priest, in every government." Repudiating the Episcopalian doctrines of divine right and passive obedience, "they knew that government was a plain, simple, intelligible thing founded in nature and reason and quite comprehensible by common sense." As reason, religion, virtue, and liberty depend on knowledge, New England's founders created public schools, funded by a town assessment, to assure that "knowledge [would be] diffused generally thro' the whole body of the people." Adams credited these measures with the high degree of "knowledge and civility among the common people" of British America in his own day, which he saw as the safeguard of their liberty. He concluded wryly, "A native of America who cannot read and write is as rare an appearance, as a Jacobite or a Roman Catholic."[16]

Adams's *Dissertation* offered a conservative defense of liberty as a patrimony already enjoyed by Americans in the 1760s. "We have a right to it, derived from our Maker," Adams maintained, "But if we had not, our fathers have earned, and bought it for us, at the expense of their ease, their estates, their pleasure, and their blood. And liberty cannot be preserved without a general knowledge among the people, who have a right from the frame of their nature, to knowledge, as their great Creator who does nothing in vain, has given them understandings, and a desire to know." The people particularly have a natural right to know "the characters and conduct of their rulers," who are "no more than the attorneys, agents and trustees for the people." Adams treated common people's understanding of their rights—and of any threats to those rights from their rulers—as a necessary safeguard of liberty.[17]

Adams urged the American press to bring abuses of power to public attention and not be intimidated by threats from royal governors. Corrupt British officials thought they could impose the Stamp Act on America, Adams's *Dissertation* contended, because they saw the colonists as "an ignorant, a timid and a stupid people." American liberty was at risk in 1765 because "We have been afraid to think." The colonists had shown too much deference to British authority. It was not enough for the people simply to reignite their love of freedom, a spirit that, "without knowledge, would be little better than a brutal rage." In the fourth installment and climax of the *Dissertation,* Adams urged the American people to reason for themselves, renew their understanding of political science, and beware of the thin edge of the wedge of tyranny: "Let us tenderly and kindly cherish, therefore the means of knowledge. Let us dare to read, think, speak and write. Let every order and degree among the people rouse their attention and animate their virtue." Adams thought the common people had a duty to consider political questions and engage in the controversies of the day. He spurred colonial intellectuals—college professors, clergymen, and lawyers—to show leadership in facilitating the spread of political knowledge: "In a word, let every sluice of knowledge be open'd and set a flowing." The young author's exuberance turned dark, as he concluded with the warning, "There seems to be a direct and formal design on foot, to enslave all America." This imposition of despotism "must be done by degrees," and the introduction of canon and feudal law through the Stamp Act was the beginning. A tax on the printed word, he concluded, had the manifest effect of curtailing the knowledge on which the virtue and liberty of the people depended.[18]

From his experience with Yankee farmers educated in township schools, Adams came to view the common people as capable of rational deliberation and sober judgment. He believed that America already enjoyed civil and religious liberty because its first settlers—inspired by a love of liberty and equipped with political knowledge—had created public institutions to secure liberty and knowledge for their posterity. It was because the common people possessed education that British America enjoyed freedom while "nine tenths of the species, are groaning and gasping in misery and servitude." Adams characterized Americans in the *Dissertation* as exceptional in their liberty and education, treating both as values endangered in 1765 by tyranny and corruption from the British government. Socioeconomic factors (such as demographic growth and abundance of arable land or naval stores) did not figure in this interpretation of America, as they had in the Webb letter ten years earlier. Having moved beyond Franklin's more demographic and economic interpretation of America's future, Adams had developed a vision of his own, defined largely in moral, intellectual, and cultural terms. Drawing on a synthesis of New England Congregationalism and Enlightenment rationalism, Adams believed that rationality depended on liberty, and liberty in turn depended on rationality. The two would rise or fall together. Determined that they would not fall in America, Adams joined the fight to educate public opinion and mobilize the people in defense of their rights.[19]

Ryerson characterizes the *Dissertation* as "a declaration of New England's political and cultural superiority that belongs to the rich literature of American exceptionalism." A thoroughgoing New England man, Adams displayed a pride in his region for its heritage of rational piety, virtue, education, and civil and religious liberty. And he wrote of New England and "America" interchangeably. By the fall of 1765, Adams had never left the confines of New England. He lacked firsthand experience with the other regions of British America. Although proud of his region and provincial in his experience, he was not bigoted against the other colonies, and lack of familiarity with them contributed to his early continentalism. Adams unknowingly projected a Yankee identity onto the colonies lying south of New England. In *Dissertation on the Canon and the Feudal Law,* he conceived of America as in effect a macrocosm of New England. Founded by Puritans fleeing Stuart tyranny, America was liberty-loving, self-governing, virtuous, churchgoing, prosperous, middle-class, and well educated. Adams identified with America against Britain during the Stamp Act Crisis in part by imagining America as New England writ large. His belief in "New England's political and cultural superiority" was as yet indistinguishable from his belief in "American exceptionalism."[20]

. . .

Nine years after repeal of the Stamp Act, Parliament retaliated against Massachusetts for the Boston Tea Party with the Coercive Acts of 1774. Among other provisions, these punitive statutes revoked the Massachusetts charter, closed the port of Boston, and placed the province under the governorship of a British general backed by British regulars. Seeking deliverance through political union with the other colonies, the Massachusetts House of Representatives held off its dissolution by Governor Thomas Gage just long enough to call for a Continental Congress, appointing a delegation that included John Adams. "A Union of the Colonies, in Sentiment and Affection [He]art and Hand," Adams wrote a friend on June 27, 1774, "is of indispensable Importance. Every Thought [ever]y Expedient for and cementing it, ought to be cherished." Adams thought of Congress as a political anchor for the moral-intellectual links binding the thirteen colonies together in such a continental union. Upon his appointment to the First Continental Congress, the Yankee lawyer felt apprehensive about his preparedness to deliberate on matters concerning all of the colonies. "I feel my own insufficiency for this important Business," he wrote fellow Massachusetts lawyer and patriot legislator James Warren on July 17, 1774. "I have not that Knowledge of the Commerce of the several Colonies, nor even of my own Province which may be necessary," Adams fretted. For all his praise of New England's public schools back in 1765, he worried, "Our New England Educations, are quite unequal to the Production of Such great Characters" as a Roman senator or British general. Ambition and necessity offset these insecurities, however, and Adams welcomed political experience in the First Continental Congress as his means of acquiring the knowledge of America and wisdom of statecraft that he needed so urgently. He imagined Congress as "a Seminary of American Statesmen, a School of Politicians, perhaps at no great Distance of Time, equal to a british Parliament, in wiser as well as better Ages."[21]

Adams was keenly aware of the limitations of his upbringing. His father, Deacon John Adams, spent his whole lifetime in Braintree, and the younger John had never before traveled farther from home than Falmouth, in the district of Maine. His departure for Congress in Philadelphia in September 1774 provided his first personal experience of America outside New England. The provincial Yankee lawyer found himself thrust suddenly on the stage of continental and transatlantic politics. Adams rose to the occasion, serving on four major committees, including that which drafted the Declaration of Rights and Grievances. During Congress's almost two-month session, he

advanced the interests of persecuted Massachusetts while striking a conciliatory tone favorable to non-Yankee delegates. Although a staunch champion
of American continentalism in 1774, he valued a continental union in no
small part from provincial motives, as the best security for the rights and interests of New England. With the conclusion of the First Continental Congress, Adams reimmersed himself in Massachusetts politics, taking his seat
in the Provincial Congress, as the Massachusetts House of Representatives
called itself on reassembling in Concord illegally, in defiance of Governor
Gage and Parliament's revocation of the Massachusetts Charter.[22]

Adams returned home from the Provincial Congress in December 1774
to find the Tory position on the current crisis represented effectively in the
Massachusetts Gazette by essays co-authored by his former friends Daniel
Leonard and Jonathan Sewall under the ungainly pseudonym "Massachusettensis." Adams took up the Whig position in a series of letters written
as "Novanglus" ("New Englander") in the *Boston Gazette* from January to
April 1775. Most of these essays were provincial in content. Adams criticized
the arguments and conduct of Tory writers in the Massachusetts press, re-
counted the long political struggle of Massachusetts Whig legislators with
former Governor Thomas Hutchinson, defended the Boston Tea Party, and
excoriated the crippling of Massachusetts's charter government by Britain's
Coercive Acts. The *Letters of Novanglus* betrayed "many signs of a deeply
provincial outlook," Ryerson argues, even as they "moved into new political
and intellectual territory."[23] In Adams's seventh essay, printed in the *Boston
Gazette* on March 6, 1775, he abruptly shifted from provincial politics to a
new constitutional conception of the British Empire as a whole. Agreeing
with Massachusettensis that there cannot be two supreme legislatures within
the same polity, Adams insisted in the March 6 essay that "our provincial
legislatures are the only supream authorities in our colonies." The Massachusetts Council and House of Representatives should be understood "in
our little models of the English constitution" as the provincial analogues to
the British Houses of Lords and Commons. Parliament had no sovereign
power over the colonies because the colonists were not represented in it. He
denied that the colonies were subject to Parliament's authority but granted
that they had consented to parliamentary regulation of trade as suiting their
own interest, a position Adams articulated in the First Continental Congress
and worked into the Declaration of Rights and Grievances.[24]

Adams went further in the seventh of his *Letters of Novanglus,* denying that the colonies were subject to the sovereign authority of the king-in-parliament. The colonists owed only personal allegiance to the king of England, under royal charters and oaths of allegiance established by provincial law. It followed that King George III "appears king of the Massachusetts, king of Rhode-Island, king of Connecticut, &c." The king bound the colonies together (and bound the colonies in turn to Britain) in a federal relation. Adams likened this arrangement to the connection of England and Scotland before the 1707 Act of Union, when both nations had their own parliament. Adams grounded his contentions in a review of the colonial charters, and for the first time his political publications gave serious consideration to colonies outside of New England, namely Maryland and Virginia. If the king alone provided the constitutional connection between the colonies and Britain, and neither Parliament nor king-in-parliament had sovereignty over the colonies, Adams reasoned that a political union of colonies providing such a continental-scale authority was required all the more urgently. "A union of the colonies might be projected," he surmised, "and an American legislature." He did not, however, consider such a continental union as incompatible with America's continued connection to Britain as a voluntary arrangement for mutual benefit. In the March 6 essay, he described the thirteen colonies as "a part of the British dominions, that is of the king of Great-Britain, and it is our interest and duty to remain so." He thought that the colonists should continue their consent to Parliament's trade regulations, "as long as she shall leave us to govern our internal policy, and to give and grant our own money." In the *Letters of Novanglus,* Adams's novanglocentric notion of America had given way to a constitutional conception of the thirteen colonies (the middle colonies and the South along with New England) as having long enjoyed federal union among themselves and legislative independence from Parliament, with the king of England binding them—and a standing American legislature sorely needed.[25]

Throughout the imperial crisis of 1765–75, Adams remained firmly persuaded that New Englanders had, since the first Puritan plantations, proven themselves capable of conceiving, implementing, operating, and preserving representative institutions with balanced constitutions, which in turn drew their authority from the people's informed consent. Adams believed that Massachusetts, under the revoked 1691 charter, already had a constitutional system that implemented the great principles of separation of powers and checks and balances, comparable favorably with the British constitution. The people of Massachusetts, along with their fellow American colonists, had long enjoyed the sovereign right to tax and legislate for themselves and had demonstrated the capacity to exercise responsibly this measure of self-government. He believed that civil liberty was not a value that New Englanders needed to gain but to conserve—or, in the case of prostrate Massachusetts, to restore. Adams concluded that the thirteen colonies were associated with one another in a *de facto* federal union, held together by the person of the king, and that a stronger union under a Continental Congress was needed to protect American liberty from Parliament—and the king's men.

The Battles of Lexington and Concord on April 19, 1775, made the long dreaded war inescapable, compelling Adams to shift the focus of his attention from provincial and regional politics back to the art of politics on a continental and transatlantic scale, a new challenge for which he was increasingly prepared intellectually. A few days after the running firefight between British regulars and Yankee militia along the road from Concord to Boston, Adams departed on his long journey to Philadelphia for service as a Massachusetts delegate to the Second Continental Congress. On May 21, 1775, the congressman wrote from Philadelphia to inform James Warren of the mobilization of Pennsylvania regiments. He inferred from the "martial Spirit" on display in Philadelphia that "America will Soon be in a Condition to defend itself by Land against all Mankind." Military mobilization by the provinces south of New England gave Adams hope that continental union would be the salvation of New England. Yankee troops encircling British regulars in Boston would not have to stand alone for long against the aroused might of the British Empire.[26]

Experience in the Second Continental Congress immediately shook that hope of deliverance from the south. On June 10, Adams wrote his friend Moses Gill, serving on the executive committee of the Massachusetts Provincial Congress, of his irritation that delegates from the mid-Atlantic and southern colonies desired the extension of a diplomatic olive branch to King George III at the same time that they approved military mobilization. "I am myself as fond of Reconciliation," Adams remarked, "if We could reasonably entertain Hopes of it upon a constitutional Basis, as any Man." Finding that the British nation was rotted through with corruption, he had become "convinced that the Cancer is too deeply rooted, and too far spread to be cured by any thing short of cutting it out entire." Humble overtures to the king were not simply hopeless but subversive of the conduct of war. "In my opinion Powder and Artillery are the most efficacious, Sure, and infallibly conciliatory Measures We can adopt," he quipped grimly. Adams had come to accept that the mid-Atlantic and southern colonies did not share the fullness of New England's commitment to victory. "However, this Continent is a vast, unweildy Machine," he observed. "We cannot force Events. We must Suffer People to take their own Way in many Cases, when We think it leads wrong—hoping however and believing, that our Liberty and Felicity will be preserved in the End, tho not in the Speedyest and Surest Manner." Having come to see British America as a whole and as regional parts, Adams adjusted his Yankee continentalism accordingly.[27]

Union with the middle and southern colonies was essential to the salvation of New England, and the regions of America would rise or fall together in this war against Britain. But, Adams concluded, the coordination of military and diplomatic efforts among the colonies would also generate political conflict, and the preservation and operation of the union would require the statesmanlike skills of tact, restraint, and compromise. On June 14, 1775, Congress created a Continental Army and general staff, formally continentalizing New England's armed revolt against Britain. A Massachusetts man, General Artemas Ward, was in command of the Massachusetts, Connecticut, and New Hampshire troops camped around Boston, and he was a natural choice to command the Continental Army. True to his matured continental vision, Adams instead nominated the respected delegate from Virginia George Washington as commander in chief, to bind the South more closely to the fortunes of New England.[28]

As Congress turned to selection of a general staff for the army, however, the question of the rate of pay in the Continental Army set off the first political conflict in Congress between New England and the rest of America. As Adams wrote Elbridge Gerry on June 18, "The pay which has been voted to all the officers, which the Continental Congress intends to choose, is so large, that I fear our people will think it extravagant, and be uneasy. Mr. [Samuel] Adams, Mr. [Robert Treat] Paine, and myself, used our utmost endeavors to reduce it, but in vain." Delegates from the more aristocratic political cultures of the mid-Atlantic and southern colonies thought that pay in the Massachusetts line was "too high for the privates, and too low for the officers, and they would have their own way." Adams wrote Gerry that those "ideas of equality, which are so agreeable to us natives of New England, are very disagreeable to many gentlemen in the other colonies." In New England, the rank and file took for granted the privilege of electing militia officers and keeping the officer corps accountable to the enlisted men. It was precisely this kind of egalitarianism that non-Yankee congressmen opposed as a threat to the subordination, discipline, and respect for the chain of command required for military effectiveness. They accordingly wanted to foster greater social distance between commissioned officers and enlisted men. On June 21, Adams fretted to James Warren, "I expect, our People when they come to know the Pay of the General officers and others, will grumble. Adams, Paine and I fought against it totis Viribus [with all our might]. But in vain. It is amazingly high. But the southern Genius's think it is vastly too low." Massachusetts pushed back, true to its comparatively egalitarian and democratic political culture, but the colonies south of New England carried the day on the issue of army pay rates.[29]

Adams was further frustrated by the prevalence and persistence among non-Yankee congressmen of vain hopes for reconciliation with the British Crown. On July 5, 1775, Congress adopted the Olive Branch Petition, reaffirming the colonists' affection for and personal loyalty to King George III, eschewing any desire for independence from the empire, and making a direct appeal for the king to open negotiations for peace and a settlement of colonial grievances. In a letter to James Warren on July 6, Adams wrote that his fellow members of Congress "are much deceived and that We shall have nothing but Deceit and Hostility, Fire, Famine, Pestilence and Sword, from Administration and Parliament." He had come to consider reconciliation as not only impossible but no longer desirable. In his first overt call for independence, Adams wrote,

> We ought immediately to dissolve all Ministerial Tyrannies, and
> Custom houses, and set up Governments of our own, like that
> of Connecticutt in all the Colonies, confederate together like an
> indissoluble Band, for mutual defence and open our Ports to all
> Nations immediately. This is the system that your Friend has aimed

at promoting from first to last; But the Colonies are not yet ripe for it. A Bill of Attainder, &c may soon ripen them.[30]

Unlike the royally appointed governors of Massachusetts and New Hampshire, Connecticut's governor was elected by the people. In urging the creation of colonial governments based entirely on popular sovereignty and entirely independent of the Crown, as well as a political union of colonies and diplomatic relations with other nations, Adams was offering his own private declaration of independence on July 6, 1775.

Adams had learned enough of statecraft to know that he could only share these views with similarly minded Yankee patriots. It was clear to him that the radical measure of complete independence was required to prevent Britain's corruption from spreading to America, and yet he observed to Warren that "the Colonies are not ripe for it." Although chagrined that the mid-Atlantic and southern colonies persisted in the folly of reconciliation, "Yet the Colonies like all Bodies of Men must and will have their Way and their Honour, and even their Whims." The other colonists would end their attachment to Britain when direct experience with Crown brutality drove them to it, as had already occurred in New England. If Yankee radicals were to push for independence before the more moderate colonists grasped the necessity of independence, Adams told Warren, the result would be "total Disunion," with the mid-Atlantic and southern colonies deserting New England and seeking a separate peace with the king's government.[31]

Adams was nonetheless convinced that Americans' civic virtue and patriotic attachment to union would sustain the war effort. The same day that he wrote Warren about the necessity of independence and the folly of reconciliation, Adams wrote Warren a second letter relating that ten companies of riflemen from the backcountry of Pennsylvania, Maryland, and Virginia were on the march to Cambridge to support the New England troops in their siege of Boston. Adams was relieved that the South was lending its strength to Massachusetts, but he suspected that one motive for dispatching the backcountry regiments was "a Secrete fear, a Jealousy, that New England will soon be full of Veteran Soldiers, and at length conceive Designs unfavorable to the other Colonies," which he considered unfounded. Two days later, Adams signed the Olive Branch Petition. As a Yankee continentalist, Adams would continually have to weigh when to stand on New England principles and when to make concessions to regional differences in values, customs, opinions, and passions.[32]

Over the nine months following Congress's adoption of the Olive Branch Petition, war provided the hard schooling necessary for Americans to transcend a narrow provincialism, forsake their attachment to Britain, and lean only on Providence and their own resources. Widely shared hopes for reconciliation faded in the fall of 1775, when King George III declined to receive the petition and declared the patriots to be in a state of rebellion. The Continental Army's siege of Boston dragged on without decision, while casualties mounted in the American invasion of Quebec. In radical New England, public opinion strongly favored independence, and popular frustration with Congress grew. James Warren wrote John Adams on March 7, 1776, "People cant Account for the hesitancy they Observe. While some Apprehend that you are startled at the measures Already taken, Others wonder why the principles and dictates of Common Sense have not had the same Influence upon the Enlarged minds of their Superiours that they feel on their own, and none can see safety or happiness in a future Connection with B[ritain] void as they are of true policy, Justice or humanity." In March, General William Howe's evacuation of British forces from Boston coincided with news from London of Parliament's Prohibitory Act, by which the Royal Navy's blockade of Boston was extended to all colonial ports, and all American commerce on the high seas was forfeited to the Crown.[33]

On March 23, Adams congratulated General Horatio Gates for the liberation of Boston. He also vented his frustration with those colonists south of New England for whom "Independency is an Hobgoblin, of So frightful Mein, that it would throw a delicate Person into fits to look it in the Face." He grumbled "that in Politicks the Middle Way is none at all. If We finally fail in this great and glorious Contest, it will be by bewildering ourselves in groping after this middle Way." Parliamentary hardliners made the "middle way" of reconciliation untenable, pushing a reluctant America toward irrevocable independence. Adams wrote,

> I know not whether you have seen the Act of Parliament call'd the restraining Act, or prohibitory Act, or piratical Act, or plundering Act, or Act of Independency, for by all these Titles is it call'd.
> I think the most apposite is the Act of Independency, for King Lords and Commons have united in Sundering this Country and

that I think forever. It is a compleat Dismemberment of the British Empire. It throws thirteen Colonies out of the Royal Protection, levels all Distinctions and makes us independent in Spight of all our supplications and Entreaties.

It may be fortunate that the Act of Independency should come from the British Parliament, rather than the American Congress: But it is very odd that Americans should hesitate at accepting Such a Gift from them.[34]

March 1776 provided an opening for the advocates of independence to make their case publicly, and Adams prepared to seize the moment.

Severing the colonies from Britain required the extirpation of Crown-appointed governorships from colonial charter governments like Massachusetts, Virginia, New York, and South Carolina. The next step toward an act of independency by Congress would be a resolution calling on all colonies to adopt new constitutions that omitted all Crown officers. As indicated in his letter to Gates, Adams was at that time working on the problem of crafting constitutions for the American states based entirely on the sovereignty of the people. It was necessary that first "each Colony should establish its own Government, and then a League [of independent states] should be formed, between them all." The obstacle to this objective was "the Reluctance of the Southern Colonies to Republican Government." So far from viewing America as New England writ large, he had become keenly sensitive to the dissonance in political culture between egalitarian New England and the more aristocratic societies of the middle and southern colonies. A "Continental Constitution for the whole" of America would, like the state constitutions, need to be "done only on popular Principles and Maxims which are so abhorrent to the Inclinations of the Barons of the south, and the Proprietary Interests in the Middle Colonies." He resolved to "get us over these obstructions" and work patiently toward the vision of a continental union of independent republics he had first communicated in June 1775 to James Warren. "Thirteen Colonies under such a Form of Government as that of Connecticutt, or one, not quite so popular," he exulted to Gates, "leagued together in a faithfull Confederacy might bid Defyance to all the Potentates of Europe if united against them."[35]

Between March 19 and March 27, 1776, Adams hurriedly outlined a model for new state constitutions that were entirely republican in character.

The North Carolina legislature was turning its attention to reform of its own government and asked its representatives in Congress to return home and bring ideas for a new constitution with them. Before departing Phila-delphia, two North Carolina delegates, William Hooper and John Penn, independently requested recommendations from Adams, so sound by then was his reputation in Congress for political sagacity. He sketched his plan for a model state government in a letter to each, submitted on March 27. At the request of Virginian delegate George Wythe, Adams composed a longer draft, writing a still longer version for Jonathan Dickinson Sergeant of New Jersey in mid-April. One draft (mostly likely the one composed for Wythe) was published as an anonymous pamphlet in Philadelphia on April 22 under the title *Thoughts on Government*. Taking the Massachusetts charter government as his starting place, Adams sketched out a template for new governments for all colonies.[36]

Adams opened *Thoughts on Government* with a review of first principles. True to the Enlightenment rationalism embedded in his rational dissent, he observed that "the happiness of society is the end of government," and "All sober enquiries after truth, ancient and modern, Pagan and Christian, have declared that the happiness of man, as well as his dignity consists in virtue." Contending that the "foundation of every government is some principle or passion in the minds of the people," he observed that "most governments" depend on the fear of the people, while some better governments appeal to the desire for "honor," neither of which are conducive to the happiness of society. Looking for guidance on the best form of government in the argu-ments of such Commonwealth and Real Whig authors as Algernon Sidney, James Harrington, John Locke, and Benjamin Hoadly, Adams concluded that "there is no good government but what is Republican." The republican form of government is the only one that depends on the people's virtue and has the people's happiness as its object. Republics require that the people possess sufficient wisdom and goodness to depute power to "a few of the most wise and good" to serve as their representatives. This representative body, the assembly, "should be in miniature, an exact portrait of the people at large." The assembly "should think, feel, reason, and act like them."[37]

Adams was keenly aware of the limitations of the wisdom and good-ness of the people and their elected deputies. A unicameral legislature, he observed, is "liable to all the vices, follies and frailties of an individual" and subject to "fits of humour, starts of passion, flights of enthusiasm, partialities of prejudice, and consequently productive of hasty results and absurd judgments." In a legislature, as in an individual person, "all these errors ought to be corrected and defects supplied by some controuling power." In 1776, as in his 1763 *Boston Gazette* essays, Adams found human nature incompatible with centralized government in general and a unicameral legislature in particular. He maintained in *Thoughts on Government,* "I think a people cannot be long free, nor ever happy, whose government is in one Assembly." His view of human nature as capable of both reason and passion, virtuous restraint and appetitive usurpation, dictated that a constitution provide structural checks and balances to prevent the abuse of power.[38]

In *Thoughts on Government,* Adams proposed a tripartite government divided into executive, legislative, and judicial branches that resembled the government of Massachusetts under its 1691 charter. He pushed for the concentration of executive power in a governor, armed with a veto over legislation, to serve as a check on the legislative branch. Once the people had formed a representative assembly, the assembly would then elect a smaller legislative body called, as under colonial governments, a council. The assembly and council would in turn elect the governor, who would serve as "an integral party of the legislature" through his use of the veto. Adams was open to an arrangement more like Connecticut's charter government in which the governor was weaker, but he thought a strong executive necessary for keeping the assembly in check. Adams favored a legislative role for the executive through an absolute veto at least as early as 1766, and he exhorted his fellow congressmen to advocate for that constitutional device in the summer and fall of 1775. As Richard Alan Ryerson observes, Adams's historical inspiration was less the royal veto of the British constitution—which no monarch had exercised since 1709—than the experience of every American provincial government: all colonial governors had an absolute veto, whether elected by the people or appointed by the Crown.[39]

The annual election of the governor would give the two legislative branches a check on abuses of executive power and any pretensions to monarchical grandeur. The other executive officers would also be elected by joint ballots of the assembly and council and subject to annual election. Adams considered it critical that every office within his proposed government be elected annually. This provision "will teach them [these great men] the great political virtues of humility, patience, and moderation, without which every man in power becomes a ravenous beast of prey." Here again,

Adams followed the precedent set by the Massachusetts Charter of 1691, by which all officers (except the royally appointed governor) were subject to annual election, a system that had in turn followed the precedent set by the original Massachusetts charter, under which all offices including the governorship were elected annually.[40]

Thoughts on Government was infused with confidence that the American people were capable of responsible self-government and suited for creating and operating independent republics—but only if their governments were crafted in such a way as to keep power in check. In addition to a tripartite division of government, a bicameral legislature, and annual elections, Adams also favored rotation in office, a militia law keeping arms in the hands of "all men," and life tenures for judges, to keep the judicial branch independent of the governor and legislatures. He again recurred to the example of Massachusetts, under both its provincial charter and original colonial charter, by encouraging all colonies to provide for "the liberal education of youth, especially of the lower class of people." He thought that creation of a public education system for each colony would be "so extremely wise and useful" that "to a humane and generous mind, no expence for this purpose would be thought extravagant." As republicanism depends on the rationality and virtue of the common people, Adams doubted that it could be sustained without the education of people too poor to provide for it themselves.[41]

Adams looked to over a century of successful self-government in Massachusetts and Connecticut for his recommendations to the other colonies. He was however a Yankee continentalist, not a New England chauvinist. His vision for America put trust in the people and leaders of each colony to craft the government best suited to their own local circumstances and regional differences. When Congress passed a motion on May 10, 1776, calling on the colonies (particularly those whose royal governors had fled) to adopt new forms of government, Adams authored a preamble to clarify the resolution, passed on May 15. His preamble urged the colonies to suppress "every kind of authority under the said Crown" and to exercise "all the powers of government . . . under the authority of the people of the Colonies," rather than the king. Adams's resolution was a *de facto* declaration of independence, and by June 7, the pump had been sufficiently primed for a resolution declaring the colonies to be states independent of Crown authority. Contributing modestly to the committee draft of the American Declaration of

Independence, his July 1 oration carried the July 2 vote of twelve colonies in favor of independence, with one abstaining. "He was our Colossus on the floor," Thomas Jefferson recalled of Adams's speech many years later, possessed of "a power both of thought and of expression which moved us from our seats."[42]

Adams had concerns for the future of self-government in the more aristocratic middle and southern colonies, but these concerns did not dim the hope—rooted in his interpretation of human nature, history, and unfolding events—that the American people were capable of civic virtue and favorable to independence. Adams's confidence that the provinces outside of New England were ready for republicanism on the model he recommended in *Thoughts on Government* soon proved well placed. Between May and December 1776, Virginia, New Jersey, Maryland, and North Carolina all adopted new state constitutions that included bicameral legislatures, independent judiciaries, and one-person executives armed with the veto, and New York followed this example in 1777.[43]

When Adams made the prophecy to his wife, that July 2 "will be celebrated, by succeeding Generations" as the birthday of an independent nation, with "Bells, Bonfires and Illuminations from one End of this Continent to other from this Time forward forever more," he insisted that it was not with irrational "Enthusiasm."[44] His vision of America as an independent, continental union was rooted in his view of human nature—both Enlightenment rationalist and dissenting Protestant—and informed by experience: New England's long record of responsible self-government, Adams's personal experience as a provincial legislator and congressional delegate, as well as recent military and political developments throughout the colonies. Ten years after the letter to Abigail, with the war won and reform of the constitutional union under consideration, Adams wrote an Irish aristocrat:

> It has ever been my hobby-horse to see rising in America an empire of liberty, and a prospect of two or three hundred millions of freemen, without one noble or one king among them. You say it is impossible. If I should agree with you in this, I would still say, let us try the experiment, and preserve our equality as long as we can.
> A better system of education for the common people might preserve

them long from such artificial inequalities as are prejudicial to
society, by confounding the natural distinctions of right and wrong,
virtue and vice.[45]

This vision of America as "an empire of liberty" rising over the North American continent, and of the common people rising with it, was indeed the
great "hobby-horse" of his life, dating from his 1755 letter to Nathan Webb
until the final public statement of his life, "Independence forever!"

John Adams first imagined America as New England in macrocosm.
By 1775, he had come to see America as a union of republics, regionally
diverse but still favorable to republican principles and open to New England's example. Within the evolution of his political thought from 1755
to 1776, commitment to both continental union and Yankee heritage remained constant. Adams's idea of America—and of the statecraft befitting a
continental-scale union of republics—can be usefully characterized as "Yankee continentalism," just as Lance Banning understood James Madison as a
"Virginia continentalist." Recently Peter S. Onuf has characterized Thomas
Jefferson's political loyalty as expanding progressively from Virginia to a confederation of self-constituted states, and ultimately to a continental republic,
while throughout maintaining Virginia's destiny as inseparable from that of
the union. Provincial continentalism may well be an interpretive concept
whose time has come. With a few exceptions like Alexander Hamilton, born
on the island of Nevis and never fully assimilated by his adopted New York,
the American national leaders styled as the founding fathers did not think
of the American union as a centralized nation-state. The cosmopolitan Benjamin Franklin was only too happy to shake the dust of Boston off his feet
for the promise of Manhattan and Philadelphia, and he was as much at
home in London or Paris as in America. But most of his colleagues—such
national statesmen as Adams, Madison, Jefferson, and Washington, along
with antifederalists George Mason, Patrick Henry, Samuel Adams, and
Mercy Warren—never entirely transcended their prerevolutionary loyalties
to province and region (nor saw the need to). They were all provincials. They
were all continentalists.[46]

Notes

1. John Adams (hereafter JA) to Abigail Adams, July 3, 1776, L. H. Butterfield et al., eds., *Adams Family Correspondence,* 13 vols. to date (Cambridge, Mass., 1963–), 2:27–28.

2. Ibid., 2:28.

3. Richard Alan Ryerson, *John Adams's Republic: The One, the Few, and the Many* (Baltimore, 2016), 25. For his description of James Madison in 1783 as a "Virginia continentalist," see Lance Banning, *The Sacred Fire of Liberty: James Madison and the Founding of the Federal Republic* (Ithaca, N.Y., 1995), 42, and Banning, "The Hamiltonian Madison: A Reconsideration," *Virginia Magazine of History and Biography* 92 (1984): 26–27.

4. JA to Nathan Webb, October 12 [?], 1755, Robert J. Taylor et al., eds., *Papers of John Adams,* 19 vols. to date (Cambridge, Mass., 1977–), 1:4–5.

5. Ibid., 1:5.

6. Ibid.

7. Ibid.; Benjamin Franklin, "Observations Concerning the Increase of Mankind, Peopling of Countries, &c," Leonard W. Labaree et al., eds., *Papers of Benjamin Franklin,* 42 vols. to date (New Haven, Conn., 1961–), 4:227–28, 233.

8. JA, diary, May 16 [17], 1756, L. H. Butterfield, ed., *Diary and Autobiography of John Adams,* 4 vols. (Cambridge, Mass., 1961), 1:27, 34. For origination of the interpretive concept of rational dissent, see Anthony Lincoln, *Some Political and Social Ideas of English Dissent* (Cambridge, U.K., 1938), 30; for an introduction to late twentieth-century scholarship on rational dissent, see Knud Haakonssen, ed., *Enlightenment and Religion: Rational Dissent in Eighteenth-Century Britain* (Cambridge, U.K., 1996); and for the centrality of Enlightenment rationalism to John Adams's worldview, see C. Bradley Thompson, *John Adams and the Spirit of Liberty* (Lawrence, Kans., 1998), chap. 1. See also Thompson, *America's Revolutionary Mind: A Moral History of the American Revolution and the Declaration That Defined It* (New York, 2019), 49–51.

9. JA, diary, July 21, May 11, 1756, Butterfield, ed., *Diary and Autobiography of John Adams,* 1:35, 26. For a recent affirmation of John Adams as a critic of aristocracy, see Luke Mayville, *John Adams and the Fear of American Oligarchy* (Princeton, N.J., 2016).

10. JA to Samuel Quincy, April 22, 1761, Taylor et al., *Papers of John Adams,* 1:48–49.

11. Ibid., 1:50.

12. JA, "An Essay on Man's Lust for Power, with the Author's Comment in 1807," [post August 29, 1763], ibid., 1:82–83; Ryerson, *John Adams's Republic,* 42–43.

13. JA, "A Dissertation on the Canon and the Feudal Law," no. 1, August 12, 1765, Taylor et al., eds., *Papers of John Adams,* 1:111; Ryerson, *John Adams's Republic,* 47–48; Thompson, *John Adams and the Spirit of Liberty,* 48–55.

14. JA, "A Dissertation on the Canon and the Feudal Law," no. 1, August 12, 1765, Taylor et al., eds., *Papers of John Adams,* 1:111–12.

15. Ibid., 1:112–14.

16. JA, "A Dissertation on the Canon and the Feudal Law," no. 2, August 19, 1765; no. 3, September 30, 1765; no. 1, August 12, 1765; ibid., 1:111–20.

17. JA, "A Dissertation on the Canon and the Feudal Law," no. 3, September 30, 1765, ibid., 1:120–21.

18. JA, "A Dissertation on the Canon and the Feudal Law," no. 4, October 21, 1765, ibid., 1:126–28.

19. Ibid., 1:123.

20. Ryerson, *John Adams's Republic,* 52, 46.

21. "Appointment of Massachusetts Delegates to the Continental Congress," June 17, 1774; JA to James Warren, July 17, 1774; JA to Joseph Hawley, June 27, 1774; "Editorial Note," Taylor et al., eds., *Papers of John Adams,* 2:98–99, 109, 101, 145–50.

22. David McCullough, *John Adams* (New York, 2001), 23; Page Smith, *John Adams,* 2 vols. (Garden City, N.Y., 1962), 1:189; Ryerson, *John Adams's Republic,* 46.

23. Ryerson, *John Adams's Republic,* 139–44, 125. For the compelling case that the Massachusettensis letters were co-authored by Daniel Leonard and Jonathan Sewall, see Colin Nicolson and Owen Dudley Edwards, *Imaginary Friendship in the American Revolution: John Adams and Jonathan Sewall* (Abingdon, U.K., 2019), chap. 6.

24. "Editorial Note"; JA, "To the Inhabitants of the Colony of Massachusetts-Bay," March 6, 1775, Taylor et al., eds., *Papers of John Adams,* 2:197, 221–22, 147, 307, 313, 315, 323.

25. JA, "To the Inhabitants of the Colony of Massachusetts-Bay," March 6, 1775, ibid., 2:320–22, 326; Ryerson, *John Adams's Republic,* 147. For Adams's federalism within the Novanglus essays, and the comparison of British America with the relation of England and Scotland before the Act of Union, see Alison L. LaCroix, *The Ideological Origins of American Federalism* (Cambridge, Mass., 2010), 84, 87–88.

26. JA to James Warren, May 21, 1775, Taylor et al., eds., *Papers of John Adams,* 3:11; Ryerson, *John Adams's Republic,* 154.

27. JA to Moses Gill, June 10, 1775, Taylor et al., eds., *Papers of John Adams,* 3:20–21.

28. JA to Elbridge Gerry, June 18, 1775, ibid., 3:25–26; John Ferling, *John Adams: A Life* (New York, 1992), 127.

29. JA to Elbridge Gerry, June 18, 1775; JA to James Warren, June 21, 1775, Taylor et al., eds., *Papers of John Adams,* 3:25–26, 43.

30. JA to James Warren, July 6, 1775, ibid., 3:62, 63n.

31. Ibid., 3:61.

32. Ibid., 3:63–64.

33. JA to James Warren, March 7, 1776, ibid., 4:45.

34. JA to Horatio Gates, March 23, 1776, ibid., 4:59.

35. Ibid., 4:59–60. For the contrast in social structure between Massachusetts and Virginia in the mid-eighteenth century, and the more egalitarian cast of Massachusetts, see Gordon S. Wood, *Friends Divided: John Adams and Thomas Jefferson* (New York, 2017), 16–20, 28–34.

36. "Editorial Note," Taylor et al., eds., *Papers of John Adams,* 4:68; Ryerson, *John Adams's Republic,* 172–74.

37. JA, "Thoughts on Government," April 1776, Taylor et al., eds., *Papers of John Adams,* 4:86–88.

38. Ibid., 4:88–89.

39. Ibid.; Ryerson, *John Adams's Republic,* 193–97.

40. JA, "Thoughts on Government," April 1776, Taylor et al., eds., *Papers of John Adams,* 4:89–90.

41. Ibid., 4:90–91.

42. Ibid., 4:90; Ryerson, *John Adams's Republic,* 183–86; "Notes on a Conversation with Thomas Jefferson," Charles M. Wiltse, ed., *The Papers of Daniel Webster: Correspondence,* 5 vols. (Hanover, N.H., 1974), 1:375.

43. Ryerson, *John Adams's Republic,* 179–80, 203–4.

44. JA to Abigail Adams, July 3, 1776, Butterfield et al., eds., *Adams Family Correspondence,* 2:28.

45. JA to Guy Claude, Comte de Sarsfield, February 3, 1786, Charles Francis Adams, ed., *The Works of John Adams,* 10 vols. (Boston, Mass., 1854), 9:546.

46. For examples of mid-twentieth-century scholarship framing early national politics in terms of a conflict between "nationalism" and states' rights or "localism," see Merrill Jensen, *The New Nation: A History of the United States during the Confederation, 1781–1789* (New York, 1950); see also Jackson Turner Main, *The Antifederalists: Critics of the Constitution, 1781–1788* (Chapel Hill, N.C., 1961), and E. James Ferguson, "The Nationalists of 1781–1783 and the Economic Interpretation of the Constitution," *Journal of American History* 56 (1969): 241–61. For a summation of Peter S. Onuf's contributions to the "federalist" interpretation of early national politics, see Alan Gibson, *Interpreting the Founding: Guide to the Enduring Debates over the Origins and Foundations of the American Republic* (2006; rpt. Lawrence, Kans., 2009), chap. 8, esp. 101–9. For his analysis of the interplay of "Virginia" and "America" in Thomas Jefferson's constitutional thought, see Onuf, *Jefferson and the Virginians: Democracy, Constitutions, and Empire* (Baton Rouge, La., 2018); see also Arthur Scherr, *Thomas Jefferson's Image of New England: Nationalism Versus Sectionalism in the Young Republic* (Jefferson, N.C., 2016). For the "Yankee nationalism" of John Quincy Adams, for which John Adams's Yankee continentalism may be considered the precursor, see Paul E. Teed, *John Quincy Adams: Yankee Nationalist* (Hauppauge, N.Y., 2006).

3 George Washington's Vision for the United States

KENNETH R. BOWLING

When Americans think of George Washington as the father of their country, they think of his practical accomplishments as commander in chief of the Continental Army, as president of the Constitutional Convention, and as president of the United States. But it is perhaps more appropriate to call him that in another sense, for, despite his inability to accept democracy or, apparently, even to write the word, Washington better than any other American revolutionary had the prescience to envision what the United States would become: an economically and religiously diverse, multiracial society that overcame its deep sectional divisions and whose enlightened federal government, seated in a large and magnificent capital, provided its citizens with cultural, scientific, and educational amenities. Washington's concern for the survival of the union was the driving force behind this forward-looking perspective; behind that was this highly ambitious man's fear that, if the union failed, along with it would go his historical reputation, something very dear to him.

Some of my argument comes from Washington's private and public letters, but most of it is based on his state papers and those his department heads submitted to Congress in his name, all but one of which survive. The one that does not, his magisterial, seventy-three-folio-page undelivered first inaugural address, is arguably the most important of them all, judging from its remnants. It survived in his papers until at least 1827, after which the historian and documentary editor Jared Sparks, with the implied encouragement of James Madison, who had prevented its delivery in 1789, began to cut it up and mail the ever smaller pieces to people requesting an example of the great man's handwriting. It belongs with the 1783 Address to the States and the 1796 Farewell Address as the most extensive and detailed statements of Washington's political views; like them, its viewpoint is centralist and stresses the necessity of supporting and maintaining the union against the forces of dissolution. Although undelivered, as president he used portions in his annual messages.[1]

Revolutions are spurred by ideologies, the American Revolution no less than those that followed in its wake. Republicanism—the belief that people were capable of virtue and self-government—is one that has been prodigiously studied. Equally important, but far less studied, was the "Rising Glory of America" concept and the related idea that empire coursed westward. These two ideologies combined to produce the utopian idea that the United States would become a republican empire with a mission to spread its form of government to the world as it fulfilled its manifest destiny to straddle the North American continent.[2]

Most of the patriot leaders and their followers had a continental vision for Britain's American colonies well before they advocated independence. In 1755, after reading Benjamin Franklin's *The Increase of Mankind*, a young John Adams imagined the "transfer of the seat of empire" to North America once the French had been driven off. That Timothy Dwight's *America* and Philip Freneau and Hugh Henry Brackenridge's *The Rising Glory of America* were both delivered at 1771 American college commencements was a sign of the times, not a coincidence. Henry Laurens of South Carolina predicted in 1775 that "a mighty empire . . . will arise on this continent" and England "cannot hinder its progress." That same year, the English clergyman Andrew Burnaby observed that "an idea, strange as it is visionary, has entered into the minds of the generality of mankind, that empire is travelling westward: and everyone is looking forward with eager and impatient expectation to that destined moment, when America is to give law to the rest of the world."[3]

It was this viewpoint and not republicanism that Thomas Hutchinson thought had spurred the American Revolution: "Speculative men had figured in their minds an American empire" prior to 1763, wrote the historian and loyalist governor of Massachusetts, "but in such distant ages that nobody then living could expect to see it." With the removal of the French that year, however, nothing existed "to obstruct a gradual progress of settlements, through a vast continent, from the Atlantic to the Pacific Ocean," and Hutchinson observed a resultant sense of grandeur and importance among his fellow colonists. Twentieth-century historians have ratified Hutchinson's opinion of the importance of that war: Merrill Jensen always began his lectures on the American Revolution by saying "You cannot understand the American Revolution without understanding the French and Indian War." John Seelye described it as "the womb of American imperialism" that "generated terrific expansionist energies," and Fred Anderson termed it "the most important event to occur in eighteenth-century North America."[4] George Washington played a major and well known role during the war that expelled the French, and it taught him more than military lessons, for it was in western Pennsylvania that Washington came to know the Alleghenies and the courses of its rivers.

Widespread American awareness of North America's advantages—its size, rapid population growth, climate, fertile soil, and other natural resources—confirmed Thomas Paine's common-sense image of the absurdity of an island ruling a continent. This was especially clear after a decade during which Parliament repeatedly restricted the growth of the North American colonies, most famously by the Proclamation Line of 1763 and the Quebec Act of 1774, but also by regulating American manufacturing, immigration, and naturalization, not to mention the long standing Navigation Acts. By July 4, 1776, enough Americans were ready for a separation from Great Britain to issue a bill of impeachment against George III. One only has to read it to understand how much the colonists resented England's attempt to stifle the rising glory of America. Better yet, read the draft where Thomas Jefferson declared that "the road to glory . . . is open to us" and "we will climb it in a separate state." Rising Glory, not republicanism, turned George Washington into a revolutionary.

By the time of the Declaration of Independence, references to the rising American Empire had deeply penetrated American popular culture. The historian-to-be David Ramsay expressed it dramatically and succinctly in his 1778 *Oration on the Advantages of American Independence*: "We have laid the foundations of a new empire, which promises to enlarge itself to vast dimensions and to give happiness to a great continent. . . . It is now our turn to figure on the face of the earth, and in the annals of the world." A year later, the *United States Magazine* editorialized that "if you would obtain an adequate idea of the empire yet in embrio, you must extend your apprehension from the bay of Hudson to the gulph of California."[5]

Just when George Washington became acquainted with Rising Glory is uncertain. But the widespread publication after 1752 of George Berkeley's "Verses on the Prospect of Planting Arts and Sciences in America" with its memorable concluding stanza, "westward the course of empire takes its way," could hardly have escaped an avid and serious reader like Washington. Certainly it was prior to his first mention of the rising American Empire in 1770. Between his pivotal speech to the army officers at Newburgh, New York, in March 1783 and his inaugural address as president in April 1789, he referred to it at least thirty times, modifying "empire" by such adjectives as "new," "great," "rising," "growing," and "extensive."[6] Joel Barlow's epic *Vision of Columbus,* which sets the background of the "new empire, rising in the west," so impressed Washington in 1787 that he purchased twenty copies for distribution. And the geographically focused Washington must have treasured his copy of Jedidiah Morse's *American Geography,* first published in 1789. Morse concluded his description of the Northwest Territory with reflections on the trans-Mississippi West. He refused to believe that Americans who settled in Spanish Louisiana would be forever lost to the United States, for "they will be Americans in fact, though nominally the subjects of Spain. . . . Besides, it is well known that empire has been travelling from east to west. . . . We cannot but anticipate the period, as not far distant, when the AMERICAN EMPIRE will comprehend millions of souls, west of the Mississippi. Judging upon probable grounds, the Mississippi was never designed as the western boundary of the American empire."[7]

The size of Washington's American empire was far more limited than that envisioned by Morse, Barlow, Hutchinson, and the newspaper and periodical literature, or by such colleagues as Franklin, Adams, Jefferson, and Alexander Hamilton.[8] He was far too practical to indulge in Pacific Ocean and California speculations. For him it stopped at the Mississippi River. Indeed, that is what he meant when he used the term "continent": "Great Britain's intent to subjugate this great continent"; paying the Continental Army veterans will preserve "the National faith & future tranquillity of this extensive Continent"; American citizens are "the sole Lords and Proprietors of a vast Tract of Continent." And, in the undelivered inaugural, Washington noted that he had received letters from all over the continent urging him to attend the federal convention.[9] His only reference to California was negative: if commerce flowed down the Mississippi instead of the Potomac, the trans-Appalachian West would mean no more to the United States than California.[10]

Washington's truncated vision of the rising American Empire resulted from his infatuation with the Potomac River. From youth he suffered from Potomac fever, a delusion-inducing obsession with the grandeur and commercial potential of the broad, westward-pointing river on which he lived. During the eighteenth century, the fever passed from generation to generation, along with the property if not the genes, of such families as the Carrolls and Johnsons of Maryland and the Lees, Masons, and Washingtons of Virginia, whose speculative landholdings on the Potomac and Ohio corridor to the West numbered in the tens of thousands of acres. Interestingly, his first use of "empire" was in conjunction with his prerevolutionary attempt to turn the Potomac River into "the Channel of conveyance of the extensive & valuable Trade of a rising Empire." Washington believed that centering an American political and commercial emporium on the Potomac would cement the union and provide a durable foundation for its survival. "The Washington Family," Edward Savage's grand painting at the National Gallery in Washington, captures that vision as well as the Rising Glory of America. No one else who suffered from the disease had Washington's political influence, and by the time Jefferson doubled the size of the United States and submerged Potomac fever under the Louisiana Purchase, Washington's commitment to Potomac River development had affected the course of American history dramatically. Washington held strong views, almost to the point of obsession in some cases, about several other aspects of the rising American Empire as well.[11]

It is not difficult to believe fellow victim and federal city promoter Samuel Blodget when he claims that he first heard Washington advocate a Potomac location for a federal seat of government at the Continental Army encampment outside Boston in 1775. By 1789, it was well understood by the leading citizens of Alexandria, Virginia, that Washington would use his clout as president to bring it to the Potomac and that their town would be included within the up to one-hundred-square-mile federal district authorized by the Constitution.[12] John Adams's often quoted aphorism that Washington had the gift of silence prevents us from detailing the evolution of his thoughts about either the nature or the location of the federal capital. One cannot find another important issue of the immediate post–Revolutionary War period on which he was so reticent. He expressed no opinion about the dual residence agreement of 1783, which called for an ambulatory government that would move between federal towns, one in the vicinity of Trenton, New Jersey, and the other near Georgetown, Maryland. But a year later, when Congress rescinded that agreement in favor of a single federal town near Trenton, he took action; it was the only time he commented on the issue until 1790, after the First Federal Congress chose a Potomac River site. An appropriation under the Articles of Confederation required a super majority, and Congressman William Grayson of Virginia, a former military aide to the commander in chief, made it his business to see that it was never achieved. Washington encouraged him from Mount Vernon: "Fixing the Seat of Empire at any spot on the Delaware, is in my humble opinion, demonstrably wrong. . . . I will venture to predict that under any circumstance of confederation, it will not remain so far to the Eastward long. . . . Time, too powerful for sophistry, will point out the place and disarm localities of their power."[13] All but one locality, that is.

Washington's role during the congressional debate that led to the Residence Act of 1790 is even less documented. His concern for discretion, and Madison's and Jefferson's willingness to honor it, masks his role. Several facts suggest that the two worked closely with the president as the political alliance leading to the Compromise of 1790 evolved. Madison had kept Washington well informed about the politics of the residence debates of 1788 and 1789. The president's aides became involved in the pre–June 1790 bargaining and showed their delight publicly in the House gallery when the bill passed. Even more indicative were his central importance to the political process, his Potomac fever, and his micromanagement of federal city development from July 1790 until his retirement and even beyond. Pennsylvania senator William Maclay was hardly alone when he summed up the matter: "It is in fact the Interest of the President of the United States, that pushes the Potowmack."[14]

Rather than trust the presidential commission created by the Residence Act, Washington chose the district's location himself and then, to the shock of many, requested a supplementary act from Congress to allow him to include Alexandria. With the specific location finally settled, he turned to the one person whom he considered capable of implementing his vision for a capital city within it, a vision that expanded as they combined their ideas. Peter Charles L'Enfant was a Continental Army officer who had first come to Washington's attention at Valley Forge during the winter of

1777–78. L'Enfant had expressed a desire to be involved with the design and construction of the seat of government in his extraordinary December 1784 memorial to Congress, calling on it to create an army corps of engineers to oversee internal improvements throughout the "new Rising Empire." The next year, he sought appointment to the commission charged with over-seeing construction of the unfunded Delaware River seat of government. When the First Federal Congress opened discussion of a location for its seat in September 1789, L'Enfant immediately detailed to Washington his inter-est in the creation of the "City which is to become the Capital of this vast Empire. . . . Altho' the means now within the power of the Country are not such as to pursue the design to any great extant it will be obvious that the plan Should be drawn on such a Scale as to leave room for that aggrandize-ment & embellishment which the increase of the wealth of the Nation will permit it to pursue at any period however remote."[15]

Washington and L'Enfant had several conversations about the nature of the city before the latter arrived at the site in March 1791. Consequently, L'Enfant knew that Washington envisioned a capital of beauty and magnifi-cence, in short, one with "éclat" where "the public buildings in size, form and elegance should look beyond the present day" and serve both as a seat of government and as a commercial and cultural center.[16] This is clearly seen in the initial city plan that L'Enfant presented to Washington in June 1791, for it included many public reservations that provided majestic aspects for such institutions as a church, a university, a theater, a hospital, an exchange, a mint, a bank, and a canal and grand dock, as well as statues, fountains, reflecting pools, pleasure walks, and extensive gardens surrounding the president's house.[17] Once L'Enfant persuaded the president to include a full six-thousand-acre tract between Georgetown, Maryland, and the Anacostia River instead of a smaller tract adjacent to either the town or the river, the president embraced size as another component of his vision, arguing that the capital of the United States should be bigger than the largest state capital, Philadelphia.[18] Although Jefferson supervised L'Enfant's initial work, the sec-retary of state indicated that ideas about the nature of the city would come from Washington. Indeed, L'Enfant maintained throughout his life that his role was "the execution *of the President's intentions.*"[19]

Washington refused to accept major changes to the L'Enfant plan and continued to support it for the rest of his life, even going so far as to require the politically influential Daniel Carroll of Duddington, the largest land owner in the federal city, to remove a house that conflicted with it. Washington invested in the city, carefully selecting lots that reflected his vision: two adjacent to the Capitol to support the political role of the city; four on the Anacostia River to support its commercial role; and, for a botanical garden to support its cultural role, all of Square 21 between what became the Kennedy Center for the Performing Arts and the twenty-acre federal reservation that he and the commissioners designated for the national university, the high ground west of 23rd Street just north of what became Constitution Avenue. One of the president's last acts in office was to order certain reservations in the federal city preserved for the use of the United States forever.[20]

Washington proved right when he predicted to his friend Sally Fairfax in 1798 that it would take a century to create the city he envisioned. When Jefferson, who had opposed the L'Enfant plan from its inception, assumed the presidency in 1801, he abandoned both it and Washington's vision of a grand capital. His successors followed suit, and the city of Washington remained for more than half of the nineteenth century merely a seat of government, unpaved, undecorated, and without the institutions and grandeur of a national capital. Washington, D.C., has never had clout in Congress, and it is only when a president or first lady asserts an interest—the Kennedys, the Johnsons, and Nixon most recently—that Congress provides for the aggrandizement of the city. The first president to do so after Washington was Ulysses S. Grant, without doubt the best friend the capital has ever had in the White House. In 1869, he stood against the powerful lobby attempting, as part of the "St. Louis, the Future Great City of the World" movement, to relocate the federal seat of government there. He routinely called the city a "capital" rather than a "seat of government," and for the next fifty years the Republican Party made the city's reconstruction physically and symbolically part of its assertion of federal supremacy. An investigative journalist, reporting on the many construction projects, recognized that the city had been planned, rediscovered the plan and laid the foundation for the resurrection of both it and L'Enfant. Today, L'Enfant and Washington would easily recognize the core of the city they founded.[21] Other aspects of Washington's vision for the republican empire he led also took decades to realize.

Although the Constitution had only granted Congress the power to issue copyrights and patents, George Washington believed the federal government should do much more in support of the arts and sciences. Indeed, he believed their development would bring the United States peace and prosperity; consequently, the intellectual advancement of the country became a national priority for him.[22] Some of this is clear in his vision for the federal capital. But it is evident elsewhere as well, most eloquently in the undelivered inaugural address when he called on Congress to take measures for promoting the general welfare: "I trust you will not fail to use your best endeavors to improve the education and manners of a people; to accelerate the progress of arts & Sciences; to patronize works of genius; to confer rewards for inventions of utility; and to cherish institutions favorable to humanity. Such are among the best of all human employments." Specifically, he called on Congress to subsidize newspapers and periodical publications by conveying them free of postage, for, as he had previously stated in a public letter, he considered them better vehicles than any other for preserving liberty, stimulating industry, and ameliorating the morals of an enlightened and free people.[23]

In his first annual message in January 1790, Washington told Congress that there is "nothing, which can better deserve your patronage, than the promotion of Science and Literature. Knowledge is in every Country the surest basis of public happiness. In one, in which the measures of Government recieve their impression so immediately from the sense of the Community as in our's, it is proportionably essential. To the security of a free Constitution it contributes in various ways." He went on to enumerate these ways. When Representative William Smith of Charleston, South Carolina, moved that the House of Representatives refer these remarks to a committee, the motion was opposed immediately as unconstitutional. The First Federal Congress's great champion of the encouragement of science, John Page of Virginia, urged his colleagues to refer the matter in order to decide the issue of constitutionality. If the committee decided in the negative, Page would consider it a defect in the Constitution that should be corrected by amendment because "on the diffusion of knowledge and literature depend the liberties of this country, and the preservation of the Constitution." The attack was a public slap at the president, and he discontinued recommending support for the arts and sciences until his eighth and final annual message in 1796 when he detailed the breadth of his vision. There he called for a national university, a military academy, manufacturing subsidies, and federally funded premiums and institutions for the promotion of agriculture. The House at least gave his recommendations cursory attention, for it referred the last item to a select committee that produced a stillborn suggestion to establish an

American Society of Agriculture with authorization to reward individuals for agricultural discoveries.[24]

Of all these proposals, the most important to Washington was a federally funded national university at the seat of government. We cannot be certain when he converted to the idea, but in all likelihood it was in the summer of 1787. James Madison proposed at the federal convention that Congress have the power to create one, but the body rejected the idea because delegates saw it as a threat to existing colleges within their states and because they knew Congress could establish one by virtue of its exclusive jurisdiction over the seat of government. The idea of such an institution might well have been a subject of conversation a month before the convention adjourned, when Washington visited Benjamin Rush, an advocate since at least 1786. Just before the convention agreed to its proposed Constitution, Philadelphia minister Nicholas Collin published an opinion piece suggesting a federal university as one of the best ways to break down sectional prejudice and thereby give "eternal stability" to the union. The argument would have electrified Washington, for he had seen the principle operate so well among the officers of the Continental Army during the Revolutionary War; whether or not he got it from Collin, he would use that argument over and over again for the remainder of his life.[25]

While Washington may have mentioned the creation of a national university in his undelivered inaugural, his earliest extant official recommendation came in his first annual message to Congress in 1790: "Amongst the motives to such an institution, the assimilation of the principles, opinions, and manners, of our countrymen, by the common education of a portion of our youth from every quarter, well deserves attention. The more homogeneous our citizens can be made in these particulars, the greater will be our prospect of permanent union." Like a Potomac capital, Washington saw the national university as an essential support for the union. Throughout his presidency, Washington's private and public letters continued to express his support for a federally funded university at the seat of government.[26]

In his Farewell Address, Washington called on Americans to support "Institutions for the general diffusion of knowledge." He had detailed his thoughts about a national university to Hamilton in an unsuccessful attempt to convince Hamilton to include direct mention of one in his draft of the address. Washington argued that it should be on a comprehensive scale, with arts, sciences, and belles-lettres, "but that which would render it of the highest importance, in my opinion, is, the Juvenal period of life, when friendships are formed, and habits established that will stick by one; the youth, or young men from different parts of the United States would be assembled together, and would by degree discover that there was not that cause for the jealousies and prejudices which one part of the Union had imbibed against another part." But his real farewell was his last will and testament in which, after elaborating at length on the importance of a national university, he attempted to generate funding by bequeathing his Potomac Navigation Company stock for that purpose.[27]

In the wake of the Farewell Address, Federal City Commissioner Alexander White suggested to Madison that the close of Washington's second term was a favorable time to bring the national university before Congress again. His recommendation, White argued, would make a greater impression than that of any future president or even his own at any earlier time in his presidency, as "it will be felt as the last request of a departing Friend." Washington agreed, even suggesting that a temporary campus could be constructed on the president's square, and the commissioners accordingly addressed a memorial to Congress. In response to lack of support in Congress after the memorial died in committee, Madison changed his strategy and asked the House merely to adopt legislation enabling a national university to accept donations—but even that failed, as once again congressmen saw it as a threat to colleges within their states.[28]

It would be more than half a century before Washington's contention about the constitutionality of federal support for the arts and sciences prevailed. In 1789 and 1790, the First Federal Congress declined to reward an American who claimed to have discovered a cure for rabies or to assist others attempting to produce an American road atlas or refine the means of determining longitude. Ironically, it was Thomas Jefferson who found the means to obtain federal funds for the arts and sciences when his passion for knowledge about the trans-Mississippi West got the better of his strict construction of the Constitution: a combination of the commerce and national defense clauses. Future presidents adopted Jefferson's solution, and the American continent, the Pacific Ocean, and the heavens above them were explored by military expeditions and institutions until creation of the U.S. Geological Survey in 1867. As to museums at the seat of government, Jefferson believed a constitutional amendment would be necessary, and in 1818 Congress refused to purchase Charles Willson Peale's museum. After 1836, it took almost ten years for John Quincy Adams, among others, to convince Congress of the constitutionality of accepting James Smithson's bequest for the creation of an institution for the diffusion of knowledge at Washington.[29]

By the time he became president, Washington had grown beyond his southern roots and adopted a middle states worldview that accepted cities, economic diversity, and financial capitalism as positives. Virginians, he thought, took themselves too seriously, and there seems little reason to question the veracity of the report that he would choose to be a northerner rather than a southerner if the union dissolved.[30] A businessman as well as a planter, Washington had long been operating a gristmill and major fishing enterprise at Mount Vernon but was slower to embrace manufacturing publicly. He first expressed an opinion about it in late January 1789 when he noted to his friend the Marquis de Lafayette that he did not support extravagant encouragements to manufacturing at the expense of agriculture; however, Washington further observed that while greater and more substantial improvements in manufacture were occurring in the United States than ever before, no diminution in agriculture had followed. In conclusion, he informed Lafayette that he had that very day ordered an American-made suit from a factory in Hartford, Connecticut, and hoped it would not be long until it became unfashionable for a gentleman to appear in anything but American-made clothing.[31]

The undelivered inaugural declared that Americans would not soon become a manufacturing people because men would rather work on farms than in shops; consequently, he believed Americans should continue to exchange agricultural staples for finer manufactured goods. On the other hand, many articles could be manufactured in the United States, especially if labor-saving machinery could be introduced. He left to Congress decisions about what encouragement should be given to particular branches of manufacturing.[32] Fresh from touring woolen and cotton factories in New England, Washington recommended the encouragement of domestic manufacturing and the importation of useful inventions from abroad in his first annual message in 1790. Congress's response led to Tench Coxe's and Alexander Hamilton's famous "Report on Manufactures" a year later. As with encouragement of the arts and sciences, Washington did not bring up the subject again until his final annual message. Still, the object was of too much consequence for Congress to ignore. While the federal government should refrain from interfering with private enterprise, national defense was an exception, and the president asked Congress to provide for federal manufacture of those items necessary for supplying the military when little hope existed that such items could be produced otherwise.[33]

Washington came to accept manufacturing as easily as he had long accepted agriculture. In fact, he went so far as to give encouragement to an industrial pirate willing to violate British statutes against the exportation of machinery and the emigration of skilled workers. In the fall of 1789, he forwarded to the governor of Virginia a proposal he had received from a British citizen offering to introduce the woolen manufactory to Virginia and suggesting that its need for labor would be a means by which gentlemen disposed to emancipate their slaves could do so and at the same time prepare them to be useful members of society. Warned by the attorney general and the secretary of state that as president of the United States he should not appear to be encouraging British subjects to commit a felony, Washington withdrew from the effort and left it to Virginia to act as it saw fit. In the 1790s, Washington became a manufacturer himself when he built a large distillery at Mount Vernon and converted his gristmill to a state-of-the-art automated system. Indeed, James Thomas Flexner argues, and I believe what little evidence there is supports him, that Washington saw manufacturing and other northern economic institutions as a viable alternative to a slave-based economy.[34]

George Washington is well known for participation in or command of military campaigns against American Indians during the Seven Years' War, the Revolutionary War, and the four-year war against the Northwest Indians in the 1790s. He should be equally well known for his outspoken support for Indian property rights, for his condemnation of the frontiersmen and land speculators who violated them, and for his proposals to civilize and integrate Native peoples into American society. Historian David Andrew Nichols describes the Federalist vision for the West, as established by Washington and his secretary of war, Henry Knox, as a "'great, respectable, and flourishing empire' where white and red gentlemen would lead their followers down the paths of enlightenment and civilization, until a future date when the nation could assimilate the surviving Indians as citizens."[35]

In September 1783, at the request of the congressional Committee on Indian Affairs, Washington, as commander in chief of the Continental Army, recommended several policies to Congress. First, it should inform those tribes that had allied themselves with the British "that their true Interest and safety must now depend upon our friendship," and that the United States, despite its right as the victorious nation, would not force them to retire with their European ally beyond the Great Lakes. Instead, the new nation would "draw a veil over what is past and establish a boundary line between them and us." Second, Congress should adopt a proclamation declaring it a felony for any American citizen to survey or settle beyond that line and to enforce it by strict orders to the army officers on the frontier. Less strongly, in order to stop the abusive practices of Americans trading with the Indians, Washington recommended that the federal government take over the Indian trade, thereby supplying Indians on much better terms than usually offered and fixing them "strongly in our Interest." Although the committee's report to Congress in some instances lifted sentences from Washington's letter, the state-kowtowing ordinance Congress eventually adopted bore little relation to Washington's recommendations. A year later, as a private citizen, he urged Congress to declare any person who marked, surveyed, or purchased land beyond the limits of what the United States had purchased from the Indians not only outlaws but "fit subjects for Indian vengeance."[36]

Well aware that a great opportunity had been wasted in the immediate wake of the Treaty of Paris, Washington moved quickly on Indian affairs when he assumed the presidency. On August 7, 1789—once Congress had established the first federal revenue system but before it had completed the organization of the executive and judicial branches or recommended constitutional amendments to the states—he submitted Secretary of War Henry Knox's report on Indian affairs to Congress with the admonition that "a due regard should be extended to those Indian tribes whose happiness, in the course of events, so materially depends on the national justice and humanity of the United States."[37]

Knox's opening statement was based on two premises: that the Indians possessed the right of soil and that a liberal system of justice should be adopted toward them. Indian lands should not be taken except by free consent or by conquest in a just war: "To dispossess them on any other principle would be a gross violation of the fundamental Laws of nature, and of that distributive justice which is the glory of a nation." "It is necessary that the cause of the ignorant Indians should be heard as well as those" of the frontier settlers; the public must enquire before it punishes and be influenced by reason, not resentment. "The dignity and interest" of the United States would be advanced by making the principle that the Indians have the right to the lands they possess the basis of the future administration of justice toward them. Any system of coercion and oppression would "stain the character of the nation" and, by implication, its leaders.[38]

At the conclusion of the report, Knox outlined administration policy. It called for an act declaring that the Indians possessed the right to the lands they inhabited and that they could not be dispossessed of them except with the express approbation of the United States. Indians should be considered as sovereign nations, not as subjects of a particular state, and only the United States should treat with them. "However painful . . . to consider," Knox argued, all the Indian tribes inhabiting the most populous and cultivated states had become extinct; if the United States did not alter the course of white-Indian relations, the idea of an Indian on this side of the Mississippi River would only be found on the page of the historian. The solution for the Washington administration was civilization, not extirpation: "Instead of exterminating a part of the human race" by our mode of settlement, we should impart to them our knowledge of cultivation and the arts. Admitting the difficulties and the time needed for this, Knox reflected that to deny that it could be accomplished "is to suppose the human character . . . to be incapable of melioration or change." Specifically, the federal government should assume the cost of supplying the Indians with livestock and the implements of husbandry. The established policy of giving individual Indian leaders medals to secure their loyalty should be expanded to include gifts of livestock.[39] Like most of Washington's visionary proposals, the report was not well received by House members, who ridiculed it as preachy. But as was almost always the case during his first term, congressional criticism was leveled at the department head and not the president.[40]

Washington's first opportunity to put his vision into practice was the 1790 Treaty of New York with the Creeks. It established a boundary line between the Creeks and the Georgian settlements, which the federal government guaranteed. Any American citizen who attempted to settle on Creek lands would forfeit the protection of the United States, and the Creeks could punish them as they saw fit. Article 12 promised that the federal government would provide the Creeks with domestic animals, implements of husbandry, and interpreters to instruct them in their use so that the Creek Nation "may be led to a greater degree of civilization and to become herdsmen and cultivators instead of remaining in a state of hunters." On August 14, 1790, Washington issued a proclamation calling on American citizens to obey the treaty. Two weeks later, he issued another calling for obedience to the Confederation Congress's treaties with the Cherokee, Choctaw, and Chickasaw. Georgians reacted quickly to what they called the "Knoxonian plan," asserting that it violated the rights of Georgia by nullifying the state's treaties with the Creeks. Washington was not about to be intimidated, and in March 1791 he officially declared the land speculator James O'Fallon an outlaw in violation of the treaty and the proclamations of August 1790.[41]

At the end of December 1790, the president addressed the Seneca Nation in response to several specific complaints carried to Philadelphia. He offered federal assistance with the nation's conversion to commercial agriculture, promised that any American accused of murdering an Indian would be tried and punished as if he had killed a white man, and, finally, as a sovereign nation, if the Seneca believed that they had been defrauded of any land after the ratification of the Constitution, Washington informed them that "the federal courts will be open to you for redress."[42]

In his annual messages of 1791, 1792, and 1793, all delivered during the war against the Northwest Territory tribes, Washington called on Congress to promote commerce with the Indians, impart the blessings of civilization to them, and send him a bill to sign that inflicted adequate penalties on Americans who, by committing outrages against Indians, infringed our treaties and endangered the peace of the union. After the war, in his 1795 annual message, Washington was even more adamant:

> The provisions heretofore made with a view to the protection
> of the Indians, from the violences of the lawless part of our frontier
> inhabitants are insufficient. . . . Unless the murdering of Indians
> can be restrained . . . all the exertions of the government to prevent
> destructive retaliations, by the Indians, will prove fruitless. . . .
> To enforce upon the Indians the observance of Justice, it is
> indispensable that there shall be competent means of rendering
> justice to them.[43]

In his annual message of 1793, Washington for the first time called on Congress, in effect, to enact a virtual federal monopoly of the Indian trade—the proposal he had made to the congressional committee in 1783 and which the twentieth-century historian of federal Indian policy Francis Paul Prucha would label a "pet scheme" of Washington's. The next year, Washington could not "refrain from again pressing upon your deliberations" the previously recommended plan for conducting trade with the Indians. A 1796 act established a nonprofit federal trading corporation, required Americans traveling through Indian Territory to have a passport, and provided fines and imprisonment for crimes against Indians and their property, including the death penalty for murder.[44]

Shortly before leaving the presidency, Washington articulated his vision with specific proposals and promised federal funding when, in August 1796, he addressed the Cherokee Nation. He began with recognition of the many years that had passed since the first Europeans came to America and the nearly fruitless attempts during that time to improve the conditions of the Native peoples. He observed,

> I have also thought much on this subject, and anxiously wished
> that the various Indian tribes, as well as their neighbors, the White
> people, might enjoy in abundance all the good things which make
> life comfortable and happy. I have considered how this could be
> done; and have discovered but one path that could lead them to
> that desirable situation. In this path I wish all the Indian nations
> to walk. It may seem a little difficult to enter; but if you make the
> attempt, you will find every obstacle easy to be removed.

The path he then detailed was commercial agriculture. By proper management the Cherokee could raise livestock not only for their own needs but also enough to sell. The United States would donate the necessary equipment and teachers to provide instruction in its use. He continued, "The advice I give you is . . . still more important as the event of the experiment made with you may determine the lot of many nations." If it succeeded, the United States "will be encouraged to give the same assistance to all the Indian tribes within their boundaries. But if it should fail, they may think it vain to make further attempts to better the condition of any Indian tribe." Washington concluded with a suggestion that the Cherokee look to the United States as a model for organizing their own government. Three months later, he made the same recommendation and promise of federal support to the recently defeated Northwest Indians, although in far less detail and, undoubtedly, far less hope that they would walk the agricultural path.[45]

None of Washington's immediate successors shared his passion about protecting Native Americans, but it was not until the presidency of Andrew Jackson that the federal government abandoned Washington's commitment to the policies of inclusion and Indian national sovereignty by forcing the Cherokees off the land where they, with almost inconceivable rapidity, had built the society and economy recommended to them by Washington.

Washington's journey from pre–Revolutionary War slaveholder to emancipator in his will has been investigated at length by such scholars as Dorothy Twohig, Henry Wiencek, Mary V. Thompson, and François Furstenberg among others.[46] My purpose here is not to repeat what they have written but to urge that, based on their evidence, it is time for historians to call Washington what he was—an abolitionist. Not a radical one to be sure, but an important one nonetheless, considering who he was and the public manner in which he freed his slaves. Washington heard the southern defense of slavery at the federal convention and read its violent attack on abolition during the First Federal Congress. Consequently, like almost all of the others who devoted much of their lives to the creation of the United States, he regarded slavery as the issue that most threatened the survival of the union, and like them, he shared in the consensus that it should be kept out of the national discourse. But by the end of his life, he had allegedly come to see "that nothing but the rooting out of slavery can perpetuate the existence of our union." But unlike many who agreed with him on the need for the abolition of slavery, he did not advocate African colonization in conjunction with emancipation. Instead, he believed that people freed from slavery should be educated and live in a multiracial republic.[47]

By the mid-1780s, Washington had begun to read abolitionist literature, correspond with European abolitionists, express his opposition to the institution privately, and advocate emancipation by state law. He had probably given up hope for state action by the time of the Constitutional Convention, and perhaps, like some of the other middle and northern delegates there, believed that one of the "expected glories of the Constitution" was "the abolition of slavery."[48] Just when he decided to free his own slaves is not clear but certainly before assuming the presidency in 1789. His two closest presidential aides stand witness to that. David Humphreys felt confident enough in Washington's intention to draft a paragraph on slavery, probably intended for the undelivered inaugural address. In this generally unknown and highly significant statement, Washington regretted his reliance on slave labor but committed himself to preparing the "rising generation for a destiny different from that in which they were born." In 1791, in assisting Washington to take measures to prevent his and the Custis dower slaves at the federal seat of government from seeking their freedom under the Pennsylvania abolition law, Tobias Lear boldly asserted to Washington that nothing should induce him "to prolong the slavery of a human being" had he not been aware of the president's intention to liberate them at some future period.[49]

That emancipation came at the front of a will that not only freed his slaves but also sought to provide for their care and education. In addition, and "most pointedly, and most solemnly," he enjoined his executors "to see that this clause . . . and every part thereof be religiously fulfilled . . . without evasion, neglect or delay." Washington felt such ironclad language necessary because his executors were his wife and other family members, most if not all of whom strongly opposed his decision. Fellow abolitionists on the other hand were delighted, and the will quickly became a widely read and celebrated document published as a pamphlet, in newspapers, and in almanacs, as well as in biographies and documentary editions.[50] To those who condemn Washington for not securing congressional abolition of slavery during his presidency, I recommend Steven Spielberg's *Lincoln,* a film about what a president had to do sixty years later to secure congressional adoption of an amendment abolishing slavery at a time when the union to which George Washington had devoted so much of his life establishing and maintaining had been broken.

Notes

The author would like to dedicate this essay to the memory of James C. Rees, whose commitment to George Washington and Mount Vernon inspired many.

The author would like to acknowledge the assistance of Mary Thompson, Amanda Isaac, Michele Lee, Pat Brady, Richard Kohn, David Silverman, Ted Crackel, David A. Nichols, John Gorney, Ellen Clark, Jack Warren, Helen Veit, and Chuck diGiacomantonio as this essay evolved, beginning with remarks made at the first annual George Washington University forum on George Washington in 2011 and concluding with its publication.

1. Undelivered Inaugural, W. W. Abbot et al., eds., *The Papers of George Washington: Presidential Series,* 17 vols. to date (Charlottesville, Va., 1987–), 2:152–73 (hereafter *PGW: Pres. Ser.*).

2. Rising Glory as a cause of the American Revolution has not been adequately studied by historians. One of the best accounts is the introduction to Marc Egnal's excellent *A Mighty Empire: The Origins of the American Revolution* (Ithaca, N.Y., 1988). See also James L. Cooper, "Interests, Ideas, and Empires: The Roots of American Foreign Policy, 1763–1779" (Ph.D. diss., University of Wisconsin, 1964). On empire, see Richard Van Alystyne, *Rising American Empire* (New York, 1960), and Durand Echeverria, *Mirage in the West* (Princeton, N.J., 1957).

3. John Adams to Nathan Webb, October 12, 1755, quoted in John Schutz and Douglass Adair, *The Spur of Fame* (San Marino, Calif., 1966), 80–81; John Seelye, *Beautiful Machine: Rivers and the Republican Plan, 1755–1825* (New York, 1991), 107–10; Laurens to Thomas Denham, February 7, 1775; Laurens to William Manning, September 23, 1775, both quoted in Egnal, *A Mighty Empire,* 14; Andrew Burnaby, *Travels through the Middle Settlements in North-America in the Years 1759 and 1760* (Ithaca, N.Y., 1960), 110.

4. Thomas Hutchinson, *The History of the Province of Massachusetts Bay: From 1749 to 1774, Comprising a Detailed Narrative of the Origin and Early Stages of the American Revolution* (London, 1828), quoted in Egnal, *A Mighty Empire,* 12–13; Seelye, *Beautiful Machine,* 103; Fred Anderson, *Crucible of War: The Seven Years' War and the Fate of Empire in British North America, 1754–1766* (New York, 2000), xv.

5. Kenneth R. Bowling, *The Creation of Washington, D.C.: The Idea and Location of the American Capital* (Fairfax, Va., 1991), 1; "Political Discourse, No. 9," *United States Magazine,* May 1779, 198, quoted in James D. Drake, *The Nation's Nature: How Continental Presumptions Gave Rise to the United States of America* (Charlottesville, Va., 2011), 159.

6. Geoffrey Keyes, *A Bibliography of George Berkeley Bishop of Cloyne: His Works and His Critics in the Eighteenth Century* (Oxford, 1976), indicates that the poem, although written much earlier, appeared in Berkeley's *A Miscellany, Containing Several Tracts on Several Subjects* (London and Dublin, 1752), and again in Joseph Stock, ed., *The Works of George Berkeley,* 2 vols. (Dublin, 1784). For newspaper printings of the poem, see as examples *Pennsylvania Evening Post* (Philadelphia), January 26, 1775; *United States Chronicle* (Providence, R.I.), May 20, 1784; *New Hampshire Gazette* (Portsmouth, N.H.), June 19, 1784; and *Independent Ledger* (Boston), September 6, 1784. The online database Founders Online, https://founders.archives.gov, allowed me to search the entire mass of Washington's papers for his use of the words "democracy," "democratic," "empire," "continent," "rising glory," "North America," and "California."

7. Amanda C. Isaac, *Take Note! George Washington the Reader* (Mount Vernon, Va., 2013), 83–84; Jedidiah Morse, *American Geography* (Elizabethtown, N.J., 1789), 468–69.

8. Washington had read the English translation of Le Page DuPratz, *The History of Louisiana, or the Western Parts of Carolina and Virginia* (London, 1774), but his extensive notes on the book focus on rivers flowing into the Mississippi rather than on the

vast territory itself. DuPratz did not include mention of Carolina and Virginia in the original French edition, published prior to the Seven Years' War.

9. For a few examples from dozens, see Washington to James Warren, March 3, 1779; Washington to Elias Boudinot, March 18, 1783, both Founders Online; and Washington, Undelivered Inaugural, *PGW: Pres. Ser.,* 2:161. Two references out of dozens (Washington to Samuel Phillips, August 10, 1783, Founders Online, and Washington, Undelivered Inaugural, *PGW: Pres. Ser.,* 2:163) that might be interpreted to include the trans-Mississippi West probably do not, given Washington's overwhelming usage of the word to mean the area east of the Mississippi.

10. California's borders in the late eighteenth century were undefined and the term could include all or parts of Arizona, New Mexico, Nevada, and Utah. Drake's excellent study on continental presumptions incorrectly concludes that Washington's continental consciousness extended to the Pacific; in part this is based on an unfortunate mistranscription of Washington's July 25, 1785, letter to David Humphreys. See W. W. Abbot et al., eds., *The Papers of George Washington, Confederation Series,* 6 vols. (Charlottesville, Va., 1992–97), 3:151 (hereafter *PGW: Conf. Ser.*). The correct transcription can be found at John C. Fitzpatrick, ed., *Writings of George Washington* (39 vols., Washington, 1931–44), 28:202–5 (hereafter *WGW*).

11. For a more detailed account of Potomac fever, see Bowling, *Washington, D.C.,* chap. 4, and Washington to Thomas Johnson, July 20, 1770, W. W. Abbot et al., eds., *The Papers of George Washington: Colonial Series* (Charlottesville, Va., 1983–95), 8:360.

12. Bowling, *Washington, D.C.,* chap. 4; Samuel Blodget, *Economica* (Washington, D.C., 1806), 22–23.

13. Bowling, *Washington, D.C.,* 15; George Washington to Richard H. Lee, February 8, 1785; Washington to William Grayson, June 22, 1785, *PGW: Conf. Ser.,* 3:332–33, 69.

14. Bowling, *Washington, D.C.,* 137, 174–75, 179, 194; James Madison to Washington, July 21, August 11, 24, September 14, 1788, *PGW: Conf. Ser.,* 6:392–93, 437–38, 469–70, 513–14; Madison to Washington, November 20, 1789, *PGW: Pres. Ser.,* 4:308–9; Samuel to Margaret Meredith, July 1, 1790, Charlene Bangs Bickford et al., eds., *Documentary History of the First Federal Congress, 1789–1791,* 20 vols. to date (Baltimore, 1972–), 20:2002 (hereafter *DHFFC*); Kenneth R. Bowling and Helen E. Veit, eds., *The Diary of William Maclay* (Baltimore, 1988), 308.

15. William to Catherine Few, January 25, 1791, Small Collections, Library of Congress, Washington, D.C.; Theodore Sedgwick to Ephraim Williams, January 24, 1791, Sedgwick Papers, Massachusetts Historical Society, Boston; Kenneth R. Bowling, *Peter Charles L'Enfant: Vision, Honor and Male Friendship in the Early American Republic* (Washington, D.C., 2002), 9–10; L'Enfant to Washington, September 11, 1789, *PGW: Pres. Ser.,* 4:15–17.

16. Paul Caemmerer, "The L'Enfant Memorials," in *The Life of Pierre Charles L'Enfant* (Washington, D.C., 1950), Appendix A, 361–410, 391 (quotation); Peter C. L'Enfant to Unknown, Undated Correspondence, Digges-L'Enfant-Morgan Papers, Library of Congress; Washington to the Commissioners for the Federal District, July 24, 1791, *PGW: Pres. Ser.,* 8:375; Washington to David Stuart, March 8, 1792,

PGW: Pres. Ser., 10:63–64; Washington to William Thornton, December 26, 1796, *WGW,* 35:348; Washington to James McHenry, May 6, 1798, W. W. Abbot et al., eds., *The Papers of George Washington: Retirement Series,* 4 vols. (Charlottesville, Va., 1998–99), 2:253 (hereafter *PGW: Ret. Ser.*).

17. C. M. Harris, "Washington's Gamble, L'Enfant's Dream: Politics, Design, and the Founding of the National Capital," *William and Mary Quarterly,* 3rd ser., 56 (1999): 542–54; Peter L'Enfant to Washington, August 19, 1791, *PGW: Pres. Ser.,* 8:439–47; Washington to Daniel Carroll of Rock Creek, December 16, 1793, *PGW: Pres. Ser.,* 14:526–27; Washington to the Commissioners for the Federal District, October 21, 1796, *WGW,* 35:248–50; Caemmerer, "L'Enfant Memorials," 389. See Don Alexander Hawkins, "Unbuilt Washington: The View George Washington Rejected," *Washington History* 25 (2013): 53–54, for an explanation of Washington's insistence that the President's House be moved west and north of L'Enfant's original location.

18. Bowling, *Washington, D.C.,* 221; Washington to the Commissioners for the Federal District, May 7, 1791, *PGW: Pres. Ser.,* 8:158–59.

19. Thomas Jefferson to Peter C. L'Enfant, April 10, 1791, Julian P. Boyd et al., eds., *The Papers of Thomas Jefferson,* 44 vols. to date (Princeton, N.J., 1950–), 20:80; Caemmerer, "L'Enfant Memorials," 372, 381, 391.

20. Washington to Daniel Carroll of Duddington, November 28, 1791, *PGW: Pres. Ser.,* 9:235–36; Washington to David Stuart, March 8, 1792, *PGW: Pres. Ser.,* 10:64; Washington to the Commissioners for the Federal District, October 21, 1796, March 2, 1797, *WGW,* 35:249, 413.

21. Kenneth R. Bowling, "From 'Federal Town' to 'National Capital': Ulysses S. Grant and the Reconstruction of Washington, D.C.," *Washington History* 14 (2002): 8–25; *American Architect* 10 (1881): 304; Washington to Sally Fairfax, May 16, 1798, *PGW: Ret. Ser.,* 2:273.

22. Isaac, *Take Note!* 4, 81.

23. Washington, Undelivered Inaugural, *PGW: Pres. Ser.,* 2:170, 172; Washington to Matthew Carey, June 25, 1788, *PGW: Conf. Ser.,* 6:355.

24. Washington, First Annual Message, January 8, 1790, *PGW: Pres. Ser.,* 4:545; John Page, speech, *Gazette of the United States,* May 5, 1790, *DHFFC,* 13:1211; Washington, Eighth Annual Message, December 7, 1796; Washington to Timothy Pickering, July 21, 1797, *WGW,* 35:314–17, 508–9.

25. Max Farrand, ed., *The Records of the Federal Convention of 1787,* 4 vols. (New Haven, Conn., 1937), 2:321, 325, 616, 620, 3:122, 362, 609; *DHFFC,* 8:7; Donald Jackson and Dorothy Twohig, eds., *The Diaries of George Washington,* 6 vols. (Charlottesville, Va., 1976–79), 5:178; Benjamin Rush to Richard Price, May 25, 1786, "A Plan for a Federal University"; Rush, "An Address to the People of the United States," *American Museum,* January 1787, 10–12; Rush to John Adams, June 15, 1789, Lyman H. Butterfield, ed., *Letters of Benjamin Rush,* 2 vols. (Princeton, N.J., 1951), 1:388, 491–95, 517; Nicholas Collin, "Foreign Spectator," *Independent Gazetteer* (Philadelphia), September 13, 1787. The best coverage of the issue is in David Madsden, *National University, Enduring Dream of the USA* (Detroit, 1966).

26. Washington, First Annual Message, January 8, 1790, *PGW: Pres. Ser.,* 4:545; Washington, Eighth Annual Message, December 7, 1796; Washington to John Adams, November 15, 1794; Washington to Edmund Randolph, December 15, 1794; Washington to the Commissioners for the Federal District, January 28, 1795; Washington to Thomas Jefferson, March 15, 1795; Washington to Robert Brooke, March 16, 1795, *WGW,* 35:316–17; 34:22–23, 59–60, 106–7, 146–49, 149–51.

27. Washington to Alexander Hamilton, September 1, 6, 1796, Farewell Address, *WGW,* 35:199–200, 204, 230; Washington, Last Will and Testament, July 9, 1799, *PGW: Ret. Ser.,* 4:481–83. For Hamilton's argument that the topic should be reserved for the final annual message, see Harold C. Syrett et al., eds., *The Papers of Alexander Hamilton,* 27 vols. (New York, 1961–87), 20:316, 317–18.

28. Alexander White to James Madison, September 26, 1796; White to Madison, December 2, 1796; Madison, Speech in the House, December 12, 1796, J. C. A. Stagg et al., eds., *The Papers of James Madison: Congressional Series,* 17 vols. (Charlottesville, Va., 1962–91), 16:401–2, 421–22, 425–26; Washington to the Commissioners of the Federal District, October 21, 1796, *WGW,* 35:248–49; Memorial, November 21, 1796, *American State Papers: Miscellaneous* (Washington, D.C., 1834), 1:153–54; Madsden, *National University,* 34–37.

29. *DHFFC,* 8:8–27; Thomas Jefferson to Charles Willson Peale, January 16, 1802, Boyd et al., eds., *Papers of Thomas Jefferson,* 36:385–86; Charles Willson Peale to Jefferson, January 1, 1819; Charles Willson Peale to Rembrandt Peale, January 6, 1819, Lillian B. Miller et al., eds., *Selected Papers of Charles Willson Peale and His Family,* 5 vols. (New Haven, Conn., 1983–96), 3:634, 673, 683; "Our History," Smithsonian Institution, https://www.si.edu/about/history.

30. George Washington to Bushrod Washington, November 9, 1787, *PGW: Conf. Ser.,* 5:422; Jefferson, Notes of a Conversation with Edmund Randolph, [after 1795], Boyd et al., eds., *Papers of Thomas Jefferson,* 28:568.

31. Washington to Lafayette, January 29, 1789, *PGW: Pres. Ser.,* 1:263–64.

32. Washington, Undelivered Inaugural, *PGW: Pres. Ser.,* 2:170–71.

33. Jackson and Twohig, eds., *Diaries of George Washington,* entries for Oct. 20, 21, 30, 5:468–69, 485; Washington, First Annual Message, January 8, 1790, *PGW: Pres. Ser.,* 4:545; Washington, Eighth Annual Message, December 7, 1796, *WGW,* 35:315.

34. Thomas Howells to Washington, July 14, 1789; Washington to Beverley Randolph, January 13, 1791, *PGW: Pres. Ser.,* 3:192–96, 7:225–28; James Thomas Flexner, *George Washington, Anguish and Farewell* (Boston, 1969), 9.

35. David Andrew Nichols, *Red Gentlemen and White Savages: Indians, Federalists, and the Search for Order on the American Frontier* (Charlottesville, Va., 2008), 201. Susan Sleeper-Smith's *Indigenous Prosperity and the American Conquest* (Chapel Hill, N.C., 2018) was published after this essay was written. While providing a badly needed explanation of the critical economic role of Native women in the Ohio River Valley, which she credits Washington with recognizing, her treatment of his involvement is as commander in chief during wartime and allows the author to ignore his role as related in this essay. Colin Calloway's comprehensive and monumental *The Indian World of*

George Washington: The First President, the First Americans and the Birth of the Nation (New York, 2018)—also published after this essay was written—gives Indians their proper importance in the early American republic and establishes how much Washington's life was interwoven with them. Calloway states that Washington's Indian policies as president were arrogant, hypocritical, and deceitful. I disagree with his assessment that "Washington's dealings with Indian people and their land do him little credit" (13).

36. Washington to James Duane, Chairman of the Committee on Indian Affairs, September 7, 1783, *WGW,* 27:133–40; Report of the Committee on Indian Affairs, October 15, 1783, Gaillard Hunt, ed., *Journals of the Continental Congress, 1774–1789,* 34 vols. (Washington, D.C., 1904–37), 25:681–94; Washington to Jacob Read, November 3, 1784, *PGW: Conf. Ser.,* 2:120.

37. Message from the President, August 7, 1789, *DHFFC,* 5:1002; Henry Knox to Washington, June 15, July 7, 1789, *PGW: Pres. Ser.,* 2:490–95, 3:134–41.

38. Report of the Secretary of War, August 7, 1789, *DHFFC,* 5:1003–7, 1116–21.

39. Ibid. Knox repeated some of these arguments in his report on the frontiers that Washington submitted to Congress on December 30, 1794.

40. Jeremiah Wadsworth, Speech in the House, January 2, 1793, *Annals of Congress, Second Congress* (Washington, D.C., 1849), 744.

41. Treaty of New York, August 13, 1790, *DHFFC,* 2:241–50; Washington, Proclamations [August 14 and 26, 1790; March 19, 1791], *PGW: Pres. Ser.,* 6:248, 342, 7:605–6; "Meeting of the Combined Society," *Augusta* (Georgia) *Chronicle,* September 25, 1790; "Metellus," *Augusta Chronicle,* November 6, 1790; "A Correspondent Observes," *Gazette of the United States* (Philadelphia), November 6, 1790.

42. Washington to the Seneca Chiefs, [December 29, 1790], *PGW: Pres. Ser.,* 7:146.

43. Washington, Third Annual Message, October 25, 1791; Washington, Fourth Annual Message, November 6, 1792; Washington, Fifth Annual Message, December 3, 1793, *PGW: Pres. Ser.,* 9:111–12, 11:344–45, 14:465–66; Washington, Seventh Annual Message, December 8, 1795, *WGW,* 34:391.

44. Washington, Fifth Annual Message, December 3, 1793, *PGW: Pres. Ser.,* 14:466; Francis Paul Prucha, *Indian Peace Medals in American History* (Madison, Wis., 1971); Washington, Sixth Annual Message, November 19, 1794, *WGW,* 34:36; Nichols, *Red Gentlemen and White Savages,* 176–77.

45. Washington to the Cherokee Nation, August 29, 1796; Washington to the . . . Representatives of the Wyandots, Delawares, Shawanoes, Ottawas, Chippewas, Potawatimes, Miamis, Eel River, Weeas, Kickapoos, Piankashaws, and Kaskaskias, [November 29, 1796], *WGW,* 35:193–98, 301.

46. See, for example, Henry Wiencek, *An Imperfect God: George Washington, His Slaves, and the Creation of America* (New York, 2003); Mary V. Thompson, "'They Appear to Live Comfortable Together': Private Lives of Mount Vernon Slaves," in *Slavery at the Home of George Washington,* ed. Philip J. Schwarz (Mount Vernon, Va., 2001), 79–109; Dorothy Twohig, "'That Species of Property': Washington's Role in the Controversy over Slavery," in *George Washington Reconsidered,* ed. Don Higginbotham (Charlottesville, Va., 2001), 114–38; and Fritz Hirschfeld, *George Washington and Slavery:*

A Documentary Portrayal (Columbia, Mo., 1997). Although this essay was completed before Mary V. Thompson published her unrivaled *"The Only Subject of Regret": George Washington, Slavery, and the Enslaved Community at Mount Vernon* (Charlottesville, Va., 2019), I had access to two of her articles as well as several conversations with her.

47. *DHFFC*, 12:283–92, 306–13, 724–832; conversation with John Bernard, quoted in Hirschfeld, *Washington and Slavery*, 78.

48. Twohig, "That Species of Property," 122; George Clymer to Benjamin Rush, June 18, 1789, John P. Kaminski et al., eds., *The Documentary History of the Ratification of the Constitution*, 34 vols. to date (Madison, Wis., 1976–), 16:804; François Furstenberg, "Atlantic Slavery, Atlantic Freedom: George Washington, Slavery and Transatlantic Abolitionist Networks," *William and Mary Quarterly*, 3rd ser., 68 (2011): 247–86.

49. Rosemarie Zagarri, ed., *David Humphrey's "Life of General Washington"* (Athens, Ga., 1991), 78; Tobias Lear to Washington, April 24, 1791, *PGW: Pres. Ser.*, 8:132.

50. Washington, Last Will and Testament, July 9, 1799, *PGW: Ret. Ser.*, 4:480–81, 491; Wiencek, *Imperfect God*, 354–55, 358; François Furstenberg, *In the Name of the Father* (New York, 2006), 84–88.

4   Agrarian Founders

Three "Rebellions" as Legitimate Opposition, 1786–1799

PAUL DOUGLAS NEWMAN

In 1813, as the Republicans and Federalists battled during the British invasion, two ex-presidents debated the political "terrorism" of the 1790s. Thomas Jefferson blamed Federalists. There was no denying "the sensations excited in free yet firm minds, by the terrorism of the day . . . and they were felt by one party only." John Adams retorted that Republicans "never felt the Terrorism of Chaises Rebellion in Massachusetts . . . the Terrorism of Gallatin's Insurrection in Pensilvania," or "the Terrorism of Fries's most outrageous Riot and Rescue." Adams then voiced his fears during wartime and knew whom to blame: "Both Parties have excited artificial Terrors and if I were summoned . . . to say upon . . . which Party had excited . . . the most terror, and which had really felt the most," Adams said, "Put Them in a bagg and shake them, and then see which comes out first."[1]

Adams had a point. For all of the continued partisanship of the "Jeffersonian" age from 1800 to 1813—the heated elections of 1800 and 1804, Aaron Burr's duplicitousness, the stresses of the embargo, and even the Hartford Convention—none of this equaled the "Age of Federalism" from 1786 to 1799 when "rebellion" surfaced again and again and again. The obvious question is why, and one obvious answer is that Jeffersonians eschewed the taxes that drew resistance. But perhaps another answer exists within the resisters themselves? Historians of Shays's, the Whiskey, and Fries's Rebellions have occasionally made brief comparisons to the others, and one even broadened his scope to include Gabriel Prosser's Rebellion, but none have squarely sought to compare all three events. This essay attempts the comparison to show the remarkable continuity of agrarian revolutionary ideology and action produced by their proximity to the Revolution in time and the immediacy of the future it portended. They shared the Revolution as a lived experience; indeed, in their minds they were still living it, fighting politically for a rapidly impending future for themselves and their children.[2]

In the days between Shays's and Fries's Rebellions, the parties were those of Jefferson and Hamilton, two founders whose hopes and fears for America's future seem diametrically opposed. Hamilton and many Federalists of 1787 and the 1790s hoped for a neo-mercantilist manufacturing future in which a powerful, centralizing, and executive-centered government won the allegiance of powerful and speculative individuals and nations through the creation of an assumed and funded national debt, redeemed at par with hard currency taxes coerced from original holders—if necessary—by a standing army. Hamilton feared the people, whose individual needs and desires might deny national prosperity, independence, and a distant future, and he demanded deference.[3]

Thomas Jefferson's Republicans, many former Antifederalists, rallied around the Constitution to subvert executive aggrandizement by demanding a balanced government. They feared the decay of virtue, the premature aging of the republic, and the demise of liberty and independence at the hands of Hamiltonianism. As for democracy, Jefferson remarked in an 1816 letter to Samuel Kercheval concerning the future of the commonwealth of Virginia, "I am not among those who fear the people. They, and not the rich, are our dependence for continued freedom. And to preserve their independence, we must not let our rulers load us with perpetual debt. We must make our election between *economy and liberty,* or *profusion and servitude.*" Republicans—many of whom as Antifederalists had opposed the adoption of the federal Constitution in 1787–88 or clamored for amendments—constructed their party as defenders of a "sacred" Constitution to identify themselves as a legitimate and loyal opposition. Lance Banning referred to this as the "Apotheosis of the Constitution."[4]

Yet in his letter to Kercheval, Jefferson admitted that at the founding, "our inexperience of self-government, occasioned gross departures in that draught from genuine republican canons." Thus, Virginia's and the U.S. government contained many unrepublican features, including upper houses and executives not elected by the people and appointed constabulary, judicial, and military officials. Indeed, Jefferson wrote, Americans had not yet penetrated to "the mother principle," that "governments are republican only in proportion as they embody the will of their people, and execute it."

Jefferson set out the desirability of a system from the bottom up based on the concept of the "ward republic," a township-like division that gives authority to a county, which gives authority to a state. Such a structure would make "every citizen an acting member of the government." The ward republican was an agrarian, the virtuous "yeoman farmer," who would claim his due proportion of political agency and guarantee an agrarian future in which the republic would age slowly and retain its independence and democratic-republican character for generations to come.[5]

Caught between the more distant futures of the Hamilton-Jefferson debate were the farmers of Massachusetts, the Upper Ohio River, and Pennsylvania's Lehigh Valley—some of America's agrarian founders. They represented quite different people. Shaysites in 1786–87 were town-dwelling Yankee mixed farmers, descendants of seventeenth-century Puritan migrants still emerging from revolutionary service and a depression. Around the Upper Ohio between 1791 and 1794, excise opponents were mainly Scots-Irish Presbyterians from Pennsylvania's and Virginia's backcountry, still fighting the Revolution's Indian war while growing and distilling corn and rye for eastern markets. In eastern Pennsylvania, direct tax protesters in 1798–99 were second- and third-generation German American (and German-speaking) farmers of wheat, barley, and oats who supported the Revolution and challenged their Quaker and Moravian Federalist leaders for local offices, citing their "Toryism."

While local conditions account for key differences, these groups shared remarkable similarities. For each the future was more immediate than for the likes of Hamilton or Jefferson. Their revolutionary legacy was the one they were living and meant to bequeath to their children with improved prospects for political liberty and economic independence. What bound these "rebellions" together were the hopes for this progression and their not-unfounded fear that some in state and national government meant to curtail this legacy. They voiced these hopes and fears by their opposition to centralized funding schemes, money and land speculation, and militarization; by their democratic mobilization; and by their agendas for reform. They each sought to "regulate" the governments *they* had created. Massachusetts Yankees called themselves "Regulators," resurrecting the prerevolutionary moniker donned by North Carolinian court closers. The "Whiskey Rebels" referred to themselves as the "Citizens of the Western Country" (though a minority advocating independent statehood styled themselves "Westsylvanians"), and they featured a prominent North Carolina Regulator among them: Herman Husband. Lehigh Valley resisters identified themselves as "The People" or the *Kirchenleute* (the patriotic Church People who had served in the War of Independence) and wore their militia uniforms or revolutionary regimentals to prove the point. All of them, even the Westsylvanians, set out to regulate the governments they had empowered.[6]

We can hear their voices through their recorded words and actions culled from three distinct phases common to each movement: petition writing and local organization, demonstration and tax resistance, and the use of the militia. Each voiced a loyal and legitimate opposition based in a shared commitment to constitutional government, and each questioned the legitimacy of the new regimes by measuring those governments against the standard of democratic participation and government responsiveness that the protesters identified with the Revolution itself. Massachusetts farmers demanded constitutional reform, and western and eastern Pennsylvania farmers demonstrated the "Apotheosis" of the Constitution by their resistance. In the end, what each group demanded was their political liberty and economic independence, and they meant to use the former to secure the latter. In the process, those regimes stained them with the shameful epithets of "Terrorism" and "Rebellion" when in truth they were democratic citizens who voiced a "popular constitutionalism."[7] As a participant in Shays's Rebellion wrote,

> We have Lately Emerged from a bloody War, in which Liberty was the Glorious prize aimed at; I Early Stepped forth in the Defence of this Country, & Cheerfully fought to gain this prize; and Liberty is Still the object I have in view when . . . I stepped forth . . . to oppose the Setting of the Court of Common pleas and general sessions of the peace. . . . I had no intention to Destroy the Publick Government but to have those Courts suspended . . . waiting to have redress of our grievances in a Constitutional way.[8]

Adam Wheeler made this public statement in Hubbardston, Middlesex County, Massachusetts, in November 1786. Earlier that year, the Massachusetts General Court, operating under the Massachusetts Constitution of 1780 and over-representative of Boston, had passed legislation to redeem state securities at par through hard-money taxes on land. Bostonians held 80 percent of the debt, 40 percent gripped in the hands of thirty-five men who either "served in the State House or were related to those who did."[9]

The men who would petition, organize, and make up the armed "Regulation" of the state of Massachusetts had recently emerged from the Revolution. While not all the participants were veterans of the American Revolution, Leonard L. Richards estimates that "the bulk of the population—85 percent or more—[were] eking out a living on small farms," and that "soldiers of the Revolution were ten times as likely to bear arms in behalf of the Regulation than in behalf of the state." That state paid soldiers for their militia service with paper money, and once back on their farms, vets used state paper currency. Hard currency was scarce during and after the war.[10]

In the spring of 1786, the towns of Athol and Acton petitioned the General Court for redress of grievances. Acton petitioners bemoaned "the Present Scarcity of money" and prayed "that the Strictest economy may be . . . Practiced in the Conduct of all our public affairs . . . [and] the General Court removed from the town of Boston to some convenient place in the Country." Athol townspeople wanted "men Chosen by the Towns" to administer the tax. Both demanded lower salaries for government officials, lowered fees for the collection of taxes, and the enactment of tender laws for in-kind payment of all debts. As historian Richards has made clear, petitioners were mostly middling farmers, not impoverished debtors, but they certainly feared poverty and tenancy. A petition from the town of Conway evinced this fear: "The mortgage of our farms—we cannot think of, with any degree of complacency. . . . To be tenants to landlords . . . and pay rents for lands, purchased with our money and converted from howling wilderness, into fruitful fields by the sweat of our brow, seems to carry with it in its nature truly shocking consequences." The towns called the counties to hold conventions to draft petitions and to call for a new state constitution. The constitution of 1780 granted that "the people have a right in an orderly and peaceful manner, to assemble and consult upon the common good, give instruction to their representatives, and to request of the legislative body . . . redress of wrongs done them and of the grievances they suffer; and the people alone have an incontestable, unalienable, and indefeasible right to institute government, and to reform, alter, or totally change the same when their protection, safety, prosperity, and happiness require it." The petitions demanded abolition of the upper house, expanded and equal representation in the lower house, annual elections, and abolition of the Court of Common Pleas and General Sessions replaced by local and elected justices.[11]

By the end of the summer, petitioning turned to regulation, first at the Hampshire County Court at Northampton. There, Luke Day and his militia "associated" themselves in writing as "Regulators" and petitioned the County Court stating, "We find sundry laws enacted by the Legislature . . . inconsistent with the principles of the Constitution and that . . . we consider ourselves to have a constitutional Right to protest. . . . We intreat your Honours to forbear doing any business . . . until . . . this county can have an opportunity of having their Grievances redressed by the General Court."[12] Just twelve years earlier, patriot communities and militia units associated to protest the Intolerable Acts in what associators perceived to be a legitimate political opposition to unconstitutional parliamentary legislation. Many Regulators had been revolutionary associators and soldiers in the War for Independence and were much more likely to join an association than to assist the state in 1786. Yet their association under the name "Regulators" was purposeful, signaling their intention to democratically restrain the unresponsive government rather than overturn it, even while preventing government operation. The "business" the Regulators sought to "forbear" was foreclosure procedures against tax delinquents that would strip them of their farms, all to pay the speculators in state securities.[13]

Soon thereafter Governor James Bowdoin summoned the militia, proclaiming the Northampton closing "a large concourse of people . . . many of whom were armed with guns, swords . . . with drums beating and fifes playing, in contempt and open defiance of the authority of this Government." A similar scene shut the Worcester court, where John Severance "addressed the people and told them they had more reason to rise against the authority of the state than we ever had against Great B." The following week at Concord, Captain Job Shattuck led the closing of the Middlesex court. The next day at Great Barrington, General John Paterson called for supporters and opponents among his troops to move to separate sides of the street: "About 150 or 200 men appeared for the Courts sitting & Seven or eight hundred men were against it." They drew up a document for the judges to sign pledging to adjourn and then "proceeded to the Gaol broke open the door, set the confined debtors at liberty." Yet there was no violence at these court closings as the leaders maintained control of their militia.[14]

Nevertheless, the General Court passed a Riot Act indemnifying officials for killing "rioters" and authorizing a forfeiture of "all their lands." It then passed a Militia Act pronouncing that any militiaman who took up arms in the court closings "shall suffer death." Finally, it suspended the writ of habeas corpus. Meanwhile, Bowdoin failed to convince his own state militia to enforce the act—most joined the Regulation—so he took subscriptions from wealthy Bostonians to hire a mercenary army from neighboring states to disband the "rebel militia." He placed General Benjamin Lincoln at its head. All this added to the Regulators' grievances, especially as some, including Job Shattuck, found themselves arrested and hauled across the state from Worcester to Boston for process. This also led to a showdown at the U.S. Arsenal in Springfield on January 25, 1787, where one of Daniel Shays's men was heard to say that the "Government meant to enslave this generation but he'd be damn'd if he thought they could do it!"[15]

When Captains Luke Day and Daniel Shays called out their militia to meet General Lincoln's army and protect the national armory from the mercenaries, Dean Lyon of Westfield said "he set out for Liberty & meant to pursue it till he obtained it." Another Regulator, Captain Joseph Harvey, though a member of the General Court, said, "He was not under oath to support injustice, & that the Doing of the Genl. Court in respect to the Public Securities was upholding injustice, & no way better than highway Robbery." Having a state assemblyman join their ranks seemed to provide a constitutional legitimacy to the Regulators' view of themselves, but so too did their own use of petition, constitutional arguments, assembly, and the militia in nonviolent delaying actions. Day and Shays mobilized these men and marched them to Springfield not to violently confront Bowdoin's mercenaries but to prevent the arms in the federal arsenal from falling into the hands of the constitutionally illegitimate army.[16]

Lincoln's army was in Worcester, while General William Shepard held Springfield. On January 20, Shepard worried to Governor Bowdoin that "acts of violence are threatened" and the next morning reported that "One of Day's Sentries wounded two of my men last night with a bayonet." On January 24, Shepard wrote that Day had a force of 800 in West Springfield, while Shays had 1,200 in Wilbraham, and "I am threatened with an attack hourly with a force much superior to mine as they exceed two thousand." Those close to Shays knew better. Ensign Israel Gates "said there would be no fighting, a majority of people would be for the mob." Likewise, Captain

James Shaw suggested that Lincoln would appear to treat with Shays and that "the people must turn out with Shays or they would have no share in the honor, that there was no danger of fighting." In fact, before dawn on the 25th, Shays penned a letter to Lincoln saying that he was "unwilling to be any way accessory to the shedding of Blood and Greatly Desirous of Restoring Peace," and requested an indemnity for all participants in "the Late Risings of the People" until the government answered their grievances and released the Boston prisoners. If granted, the "people now in arms in Defence of their Lives and Liberties will Quietly Return to their respective habitations patiently Waiting and hoping for a Constitutional Relief from the Insupportable Burdens they now Labour under." The letter did not reach Lincoln, and hours later General Shepard marched his troops to the arsenal.[17]

Later that morning, Shepard ordered his canon, filled with grape shot, to fire into the middle of Shays's line. Three men died instantly, and this "put the whole column in utmost confusion" as Shays's men fled pell-mell. According to Shepard, the three deceased men's muskets "were all deeply loaded," yet "there was not a single musket fired on either side." This fact, combined with the letter Shays penned that morning and his troops' statements that they in no way expected to see fighting at Springfield, make clear that Shays had no intention of overthrowing the government, and, despite the words and actions of some hotheads, his men were generally surprised to have been fired upon. They sought to protect the national armory, seek redress of grievances, petition the government, and initiate a new constitutional convention. Lincoln's army pursued and subdued scores of Regulators in the ensuing weeks. The government held trials; a new governor issued pardons; two lesser fish hanged; thousands, including Shays, disappeared to Vermont. The Regulation fizzled but not before they had espoused clear republican principles, established extralegal republican institutions, and framed their resistance beneath the banner of "constitutionalism."[18]

No less a figure than Alexander Hamilton used the specter of Shays's Rebellion in the *Federalist Papers* to advocate for a centralized federal republic, with a standing army capable of suppressing "actual insurrections and rebellions." Then as secretary of the treasury, he composed his report on public credit that led to the assumption plan, a national debt combining state and national securities, funded indefinitely by excise and customs duties, and the creation of the Bank of the United States to manage it all. Popular resistance to the "Funding System's" incursions on liberty was as immediate as Thomas Jefferson's opposition in the cabinet as national parties began to emerge.[19]

A representative body of six Upper Ohio counties of Pennsylvania and Virginia, meeting at Parkinson's Ferry in August 1794, charged that "the taking of citizens of the United States from their respective vicinage, to be tried for real or supposed offenses, is a violation of the rights of citizens, is a dangerous and forced construction of the Constitution, and ought not under any pretense whatever, to be exercised by the judicial authority."[20] They were protesting warrants for excise violators returnable to Philadelphia, hundreds of miles away. At a 1794 liberty pole in Northumberland County, a Pennsylvanian named "Stockman" said, "The Excise Law was dangerous and oppressive & permitting [it] to exist would be the cause of other taxes, more oppression." The Congress who passed it were "a lot of Damned Rascals," and "he told them there was a regular mode of redress by the constitution. . . . They had petitioned but could get no redress, that they would have a land tax & then all would be regular." Before erecting the pole, the crowd procured "silk for the flag" on which "they put Liberty, Equality of Rights, a Change of Ministry, and No Excise." When challenged on the "Change of Ministry" slogan aimed at George Washington, one participant said that "the President might kiss his backside." Like their Massachusetts counterparts to the north, western Pennsylvanians were still in pursuit of liberty after the Revolution, even after the adoption of the federal Constitution. For them, as for the Shaysites, taxes were but one threat among many to their liberty.[21]

Why would outraged taxpayers in Pennsylvania, mobilizing against a 1791 federal excise on whiskey, mount a "rebellion" against the U.S. government after seeing what Massachusetts had done to the Shaysites, with two executed and thousands forced to flee their homes never to return? For one thing, they sought to regulate a different government, one in which they had local champions for the reforms they sought, such as Senator Albert Gallatin, Representative William Findley, District Judge Alexander Addison, and local lawyer Hugh Henry Brackenridge. For another, they also had the Bill of Rights, especially the First Amendment guarantee of free speech, assembly, and petition that they thought would make the difference. Moreover, it was their own William Findley who had opposed the Constitution's undemocratic character at the Constitutional Convention and pushed for a bill of rights during the state ratification process. Like the Massachusetts

Regulators, they thought they had constitutional rights and protections, and that through democratic mobilization they could assert those rights and regulate a government that sought to aggrandize its resources through taxation for redistribution to wealthy eastern speculators in public securities.

By 1790, the Forks of the Ohio was home to about a thousand settlers, and they sat in the middle of a population of about seventy thousand corn and rye farmers in the Upper Ohio drainage of western Pennsylvania and northwestern Virginia. Most were descendants of a wave of Scots-Irish Presbyterian immigrants from the middle third of the eighteenth century. Their forebears—some from the colony of Pennsylvania, others from Virginia—had engaged resident Indians in a vicious, decade-long war when they poured into the region after the fall of Fort Duquesne in 1758. They continued the war with the Indians for the Ohio Country during the Revolution and into the decade that followed. Meanwhile, just before the American Revolution, during the 1774 "Dunmore's War," they had battled one another over which colony would govern them: Virginia or Pennsylvania. From 1775 to 1783, they made three attempts to become a separate colony, then state (and some even envisioned a nation) of "Westsylvania." King, Parliament, the Continental Congress, and finally the state of Pennsylvania quashed these attempts.[22]

Because the U.S. government had failed to negotiate with Spain the right to navigate the Mississippi through New Orleans, Upper Ohio farmers had to ship their grain overland to Philadelphia to market, a long and costly journey. Some farmers held title to their lands from Pennsylvania, others farmed as squatters, and still more were tenants to local or distant landlords. Great tracts of land in their midst stood unimproved, held by land speculators waiting for the frontier Indian War to end for the market to turn upward. Almost none shipped grain out of the region; instead, they distilled it into whiskey to increase its value and absorb the cost of shipping. By 1790, the Upper Ohio was home to 25 percent of the nation's stills, between 1,200 and 1,300. Most farmers did not own a still, and thus paid half of their grain as the price for distillation. The excise created two classes of stills, but three taxable classes. The first class was the large distillers, with stills measuring in the hundreds of gallons of capacity. They could pay a flat annual rate and reduce the proportion of their tax by increasing production, which also drove down prices by increasing supply. The largest capacity distillery in the country belonged to none other than George Washington and operated on his Mount Vernon estate. The man who signed the Excise Act into law stood to be its biggest beneficiary. The second class included small distillers who paid a tax by the gallon. For them, the regressive tax inhibited increased production. To cover their costs, they charged higher prices for distillation to those without stills, passing the burden downward to what amounted to a third, and most numerous and most economically tenuous, class.[23]

Meanwhile, the frontier Indian war reignited by the American Revolution raged on; between 1783 and 1790, Delaware, Shawnee, and Seneca Indians killed, wounded, or captured 1,500 settlers in the Upper Ohio Valley and took more than 2,000 horses. The U.S. government pushed the settlement line southwest through purchases at the Treaties of Forts Stanwix and McIntosh in 1784 and north from Pittsburgh with the Treaty of Fort Harmar in 1789. But by 1794, the government had still not allowed settlers to move onto the "Erie Triangle" tract. Over that period, historian Thomas P. Slaughter has estimated that the national government devoted over five-sixths of its operating budget to a western war with Ohio, Miami, and Maumee Valley Indians but ineptly misspent it in one debacle after another, staffed by western volunteers who were ill-trained and ill-equipped. As late as March 1794, for example, General Anthony Wayne complained that his men could not see or hear to fight because "the hats [supplied] are very little better than stiffened blankets which when the least wet droops over the ears and eyes of the men." Settlers and Indians continued to attack one another around the Forks of the Ohio through 1794. For western Pennsylvanians, the first key to their liberty was the ethnic cleansing of the land from the Forks north to Lake Erie and west across Ohio, and after that the opening of the Mississippi to their trade. This was the backdrop to the resistance to the excise, which funded a debt held by easterners instead of paying for a professional army capable of defeating the Indians and opening the land. Threats to western life and liberty were immediate yet seemingly ignored by easterners. Of course, conversely, threats to Indian life and liberty were greater still.[24]

Resistance to the excise began when the Pennsylvania legislature passed a resolution on June 22, 1791, to instruct its U.S. senators to oppose the excise bill because it was "on principle subversive of peace, liberty and the rights of the citizens." The bill passed over the opposition of western Pennsylvania senator William Findley, but the leading citizens of Allegheny, Washington, Fayette, and Westmoreland Counties met on September 7 at Pittsburgh and drafted a number of resolutions airing their grievances to the Pennsylvania legislature and U.S. Congress. First, they condemned the funding scheme as "hasty strides" toward "all that is unjust and oppressive," noting particularly "the exorbitant salaries of officers; . . . unreasonable interest of the public debt" that makes "no discriminations between the original holders [soldiers and farmers] and the transferees [speculators]" and constitutes "a capital of nearly eighty millions of dollars in the hands of a few; . . . the act of establishing a National Bank"; and "the excise," which "will discourage agriculture . . . and fall heavy . . . upon the western part." They further railed against speculators and argued for a tax on unimproved lands. Washington County offered a resolution to treat excise officials "with contempt," but the committee declined. The day before, sixteen Washington men dressed as women attacked excise man Robert Johnson, shaved his head, and gave him a liberty jacket of tar and feathers—a replay of "Skimmington" treatments the Sons of Liberty had doled out in the 1760s and 1770s.[25]

In 1792, the same committee wrote a remonstrance against the structure of the excise arguing that "the circumstances of our agriculture, our want of markets, and the scarcity of a circulating medium . . . will bring immediate distress and ruin on the Western Country. We think it our duty to persist . . . in every other legal measure that may obstruct the operation of the law until we . . . obtain its total repeal." The group then named a committee of correspondence to warn any who may "accept offices for the collection of the duty . . . we will consider such persons as unworthy of our friendship . . . and upon all occasions treat them with that contempt they deserve." They added that the tax "operates in proportion to the number and not to the wealth of the people." They again demanded a progressive tax on improved and unimproved lands. Similarly, at a liberty pole raising, a protester proclaimed that "they had petitioned but could get no redress, that they would have a land tax & then all would be regular." These words and actions were all deeply rooted in the "Spirit of '76."[26]

In July, Washington County residents busied themselves forming associations, pledging noncompliance, and warning excise officials. General John Neville—a large distiller, nexus of a web of military contractors, and excise official for Washington County—advertised his headquarters as a public house, "The Sign of the President's Head." Public houses in the eighteenth century frequently identified themselves to their clientele by using signs without words, usually painted symbols such as an oak tree or two foxes or the like. In this case, the signboard featured a cameo silhouette of

George Washington's profile. Soon after, the so-called Mingo Creek militia, "painted as Indians," surrounded William Faulkner's tavern and "filled with bullet holes . . . the sign of the President's head," in effect executing the effigy of President Washington. Washington County associators were simultaneously battling invading and peaceful Indians while General Arthur St. Clair waged a losing effort in Ohio. Earlier, Fayette associators with "blackened faces" burned the home of official William Wells, while Washingtonians burned General Neville in effigy. By painting themselves "as Indians," citizens of the western country combined their resistance to the excise with their frustrations over an inept Indian war, at the same time mimicking the revolutionary-era ritual dress of the Sons of Liberty at the Boston Tea Party in 1773 and the "Black Boys" of the Pennsylvania frontier in the 1760s.[27]

These comprised the principal cases of violence, mostly symbolic and the work of groups beyond the immediate control of the leadership, reminiscent of colonial "rough music" in the years before the Revolution and connected to the immediate issue of Indian removal. As in Massachusetts, leaders maintained control by using the militia. Even in the hottest bed of resistance, Washington County, there was order and the self-perception of legitimate opposition. There was violence, yes, but this was no French Terror.

Two years later in 1794, Judge Alexander Addison of Washington County wrote to Governor Thomas Mifflin that he had "endeavored to inculcate constitutional resistance, which is alone justifiable in a free people." Folks there had formed "Democratic Societies" following easterners in the wake of Citizen Edmond Genet's visit. The Mingo Creek Democratic Society wrote a constitution in February, the "Constitution of Hamilton's Districts," that divided the county by its militia districts wherein citizens—free men of at least eighteen years—elected representatives to a monthly council to review the activity of Congress and Pennsylvania's legislature; nominated men for state and national office; acted as local arbiters for civil matters before proceeding to court; oversaw teachers and introduced the Bible into schools; and made "all Laws which shall be necessary" for those powers. This was quite nearly the formulation for a "ward republic" that Thomas Jefferson devised twenty-two years later in his Kercheval letter. They also drafted a remonstrance to the president and Congress that connected three issues: "the navigation of the river Mississippi . . . the protection of our territorial rights" against Ohio Indians, and regarding the excise, "if the intent of the custom America requires is that we should be kept in poverty it is unreasonable from such poverty to exact contributions." Opponents across the West objected to warrants returnable to distant Philadelphia.[28]

In May, Congress amended the excise to allow for local process, but days before the revision took effect, Secretary Hamilton secured warrants returnable to Philadelphia. It was July 15 when U.S. marshal David Lenox along with General John Neville served papers to William Miller for failure to register his second-class still. Word had already reached Mingo Creek that they were "taking away people to Philadelphia." Dr. Absalom Baird's militia was mustering to join General Anthony Wayne in the Ohio Indian War and instead marched to Neville's house to protest where Neville fired and killed Oliver Miller (probably William Miller's father). The next day, five hundred marched to Neville's to seize the warrants, at which point he and seventeen regulars from Fort Fayette fired on the crowd, killing prominent protestor Andrew McFarlane. Neville and the soldiers surrendered when the militia set fire to his buildings. About ten days later, a circular appeared, distributed to all militia officers of the four counties, stating, "You are then called upon as a citizen of the western country to . . . march" your companies "to Braddock's field" on August 1 to secure the weapons in the federal arsenal at Fort Fayette in Pittsburgh. A minority now clamored for independence, principally Washingtonians reviving the 1770s attempt to form "Westsylvania." Most at Braddock's Field wanted to keep the arsenal's weapons out of the hands of U.S. government forces while they awaited local trials and repeal of the excise—as had the Massachusetts Regulators when they defended the Springfield Armory from Governor Bowdoin's militia eight years earlier. A few days before the rendezvous, the leaders learned that the weapons were destined for Wayne and the Indian War, and thus decided to simply march the five-thousand-man army in front of Fort Fayette instead. Even Washingtonians agreed and abandoned the idea of Westsylvania in favor of a fortified U.S. war on Ohio Indians. When state and federal authorities began to negotiate with the westerners, most through their committees decided to listen. Judge Alexander Addison thus delivered a charge to the Washington County Grand Jury in a plea for peace and to quiet the radical minority's call for an armed revolution: "Suppose us then a separate People, what prospect have we of being able to secure those objects, which are essential to the prosperity of this country, and so far more consequence than the repeal of the excise law? Shall we, at our own expence, subdue the Indians, seize the western posts and open the Mississippi? . . . The continuance of our union with the United State may therefore, in a short time, secure us all our favorite objects."[29]

Addison turned out to be exactly right when news of Wayne's victory at Fallen Timbers soon arrived, followed by news of the Jay and Pinckney Treaties the next year—clearing British soldiers of western posts, opening the British West Indies to American grain, and opening the Spanish port of New Orleans to American exports. In the autumn of 1794, most "Citizens of the Western Country" and "Westsylvanians"—knowing of Wayne's victory and of the federal government's negotiations with Britain and Spain—agreed with Addison and through their committees voted to submit to the laws. Nevertheless, Hamilton and Washington marched a federalized militia more than ten thousand strong into the region to make more than one hundred arrests. Thousands fled downriver to Kentucky. The United States convicted two men of treason and sentenced them to death. Washington granted amnesty and pardons to nearly all—including the condemned—but not before condemning the "self-created societies" and their Republican supporters in a polarizing, partisan attack. No one hanged this time, but the army of federalized militia killed two in Carlisle in September 1794 when they stopped to tear down a liberty pole, and they took Herman Husband to Philadelphia for trial and jailed him for a year. After the court dropped the charges, a weakened Husband died of pneumonia trying to return home. Many refused to answer their state's draft to join the force. In Hagerstown, Maryland, the mostly German residents defied this draft. Governor Thomas Sim Lee sent in a militia force of 800 to occupy the town and make over 150 arrests. But thousands did go, and they forced more than two thousand western Pennsylvanians to flee their homes and move into the newly won Ohio Country and Kentucky following Wayne's victory.[30]

From Pennsylvania's Lehigh Valley, Captain John Fries and a handful of his Bucks County militia unit answered the call for Washington's draft and marched west, but Pennsylvania Secretary of the Commonwealth Alexander James Dallas lamented that not a single man would answer from neighboring Northampton County, "as the matter is they are called to fight against their own fellow subjects." One militia captain reportedly told his men that "he would be damned if he would go, and every man that did go was a damned fool!"[31]

* * *

When Henry and Peggy Lynn Hembolt raised a liberty pole in December 1798, they attached a flag reading "The Constitution Sacred, No Gagg Laws, Liberty or Death!"[32] The Hembolts opposed a collection of congressional legislation preparing the nation for a war with France: the Sedition Act criminalizing political dissent; Alien Acts, designed to undercut urban-based Republican opposition; $10 million in military spending including a stand-ing army; a loan of $6 million from the Bank of the United States; and a "Direct Tax on Lands, Dwelling Houses, and Slaves" and a "Stamp Act" to tax legal documents, all to fund the other spending. Western Pennsylvanians preferred a progressive "land tax" over the excise earlier in the decade, and while Hamilton's direct tax progressively rated homes, it still regressively taxed farmers' improved land more heavily than speculators' unimproved investments.[33]

The German-speaking farming men and women of the Lehigh Valley were second-, third-, and fourth-generation Americans from the Palatinate. They were overwhelmingly Lutheran and Reformed in their religion. Living among them were German-speaking Moravian Brethren and Schwenkfelders, paci-fist sectarians who founded the Pennsylvania towns of Bethlehem, Emmaus, and Nazareth. Town-dwelling English pacifistic Quakers controlled the poli-tics of Bucks and Northampton Counties from Newtown, Quakertown, and Easton. The German Lutherans and Reformed distinguished themselves from their sectarian neighbors, who refused service in the Revolutionary War or to take the test oath to the state. The Lutherans and Reformed branded them *Sektenleute*—sectarian people—and joined with English-speaking patriots to push the pacifists from power. They called themselves the *Kirchenleute,* "the Church People." They wore their revolutionary service as a badge of honor and celebrated equal citizenship with their English neighbors, and they dis-dained the Sektenleute who joined the Federalist Party and reassumed control of local politics in the 1790s. The Kirchenleute farmed and milled grain for the local, national, and international flour market on modest farms. In the five townships of heaviest resistance, the average farm was about 100 acres, the largest no more than 300, but the 648 male heads of households were fathers to nearly 5,000 children. These were middling farmers, not poor rabble but men who feared for their children's immediate economic futures and the burden that taxes would place on improved property to fund an unnecessary war. In 1798, the Adams administration appointed Federalist Sektenleute to assess and collect the direct tax during an election season when the Kirchenleute fought to retake local offices, and Republican assemblymen and congressmen recruited their votes for the Republican Party.[34]

The Kirchenleute still resented those who had refused to serve, and they resented the new laws coming from the Federalist-dominated Congress. As middling farmers with large families in a shrinking eastern land market, they felt vulnerable in the face of a regressive land tax. So, like the Massachusetts Regulators and the Pennsylvania Citizens of the western country, the Kirchenleute set out to regulate a government that they felt they had created. Why would they engage in "rebellion" when dozens of them, principally the man whose name adorns the movement, John Fries, saw firsthand what the U.S. government would do to a population who defied a federal tax? Like the "Whiskey Rebels," they thought that they were engaging in legitimate constitutional opposition to a money scheme that would enrich the shareholders of the Bank of the United States by appropriating the resources of average farmers through a tax that skipped over land speculators. They would add the Second Amendment to the First when acting, using their active Pennsylvania militia units and wearing their regimentals to display their legitimacy. Their leaders were more careful than those in western Pennsylvania had been, and they purposefully prevented the types of interpersonal violence exacted on excisemen. Moreover, they too had local champions in the federal government cheering them on, encouraging them to resist.[35]

In October 1798, Republican politicians campaigned in the region for Congress and the Pennsylvania Assembly. State representative Jonas Hartzell, a Democratic-Republican, warned, "If a War should break out, we would then show [the Federalists] who *The People are,* we're *the People!*" U.S. Representative Blair McClenachan, also a Democratic-Republican, claimed that Federalists "wished to oppress the people" with the "Tax Law . . . 'til they got all their lands and they would lease it out again to the people for their life," yet "if the people were to oppose it, it might yet be altered." At that point the petitions began. One from Northampton signed by 1,100 announced that the legislation was "contrary not only to the spirit but to the letter of the Constitution." Another revealed not only the petitioners' attachment to the Constitution but the yeoman and revolutionary character of their resistance. "That while we are warmly attached to the Union," they affirmed, "we cannot but express our concern at several acts passed in the last two sessions of Congress: 1. The law for erecting a standing army." Here they objected to the Provisional Army Act and the augmentation of the "New Army" by thousands of professional soldiers, while assuring and reminding Congress that "we [the militia enshrined in the Second Amendment] are ready at any call, to defend our country against any foreign enemy or domestic insurrection." They opposed the Alien and Sedition Acts, which produced "more disunion than union" by contradicting the First Amendment. They disputed "the inconvenience of procuring and using stamped paper" and suggested that "the name of a Stamp Act [was] odious to most Americans." Last, they objected to the direct tax because "it is now well known, that the owners of Houses in Pennsylvania will pay much more in proportion to the value of their property than the holders of uncultivated lands." The tax punished those who virtuously improved their property and allowed speculators to continue their self-interested pursuits without subjection to the public interest. This last grievance was less concerned with the letter than the "Spirit" of the Constitution. The petitioners were being taxed not to fund a previous war's debt (and its speculators) like Massachusetts Regulators and the Western Citizens but to pay for a potential war against their revolutionary ally France and a political war waged by Federalists against their legitimate constitutional opposition—all this while enriching purchasers of public securities and investors in the Bank of the United States.[36]

When the Federalist-appointed Sektenleute assessors began their rounds, Kirchenleute militias formed associations that crossed township and county borders. Signers pledged to resist the assessment of their homes, to refuse to do business with assessors, and to boycott or pressure any neighbors who complied with the assessors until they heard from Congress about their petitions. While Thomas Jefferson and James Madison were authoring the Kentucky and Virginia Resolutions, contending that states could determine the constitutionality of a federal law, the Kirchenleute argued that *the people* held that right and used the militia as the Second Amendment arm of popular nullification within their conception of popular constitutionalism. A majority of Lehigh Valley Associators were Revolutionary War veterans or the sons of veterans, and so donned their own or their fathers' regimentals. Many militia captains, including John Fries, had answered Pennsylvania's call to put down the Whiskey Rebellion, witnessed the power of an army suppressing a Regulation marred by violence against officials, and determined to control their men. Thus, in the Lehigh Valley the resistance was milder than in the Ohio.[37]

Seventeen Lehigh township residents in Northampton bound themselves in an association of resistance, and ordered assessor "Friend Henry Strauss": "You shall cease to measure the Houses until further orders; and if it must be done, we will ourselves elect a sober and fit man to do the business in our Township." Echoing the Massachusetts Regulators, Bucks County tavernkeeper George Mitchell informed assessor Samuel Clark that "the people were dissatisfied that their assessor was appointed without their having a choice; for they wished to choose themselves." Back in Northampton, some Upper Milford and Macungie militia gathered at Captain Henry Jarret's Millerstown home on Christmas Day, where Henry Shankweiler declared that "he would not suffer his house to be appraised by anybody that had been a Tory in the Last War." Many others present agreed but added that "they were willing to pay a land tax if it was laid as they had petitioned Congress." Jarret then redirected the men from the tax collector to the laws when he sent them outside to fashion a liberty pole, commanding that "they should never take up with the Stamp Act, if they did they would be sold for slaves." Jarret "ordered them to take off their hats, ride around the pole, and huzzah for liberty." The men fell in, "and they cursed and swore that they would rather die than submit to the Stamp Act and House Tax Law which was Slavery and Taking the Liberty Away!" The Spirit of '76 lived in 1798.[38]

In January and February 1799, militia units warned off assessors and occasionally threatened violence, but Captains Fries and Jarret maintained order, and there were no acts of violence comparable to the bayoneting near Wilbraham, Massachusetts, or the "liberty jackets" applied to excise officials in the Upper Ohio. Still, U.S. marshal William Nichols came to the Lehigh Valley in February and began making arrests, keeping the prisoners at a Bethlehem tavern while gathering them all for transport to Philadelphia sixty miles away to be tried for obstructing process. On March 7, Fries and Jarret assembled several hundred militia to march in uniform to Bethlehem to bail out the prisoners and to demand local trials per the Sixth Amendment to the U.S. Constitution. Outside the tavern, Fries rallied his men: "All those people who were Tories in the Last War mean to be the leaders, they mean to get us quite under, they mean to make us Slaves!" He negotiated with the marshal to bail out the prisoners, claiming they had "no objection" to the prisoners' trial, as long as "they were tried in their own courts and by their own people," but the marshal held fast. Nichols warned Fries that the government would send an army to quell this insurgency, but Fries shot back that the soldiers would join the people. After hours of failed negotiation, a crowd as large as the militia gathered demanding the prisoners' release. The leaders could control their men but feared the crowd and determined to act quickly. Fries then disarmed himself and agreed to lead his Bucks County men into the tavern but first warned them, "Please, for God's sake, don't fire except we are fired on first!" Fries's armed men pushed through the marshal's armed posse and secured the prisoners without a shot fired or even a punch thrown.[39]

Nevertheless, Federalists in Philadelphia branded Fries's people "rebels" and within weeks a federalized patchwork of state militias occupied the region, arrested more than one hundred principals, and hauled them to Philadelphia for trials. President John Adams followed George Washington's precedent and pardoned Fries and two others convicted of treason. Adams revealed his decision at the last minute, after the condemned had watched from their cells as the carpenters constructed the hangman's scaffold. The only death was David Schaeffer. He died of yellow fever while in the Philadelphia jail awaiting his trial in the summer of 1799. Unlike Massachusetts and the Upper Ohio Valley, there was no mass exodus of resisters from the Lehigh Valley. John Fries and Henry Jarret lived out their lives there, though there would not be land or opportunity enough for all their children to do so.[40]

While only Shaysites identified themselves specifically as Regulators, all three events were eighteenth-century Regulations, each viewed itself as a legitimate and constitutional opposition, and each was tarred as "rebellion" by those who sought to delegitimize them and their grievances and to impose onerous taxes on them. Despite significant ethno-religious and geographic differences, these three Regulations shared remarkably similar words, tactics, and goals. Each audibly pronounced agrarian hopes and fears for the future of the American experiment of democratic participation in republican governance. Each sought to exercise political liberties won in the Revolution or secured by the Bill of Rights to ensure economic independence. Each mobilized Revolutionary War veterans in an attempt to regulate a government funding scheme to redirect wealth from farmers to wealthy speculative lenders, landjobbers, and politicians. Each justified their opposition using revolutionary language; used the right of petition to demand redress of grievances; employed revolutionary techniques of ritualistic violence and threats against taxmen; used local militia to organize resistance; manufactured local extralegal institutions—county conventions, democratic societies, associations—to assert local control and claim authority to govern themselves; and through those organizations and the militia controlled and channeled the anger of the people into avenues that each movement believed to be "constitutional." Massachusetts Regulators sought to make a fair constitution based in republican and democratic principles—demanding equal representation, an accessible capital, the writ of habeas corpus, and the right to petition—to replace the 1780 document lacking these features crafted in a winter when snow-packed roads blocked their participation. Citizens of the western country also believed they were underrepresented in the federal republic and demanded congressional redress of constitutional grievances from a centralizing executive. Kirchenleute patriots protested the unconstitutionality of the Alien and Sedition Acts and claimed that the direct tax violated the "spirit" of the Constitution. Each claimed that the long transport of prisoners to Boston and Philadelphia for trials was unconstitutional.

Their agrarian fear for the future of the republic (either the commonwealth of Massachusetts or the United States) was that moneyed men and the administrations and legislatures they controlled would doom republicanism. But unlike Jefferson's and Madison's fear of a slow "liberticide" at the hands of the Hamiltonian conspiracy, these agrarians' fear for themselves was that these policies would quickly spell the end of their actual or intended economic independence to own some ground and market some crops for a profit, and then to pass the land on to their progeny. Each witnessed the contraction of political liberties and feared the consequent loss of economic independence, and each was willing to secure their own liberty and independence at the expense of others. In Massachusetts, the Regulators demanded it at the expense of the holders of the state war debt. In Pennsylvania, the Citizens demanded it at the expense of Ohio Indians, while the Kirchenleute grabbed it at the expense of the Sektenleute. Their means toward achieving these ends was the political participation afforded by the Revolution and protected by the Constitution and its Bill of Rights—in Jefferson's words, making "every citizen an acting member of the government."

So we return to Jefferson, who was on the losing side of an 1813 argument with John Adams. Adams was right. Both parties had been guilty of "political terrorism. He was also right that Jefferson "never felt the Terrorism of Chaises Rebellion . . . the Terrorism of Gallatin's Insurrection," or "the Terrorism of Fries's, most outrageous Riot and Rescue." Adams may have been right because Jefferson's administration and party eschewed debt-creating and funding schemes designed to redistribute wealth from agrarians to speculators that provoked popular constitutionalists to regulate. Jefferson and Madison by this time had themselves led the nation for three terms without facing a "rebellion," outside of the abortive Hartford Convention. So, in this respect, Jefferson certainly comes out on top of the argument with Adams. However, Adams's jibe may have got Jefferson to thinking, or at least to rethinking his 1787 quip that the "tree of liberty must be refreshed from time to time with the blood of patriots and tyrants," and to ruminate more thoughtfully and productively as he did in his "ward republics" letter to Kercheval in 1816. Yet even in that eloquent postulation about the ideal future of the republic of the commonwealth of Virginia, Jefferson got it only partially right about the founders' past when he said "*our* inexperience of self-government, occasioned gross departures in that draught from genuine republican canons." Perhaps *his* inexperience had this result, but these three sets of agrarian founders prove that they understood clearly—long before Jefferson's 1816 postulation of the "mother principle"—that "governments are republican only in proportion as they embody the will of their people, and execute it." The protesters had made their "election between *economy* and *liberty,* or *profusion* and *servitude*" and had determined not to "let [their] rulers load [them] with perpetual debt."[41]

Adams of course was also wrong about his castigation of these three events as acts of "Terrorism," "Rebellion," and "Insurrection," or minimized as "Outrageous Riot and Rescue." Even though the "friends of order" put each movement in its place, branding them traitors, insurrectionists, and rebels, each movement by their words and actions—as a self-conceived legitimate and constitutional opposition—extended their liberty, their independence, and their republic as far into their future as they possibly could. They won significant victories. They regulated their governments, pushing them to change tack. Shaysites did not force a new constitutional convention, but they pushed James Bowdoin out of office. Governor John Hancock subsequently issued pardons, and the new government loosened its taxes and expanded tender laws to ease the economic strain. Citizens of the western country did not secure the repeal of the excise, but their pressure convinced the federal government to let it expire, partially uncollected. Moreover, it was western insistence after 1791 that led Congress to better outfit Anthony Wayne's army for the 1794 campaign that led to Fallen Timbers and the Treaty of Greenville, and the negotiations for the Jay and Pinckney Treaties to open the Ohio country and the port of New Orleans. The Kirchenleute took local office, cheered peaceful diplomatic negotiations with France, helped turn Pennsylvania for Republicans in the "Revolution of 1800," and ensured the repeal of the Sedition Act. Moreover, each group vindicated the people's right to free speech and assembly: Shays's Regulation may have inspired Antifederalists to demand the inclusion of these rights, while the Pennsylvania movements assumed and asserted them through an agrarian "Apotheosis of the Constitution." These three movements were not solely responsible for all these victories, of course, but they all played integral roles in vocalizing dissent from the self-aggrandizing policies of elites at the expense of the revolutionary generation of American farmers. These victories gave governments pause about enacting new funding schemes in the nineteenth century, and as a result, Regulation movements using popular constitutionalism were not necessary over the following fourteen years as they had been in the first fourteen. Through these victories, these agrarians proved themselves to be the "other founders" and successfully, if only momentarily, proclaimed, "We're the People!"[42]

Notes

The author wishes to express his gratitude for assistance in the course of developing, researching, and writing this essay: Emily McGaha, Joseph Heffley, Ryan Bixby, Bethany Winters, Thomas Kiffmeyer, John Craig Hammond, David Nichols, Todd Estes, Peter S. Onuf, Robert McDonald, the library and archives staff of the University of Pittsburgh at Johnstown, the University of Pittsburgh, the Western Pennsylvania Historical Society, the Historical Society of Pennsylvania, the Massachusetts Archives, the Massachusetts Historical Society, the American Antiquarian Society, and the Carnegie Library of Pittsburgh. Most important are Lance and Lana Banning, without whose patient guidance and gracious care neither this essay nor my career would have been possible.

1. Thomas Jefferson to John Adams, June 15, 1813; Adams to Jefferson, June 30, 1813, Lester J. Cappon, ed., *The Adams-Jefferson Letters: The Complete Correspondence between Thomas Jefferson and Abigail and John Adams* (Chapel Hill, N.C., 1987), 331–33, 346–48.

2. On Shays's Rebellion, see Robert J. Taylor, *Western Massachusetts in the Revolution* (Providence, R.I., 1954); Marion L. Starkey, *A Little Rebellion* (New York, 1955);

David Szatmary, *Shays' Rebellion: The Making of an Agrarian Insurrection* (Amherst, Mass., 1980); Robert Gross, ed., *In Debt to Shays: The Bicentennial of an Agrarian Rebellion* (Charlottesville, Va., 1993); Leonard L. Richards, *Shays's Rebellion: The American Revolution's Final Battle* (Philadelphia, 2002); and Sean Condon, *Shays's Rebellion: Authority and Distress in Post-Revolutionary America* (Baltimore, 2015). On the Whiskey Rebellion, see Leland Baldwin, *Whiskey Rebels: The Story of a Frontier Uprising* (Pittsburgh, 1939); Dorothy E. Fennell, "From Rebelliousness to Insurrection: A Social History of the Whiskey Rebellion, 1765–1802" (Ph.D. diss., University of Pittsburgh, 1982); Thomas P. Slaughter, *The Whiskey Rebellion: Frontier Epilogue to the American Revolution* (New York, 1986); William Hogeland, *The Whiskey Rebellion: George Washington, Alexander Hamilton, and the Frontier Rebels Who Challenged America's Newfound Sovereignty* (New York, 2006); and Terry Bouton, *Taming Democracy: "The People," the Founders, and the Troubled Ending to the American Revolution* (New York, 2007). On Fries's Rebellion, see W. W. H. Davis, *The Fries Rebellion of 1799* (Doylestown, Penn., 1899); Louis Weinstein, "The Fries Rebellion" (M.A. thesis, Temple University, 1939); Dwight Henderson, "Treason, Sedition, and Fries Rebellion," *Legal History* 40 (1970): 308–17; Kenneth Keller, "Diversity and Democracy: Ethnic Politics in Southeastern Pennsylvania, 1788–1799" (Ph.D. diss., Yale University, 1971); Peter Levine, "The Fries Rebellion: Social Violence and the Politics of the New Nation," *Pennsylvania History* 40 (1973): 241–58; Sue Taishoff, "Parties, Political Culture, and Latent Values: The Fries Rebellion and Partisan Behavior in Southeastern Pennsylvania" (M.A. thesis, University of Virginia, 1973); Derek C. Smith, "The Fries Rebellion: Ideology and Insurrection in the Early American Republic" (M.A. thesis, Claremont Graduate School, 1995); all of the essays by Terry Bouton, Robert Churchill, Owen S. Ireland, Paul Douglas Newman, Simon Newman, and Whit Ridgeway in the special issue of *Pennsylvania History* 67 (Winter 2000); and Paul Douglas Newman, *Fries's Rebellion: The Enduring Struggle for the American Revolution* (Philadelphia, 2004). There are only three works that make any comparisons, and only one specifically, among Shays, Whiskey, and Fries, and that is a study in political science by George E. Connor, "The Politics of Insurrection: A Comparative Analysis of Shays', Whiskey, and Fries' Rebellions," *Social Science Journal* 29 (1999): 259–79. Bouton's *Taming Democracy* compares the Whiskey to Fries's Rebellion, and Simon Newman makes another comparison in "The World Turned Upside Down: Revolutionary Politics, Fries' and Gabriel's Rebellions, and the Fears of the Federalists," *Pennsylvania History* 67 (Winter 2000): 5–20.

3. The literature on the First Party System is large, and Lance Banning still sits squarely at its center. Some important works among many are Lance Banning, *The Jeffersonian Persuasion: Evolution of a Party Ideology* (Ithaca, N.Y., 1978); Stanley Elkins and Eric McKitrick, *The Age of Federalism: The Early American Republic, 1788–1800* (New York, 1993); Joyce Appleby, *Capitalism and a New Social Order: The Republican Vision of the 1790s* (New York, 1984); and James Rogers Sharp, *American Politics in the Early Republic: The New Nation in Crisis* (New Haven, Conn., 1993).

4. Thomas Jefferson to Samuel Kercheval, July 12, 1816, Paul Leicester Ford, ed., *The Works of Thomas Jefferson,* 12 vols. (New York, 1904–5), 10:37. Drew McCoy, *The*

Elusive Republic: Political Economy in Jeffersonian America (Chapel Hill, N.C., 1980), famously made the argument that Jeffersonian political economy intended to extend the republic through time by extending it across space to ensure an agrarian future. Lance Banning, "Republican Ideology and the Triumph of the Constitution," *William and Mary Quarterly,* 3rd ser., 31 (1974): 167–88, contains his apotheosis argument.

5. Jefferson to Samuel Kercheval, July 12, 1816, Ford, ed., *Works of Thomas Jefferson,* 10:37.

6. Terry Bouton makes the case that both the Whiskey and Fries's Rebellions were in the vein of eighteenth-century regulation movements in *Taming Democracy.*

7. Excellent works on popular constitutionalism include Larry D. Kramer, *The People Themselves: Popular Constitutionalism and Judicial Review* (New York, 2004), and Robert Churchill, "Popular Nullification, Fries's Rebellion, and the Waning of Radical Republicanism, 1798–1801," *Pennsylvania History* 67 (2000): 105–40. I tend to expand the definition of popular constitutionalism from popular movements restraining the courts to include the specific use of constitutions—state, national, and of their own creation—and the invocation of constitutional protections and liberties by average people to secure republican and democratic rights and privileges they believed were their due.

8. Adam Wheeler to the Town of Hubbardstown, November 7, 1786, Shays' Rebellion (hereafter SRB), box 1, folder 3, American Antiquarian Society, Worcester, Mass.

9. Richards, *Shays's Rebellion,* 16–17, 75.

10. Ibid., 4, 111.

11. Athol Petition, May 5, 1786; Acton Petition, June 1786, SRB, box 1, folder 2; Richards, *Shays's Rebellion,* 53–61, 92–108; *Massachusetts Gazette,* January 20, 1784, cited in Szatmary, *Shays' Rebellion,* 33; Constitution of Massachusetts, part 1, arts. XIX, VII; Jon Worthington, interview, Witness Notebook, Robert Treat Paine Papers (hereafter RTPP), Minutes of Criminal Trials, 1781–1789, microfilm 17, Massachusetts Historical Society (hereafter MHS), Boston.

12. Northampton Petition, August 29, 1786, A180:318, Massachusetts Archives, Boston (hereafter MA). For a similar petition, see Petition of Regulators at Worcester, September 6, 1786, A180:190, MA. See also Dracut, September 25, 1786; Bedford, October 16, 1786, SRB, box 1, folder 2, and Greenwich, January 16, 1787, SRB, box 1, folder 3.

13. William Pencak, "'The Fine Theoretic Government of Massachusetts Is Prostrated to the Earth': The Response to Shays's Rebellion Reconsidered," in Gross, ed., *In Debt to Shays,* 121–44; Richards, *Shays's Rebellion,* 109–13.

14. Governor James Bowdoin's Proclamation of September 2, 1786, A180:189, MA. Another description is in A180:318, Account of Northampton Court Closing, August 29, 1786, A180:318. Captain Joseph Slate, interview, RTPP, Shays' Rebellion Papers, 1786–88, microfilm 17; Minutes of the Middlesex Convention, Concord, Mass., September 12, 1786, A180:318, MA; Caleb Hyde to Bowdoin, n.d. (less than a week after September 13, 1786), A180:190, MA.

15. Richards, *Shays's Rebellion,* 17–18; Szatmary, *Shays' Rebellion,* 84; Sam Lyman, interview, RTPP, Shays' Rebellion Papers, microfilm 17.

16. Dan Taylor, C. Kingsley, Saul Fowler, Dr. Elijah Clarke, RTTP, Shays' Rebellion Papers, microfilm 17.

17. William Shepard to James Bowdoin, January 20, 1787; Shepard to Benjamin Lincoln, January 21, 1787; Shepard to Bowdoin, January 22, 24, 1787, A180:318, MA; Shepard to Lincoln, January 24, 1787, Shays Rebellion Papers, MHS (hereafter SRP); Dr. Samuel Merrick, Oliver Cattin, John Ferry, interviews, RTPP, Shays' Rebellion Papers, microfilm 17; Daniel Shays to Lincoln, January 25, 1787, SRP.

18. William Shepard to James Bowdoin, January 26, 1787, A180:318, MA; Benjamin Lincoln to Bowdoin, January 26, 1786, SRP; "Mrs. Miller of Colerain," interview, RTPP, Shays' Rebellion Papers, microfilm 17.

19. *The Federalist,* ed. Jacob E. Cooke (Middletown, Conn., 1961), no. 6, 35.

20. Meeting at Parkinson's Ferry, August 14, 1794, *Pennsylvania Archives,* ser. 2, vol. 4 (Harrisburg, Penn., 1890), 159–60 (hereafter *PA*). For a description of the Whiskey Rebellion as a Regulation movement, see Bouton, *Taming Democracy,* chap. 10, passim.

21. Depositions of Christian Yentzer, December 27, 1794; Rosewell Douty, December 27, 1794; Benjamin Young, October 10, 1794; William Brady, October 25, 1794; William Wilson, October 20, 1794; John Mason, December 22, 1794, Rawle Family Papers (hereafter RP), box 5, folders 5–6, Historical Society of Pennsylvania (hereafter HSP), Philadelphia.

22. Baldwin, *Whiskey Rebels,* 30, 38, 106–9; "Memorial of the Inhabitants of the Country West of the Allegheny Mountains," 1776, Jasper Yeates Collection, HSP.

23. On the operation of the excise, see Baldwin, *Whiskey Rebels,* 68–73, 106–9, and Slaughter, *Whiskey Rebellion,* 148–49.

24. Slaughter, *Whiskey Rebellion,* 93–94, 105–7; Solon J. and Elizabeth Hawthorn Buck, *The Planting of Civilization in Western Pennsylvania* (Pittsburgh, 1939), 199–203. Also useful is Hogeland, *The Whiskey Rebellion.* Anthony Wayne to Henry Knox, March 10, 1794, RP, box 6, folder 5. On Harmar's and St. Clair's defeats and other Indian successes between 1789 and 1794, see Slaughter, *Whiskey Rebellion,* 94–107, and Randolph C. Downes, *Council Fires on the Upper Ohio* (Pittsburgh, 1968), 310–37. Settlers and Indians continued to attack one another around the Forks; see the correspondence between Knox and Isaac Craig at Forts Pitt and Fayette from March 24, 1791–June 27, 1794, Major Isaac Craig Papers (hereafter CP), Carnegie Library of Pittsburgh: Knox to Craig, March 24, 1791; Craig to Knox, March 25, 1791; Craig to Knox, March 31, 1791; William Shepard to Craig, May 4, 1791; Craig to Knox, May 19, 1791; Craig to Knox, March 31, 1792; Craig to "Captain Cass," April 7, 1792; Craig to Joseph Howell, May 25, 1792; Craig to Knox, May 25, 1792; Craig to Knox, June 1, 1792; Craig to Knox, March 30, 1793; Craig to Knox, May 31, 1793; Craig to Knox, June 7, 1793; Craig to Knox, June 14, 1793; William Wilson to James Brison, July 8, 1793; Benjamin Lincoln to Craig, August 23, 1793; Craig to Knox, June 6, 1794; Craig to Knox, June 13, 1794; Knox to Craig, June 21, 1794; Craig to Knox, June 27, 1794.

25. Pennsylvania House Resolution, June 22, 1791, *PA,* 16; First Pittsburg Meeting, September 7, 1791, *PA,* 16–18; Baldwin *Whiskey Rebels,* 82; Slaughter *Whiskey*

Rebellion, 113; James Brison to Thomas Mifflin, November 9, 1791, *PA,* 38–39. The literature on Skimmington treatments and ritualistic violence during the American resistance to parliamentary taxes and Regulations is large, but Brendan McConville's idea of an "American Terror" is useful for understanding the western Pennsylvanians' sense of violence as a legitimate "revolutionary" tool of political expression; see McConville, *The King's Three Faces: The Rise and Fall of Royal America, 1688–1776* (Chapel Hill, N.C., 2006).

26. Second Pittsburg Meeting, August 21, 1792, *PA,* 25–26. On the operation of the excise, see Baldwin, *Whiskey Rebels,* 68–73, and Slaughter, *Whiskey Rebellion,* 148–49. Depositions of Christian Yentzer, December 27, 1794; Rosewell Douty, December 27, 1794; Benjamin Young, October 10, 1794; William Brady, October 15, 1794; William Wilson, October 20, 1794; John Mason, December 22, 1794, RP, box 5, folders 5–6.

27. Baldwin, *Whiskey Rebels,* 84–85, 90–91; Slaughter, *Whiskey Rebellion,* 114–15, 150–51. On James Smith's "Black Boys," see Patrick Spero, *Frontier Rebels: The Fight for Independence in the American West* (New York, 2018).

28. Alexander Addison to Thomas Mifflin, November 4, 1792, *PA,* 30–33; Eugene P. Link, *The Democratic-Republican Societies, 1790–1800* (New York, 1942); Jeffrey A. Davis, "Guarding the Republican Interest: The Western Pennsylvania Democratic Societies and the Excise Tax," *Pennsylvania History* 67 (2000): 43–62; Matthew Schoenbachler, "Republicanism in the Age of Democratic Revolution: The Democratic Societies of the 1790s," *Journal of the Early Republic* 18 (1998): 237–61. Schoenbachler wrote this essay in a seminar with Lance Banning in 1992, the same seminar in which I wrote "Fries's Rebellion and American Political Culture, 1798–1800," *Pennsylvania Magazine of History and Biography* 119 (1995): 37–73. The Constitution of Hamilton's Districts, February 28, 1794; Remonstrance from Hamilton's Districts to the Congress of the United States, 1794, RP, box 5, folder 2.

29. John Gibson to Thomas Mifflin, July 18, 1794, *PA,* 58–60; Isaac Craig to Henry Knox, July 18, 1794, CP, IIB 201–2; Baldwin, *Whiskey Rebels,* 110–17; Slaughter, *Whiskey Rebellion,* 177–79; Call to Braddock's Field, July 28, 1794, *PA,* 67; Craig to Knox, August 3, 1794, CP, IIB 213–14; Bouton, *Taming Democracy,* 232–35. For Alexander Addison's speech, see *PA,* 201–9.

30. Slaughter, *Whiskey Rebellion,* 205–22; Bouton, *Taming Democracy,* 214–43.

31. Report of Alexander Dallas, January 16, 1795, *PA,* 237–38; Jacob Rush to John Craig, October 2, 1794, RP, box 5, folder 4. On resistance in Northampton, see Lawrence Erb to William Rawle, September 15, 1792; Isaac Richardson to James Collins, September 24, 1792, RP, box 5, folder 2.

32. Much of what follows is derived from my 1996 dissertation, guided by Banning, "The Fries Rebellion of 1799: Pennsylvania Germans, the Federalist Party, and American Political Culture" (Ph.D. diss., University of Kentucky, 1996); *Fries's Rebellion: The Enduring Struggle for the American Revolution* (Philadelphia, 2004); and "Fries' Rebellion," *Encyclopedia of International Protest and Revolution,* ed. Immanuel Ness (New York, 2009), 1–3.

33. Deposition of John Romig, January 29, 1799, RP. When I conducted my Fries research, Rawle's Whiskey Rebellion and Fries's Rebellion Papers were mounted in two bound volumes titled "Insurrections in Pennsylvania." They have since been removed and placed in acid-free folders and boxes. Fries references are searchable by date.

34. Newman, *Fries's Rebellion*, 30–36; for statistical data, see pp. 32–35.

35. Ibid. This is culled from chapters 1–3.

36. Depositions of Andrew Schlichter, April 6, 1799; John Jarret, April 10, 1799; Henry Ohl, April 27, 1799, RP; *Annals of Congress*, 5th Cong., 3rd sess., 2795 (to see all petitions, 2785–3002); *Oracle of Dauphin and Harrisburg Daily Advertiser,* January 23, 1799.

37. See Saul Cornell, *A Well Regulated Militia: The Founding Fathers and the Origin of Gun Control in America* (New York, 2006), chaps. 1–2, passim.

38. "Lehigh Association," draft, January 28, 1799, RP; Thomas Carpenter, *The Two Trials of John Fries* (Philadelphia, 1800), 68; Deposition of John Fogel Jr. before Judge William Henry, January 29, 1799, RP; Examination of Henry Shiffert before Judge Richard Peters, April 14, 1799, RP; Deposition of Philip Wescoe, recorder and date unknown, RP.

39. A Deposition of Phillip Schlough before Judge Richard Peters, April 15, 1799, RP; Testimony of John Barnet, Carpenter, *Two Trials,* 30. See also Newman, *Fries's Rebellion,* 112–41.

40. Deposition of Phillip Schlough, April 15, 1799, RP; Carpenter, *Two Trials;* Testimonies of Joseph Horsefield, 43; John Barnet, 30; William Nichols, 40; William Thomas, 187; Cephas Childs, 73–79; William Barnet, 30; George Mitchell, 66; John Roderock, 70–73, RP.

41. Thomas Jefferson to William Stephens Smith, November 13, 1787, Julian P. Boyd et al., eds., *The Papers of Thomas Jefferson,* 44 vols. to date (Princeton, N.J., 1950–), 12:356; Jefferson to Samuel Kercheval, July 12, 1816, Ford, ed., *Works of Thomas Jefferson,* 10:37.

42. See Woody Holton's *Unruly Americans and the Origins of the Constitution* (New York, 2007).

5 The Sovereign People

Indians, Treaties, and the Subversion
of the Founders' Colonialist Vision

DAVID ANDREW NICHOLS

Half a century ago, in her comparative study of the American and French Revolutions, Hannah Arendt observed that the first of these upheavals had many exceptional features, among them the Americans' tendency to bind down the radical tendencies of their Revolution with rules, laws, and written constitutions. Subsequent scholars have chipped away at the notion that the American Revolution was exceptional, but it remains true that it became a more legalistic and document-bound episode than many other national revolutions. Of the documents on which the revolutionary generation rested the legitimacy of their new state, some of the most important—to the revolutionaries, if not to their descendants—were the treaties they drafted and negotiated with other nations. These were their ticket to admission into what Leonard Sadosky has called the "Westphalian system," a creation of seventeenth-century European nation-states who predicated sovereignty on recognition by other nation-states. The Second Continental Congress developed a model treaty for its diplomats early in the War for American Independence, and American ministers devoted years of effort to negotiating treaties of amity with European powers, not only to obtain resources but also to prove their new nation respectable and "treaty-worthy."[1]

In his discussion of the United States' "Westphalian" aspirations, Sadosky notes that Americans concurrently sought to curtail the sovereignty and resources of another group of nations, namely Native American ones. Revolutions are both creative and destructive acts, and one of the things the American revolutionaries wanted to eliminate was the Native American presence within their new nation. This is not to say the founders of the

United States were genocidaires, but rather that they believed that nomadic (or allegedly nomadic), ungoverned, and easily manipulated people had no place in a republic of orderly, independent, virtuous farmers. Some hoped that Indians would simply die out as white settlements grew; some wanted the U.S. government forcibly to expel Native Americans from the country; some wanted to convert Indians into English-speaking commercial farmers and absorb them into the general population.[2]

None of these views was exceptional in world-historical terms. They were in fact typical of the "settler-colonialist" regimes that modern scholars have been identifying and comparing since the 1990s. Settler-colonialists, Lorenzo Veracini observes in a transnational survey of the type, carried with them from the mother country a conviction of their own special status and arrogated to themselves special virtues that their metropolitan kinsmen had lost, a "provincial" superiority complex that the American revolutionaries certainly displayed. They presumed that their status and virtues entitled them to self-rule and even independence, a claim shared by fifteenth-century Genoese colonists, nineteenth-century *voortrekkers,* and British North Americans. They developed a national narrative stressing their own collective virtues and their injury by unprovoked external enemies, adversaries whom, in the form of Indian war parties and British armies, the American colonists' independence war had certainly supplied. More importantly, they viewed themselves as so vastly superior to the indigenous inhabitants of their new homelands that the indigenes might as well not exist. Settler-colonialists developed many strategies of elimination, including actual extermination, deportation, confinement, and assimilation. All of these strategies white Americans would employ at one time or another against Native Americans.[3]

Post-revolutionary Americans' expansionist goals and justifications were not exceptional, but the means they used to acquire Native American land and relocate or assimilate Indian peoples were. The primary instrument of American colonialism, as Dorothy V. Jones observed nearly forty years ago, was not the army but the treaty. This "technology of empire," to borrow Lisa Ford's term, was old in Washington's day and archaic by Andrew Jackson's, and other British settler-colonies, like Australia and South Africa, employed them very rarely in their dealings with indigenous peoples. The U.S. government, by contrast, negotiated nearly four hundred ratified treaties with Native Americans between 1778 and 1871, and however much their white negotiators resorted to coercion or fraud, many modern Indians consider these documents the bedrock of their sovereignty.[4]

Early U.S. officials resorted to treaty-making with some reluctance. Many believed they should simply dictate terms to Indians at gunpoint or by statute. Many federal treaty commissioners were themselves current or former army officers, who sometimes did negotiate with their Native counterparts while backed by bayonets. At the 1784 Treaty of Fort Stanwix, Connecticut militia General Oliver Wolcott and Continental Army Colonel Richard Butler (along with Congressman Arthur Lee) intimidated Iroquois chiefs with an escort of 150 soldiers and an unconditional demand for their submission. "You are a subdued people," Lee declared, "overcome in a war which you entered into with us. . . . You now stand out alone against our whole force." Eleven years later, General Anthony Wayne ordered the defeated captains of the United Indian confederacy to meet him at his headquarters in Greenville, Ohio. Supported by the muskets and cannon of the Legion of the United States, Wayne was able to adopt a magnanimous posture, but he still dictated to his "guests" a large and binding land cession (two-thirds of present-day Ohio) and peremptorily refused an attempt by Little Turtle (Miami) to modify it. Most notoriously, in 1814 General Andrew Jackson forced the *micos* of the Creek confederacy, several dozens of whose towns Jackson's army had just destroyed, to sign away 23 million acres of Creek land in present-day Alabama and Georgia. "Our friends will sign the treaty," the general declared, "our enemies"—whom Jackson had already promised to annihilate—"must depart." His "friends" signed.[5]

Jackson criticized the practice of signing treaties with people he considered barbarians, and whom he believed federal laws should suffice to control. "I do think it not only useless but absurd," Jackson wrote John Calhoun in 1820. Actions, however, would speak more loudly than words: as a civilian, Jackson served as the principal negotiator of half a dozen treaties in which he used bribery and veiled threats of coercion rather than naked military force. As president he signed seventy more, a record for a sitting chief executive. What drove President Jackson and other eighteenth- and nineteenth-century Americans to employ this archaic "technology" was necessity. War, like the United Indian War of the 1790s and the Creek War of 1813–14, was expensive. Their national government began its existence as an Atlantic-oriented fiscal-military state with limited resources, and treaties that acknowledged some degree of Native sovereignty and procured Indian consent were less expensive ways to secure the frontier and procure land cessions than military force. Even as late as the 1830s, the U.S. government would have been hard pressed to undertake so massive a project as Indian Removal, which involved the relocation of 90,000 people and cost over $100 million, without the consent of at least some of the people it sought to relocate. Moreover, as Henry Knox observed in 1789, treaties offered the federal government a solution to the problem of divided sovereignty within the American federation. The Constitution of 1787 granted the U.S. government only limited authority over Indian relations, and the Northwest Ordinance ensured that new states controlled by Indian-fearing settlers would soon enter the union and challenge the federal government's Indian policy. The U.S. government did enjoy, however, the exclusive right to negotiate treaties, and so long as it resolved issues like political alignment or land sales through these instruments, the states could not challenge it.[6]

Treaties, because they are at least nominally voluntary agreements, strengthened the political position of Native Americans. They allowed Native leaders to negotiate better terms (e.g., more money, technical assistance) for land cessions, granted the United States the right to build roads in Indian country but gave indigenous peoples control over the inns and ferries thereon, and during the Removal era permitted some Native peoples to remain in the eastern states on family allotments or small reservations. Just as importantly, the process of treaty-making encouraged American Indians to develop their own thinking about the meaning of sovereignty. Treaties grew from products of dialogue between federal officials and Indian leaders, and as several generations of Native American chiefs and captains negotiated these documents, they also synthesized a new concept of Indian sovereignty. For Natives, sovereignty came to mean control of a bounded communal land base, self-selected government, and recognition of tribal leadership by the American sovereign. These concepts survived long after the Senate approved the last Indian treaty in 1871. American officials of the revolutionary generation wanted to behave like settler-colonialists, forcing Indians to assimilate or emigrate, but the treaty system obliged them and their successors to accept what Lauren Benton calls "layered sovereignty" and a "plural legal order," and to make a place in their continental empire for people they would have preferred to subjugate.[7]

. . .

For Native Americans, treaties retained a cultural and political importance even greater than the value white Americans placed on them, confirming signatories' collective political identity and "treaty-worthiness." To begin with, signed treaties were legal superstructures supported by a ceremonial infrastructure that the Woodland and Plains Indians had been building for centuries. For American Indians, a "treaty" did include the signed and ratified agreement itself, though they were sometimes skeptical about whether their translators accurately explained the "pen-and-ink work" to them. The Menominees proved that such skepticism was well founded when in the 1830s they insisted they had never consented to a treaty clause that allowed the president to demand further land cessions at his pleasure. Their Ho-Chunk neighbors similarly suffered from a deceptive 1837 treaty clause that their translator told them would provide eight years to prepare for Removal when the written treaty said "eight months." More important than written documents were the rituals whereby Indian leaders sacralized the treaty ground, the ceremonial exchanges that took place there, and the speeches that American and white diplomats made.[8]

Most Indian nations regarded oral addresses as the substantive core of treaty conferences and indeed more important than written treaties, a point the Wyandot half-king made in 1786 when he demanded that the United States stop its surveys north of the Ohio River. The chief simultaneously affirmed his support for his nation's recent Treaty of Fort McIntosh and insisted that "not one word be altered" of that agreement. This puzzled American officials, since the written treaty had included the large land cession that surveyors were now marking, but as federal commissioner Timothy Pickering later observed, the *speeches* at the Fort McIntosh treaty conference had "said nothing about land." Certainly, Native Americans devoted considerable time and resources to ensuring that everyone understood these speeches: they spaced out addresses over the course of several days or weeks, spoke slowly and with time for translation, and in many cases accompanied their talks with special aides-memoirs, wampum. These shell or glass beads, strung onto strings or woven into elaborate belts, represented a large investment of community labor and as such constituted valuable symbolic tokens. They helped speakers certify the solemnity of their words and helped listeners remember past speeches as well. The use of wampum had spread from the Northeast to the Great Lakes and the Southeast by the late eighteenth century: Cherokee and Chickasaw diplomats gave white wampum strings at the 1785–86 Hopewell conference, and Arthur St. Clair's failure to bring adequate wampum to the 1788–89 Fort Harmar conference became a fatal faux pas.[9]

White Americans generally considered *written* treaties the culminating products of diplomatic conferences, but they did not disregard the speeches that white commissioners and Native American leaders delivered. American officials regarded these as a dialogue about treaty terms, such as boundaries and annuities, and they took care to record the proceedings in writing, while Indian leaders like Puckshunnubbee (Choctaw) often requested copies of these transcripts, which literate Indians could read for their kinsmen. Speech-making served another purpose for Indian chiefs and captains: it allowed them to identify the sources of their political power and to assert both individual and collective authority. At the Hopewell conference in 1786, Chickasaw leaders Piomingo (Mountain Leader) and Mingatushka grounded their authority in their maternal lineage, presenting the American commissioners with a medal owned by "the daughter and mother" of some of the "great men of our nation." This indicated that American commissioners were treating with leading families as well as individuals, and introduced a female presence to a male gathering, an important consideration for indigenous peoples who associated femininity with diplomacy. Other Native American leaders traced their political power to their particular polities or communities. At the 1795 Greenville conference, the leaders of the defeated United Indian confederacy signed a peace treaty as members of specific nations or towns, or used pictograms identifying their particular clans, while at later treaties Ojibwa *ogemaa,* or town chiefs, spoke very deliberately about the towns and territories they represented and asserted that these communities were the sources of their authority and strength.[10]

As these examples indicate, many Native Americans still identified themselves more with their towns and kinship groups than with their nations. Americans increasingly took advantage of these divisions. At the 1820 Doak's Stand conference, for example, Andrew Jackson and Thomas Hinds threatened to seek a land cession from the Choctaws who had emigrated west of the Mississippi River unless their eastern kinsmen agreed to make one instead, and between 1821 and 1834 treaty commissioners obtained virtually all of the Potawatomis' extensive land claims by negotiating with different bands and playing ambitious chiefs off against one another. Treaties also, however, provided chiefs and captains with the opportunity to assert identity in larger, transnational groups. At Greenville, for instance, Odawa, Ojibwa, and Potawatomi speakers indicated to General Anthony Wayne that their "Three Fires" cultural league would persist after the disbanding of the larger Northwest confederacy, and at the Detroit conference following the War of 1812, the Wyandot captain Tarhe (the Crane) reminded General William Henry Harrison of the unity of the "four tribes" (Delawares, Senecas, Shawnees, and Wyandots) who had fought alongside American troops. One suspects, since Indian leaders made these assertions at the ends of wars in which Native American confederacies had been defeated, that they were not trying to revive these older confederations. Rather, they were asserting the sovereign right of their people to maintain friendships, cultural leagues, and alliances with other Indian nations, even if they had renounced their right to negotiate with other European nation-states.[11]

Indians used treaty conferences as venues where they could make and record agreements in their own words and strengthen bonds with other Indian nations. Such conferences also gave them the opportunity to renew their peoples' collective identities and form or strengthen bonds between their people and their fictive American parent, or "Father." Native American men and women first took ceremonial possession of the treaty ground with social and military dances in which white commissioners sometimes joined or into which Indian performers incorporated them. At the 1802 Fort Wilkinson conference, for example, Creek dancers performed an eagle-tail dance for federal commissioners Benjamin Hawkins, Andrew Pickens, and James Wilkinson, touching them with white eagles' wings before seating them on white deerskins in front of a white pole. (To emphasize the chromatic dichotomy between whiteness, the color of peace, and the color red, which they associated with war, Creek *micos* broke a red-painted bow and arrows in front of the commissioners.) Chiefs incorporated their warriors into these ceremonies of possession by staging war dances, lacrosse games, and the "ball plays" of the Native Southeast. They used metaphorical language to assuage the fears and ill feelings of the conferees, declaring that their words would open one another's eyes and ears and dry their blood and tears, or calling attention to the brightly burning conference fires and the good omens that attended the meeting. The Wyandot captain Tarhe in 1815 noted that these words were sacred, calling them "the emblematic language that the Great Spirit gave to his children." Legal scholar Robert A. Williams Jr. notes another important purpose of these metaphors: they served a "jurisgenerative" function, demonstrating the common humanity of both parties by asserting that they shared one another's suffering and hope, thereby laying the groundwork for "a binding treaty relationship of law."[12]

Indians' wealthier American "fathers"—a term that the Woodland Indians used to denote avuncularity, not paternal authority—were then supposed to play their particular role and complete the bond by displaying hospitality to the men and women who attended the conference and distributing gifts at its end. At the 1815 Detroit peace conference, Odawa speaker Ouquenogsch declared that William Henry Harrison's talk of peace made him smile but that "both his face and his heart would smile more if his belly was full." Throughout the 1780s and 1790s, even when the treasury was low or empty, American commissioners provided food and drink for Native American conference guests. At the 1809 Fort Wayne conference, Harrison supplied his 1,400 Lakes Indian guests with 870 quarts of whiskey, perhaps hoping to fuddle the Miamis and Delawares with alcohol, though the attending chiefs would not necessarily have seen his gesture in this light. Ojibwas and other Lakes Indians referred to liquor as "milk," viewing it not only as a foodstuff and medicine but as a symbol of the quasi-familial bond that treaties renewed.[13]

Treaties were also opportunities for Americans to demonstrate generosity, and distribution of presents became one of the crucial components not only of treaty councils but of treaties themselves. Henry Knox and the members of Congress agreed in 1787 that the U.S. government could use gifts of clothing, metalwares, firearms, and other goods to pay Indians for land cessions, and shortly thereafter he and federal commissioners introduced the concept of annuity payments into federal Indian policy. Beginning with the Treaties of New York and Holston (with the Creeks and Cherokees, respectively), the president and Senate promised annual distributions of merchandise or cash to Indian nations whose lands or allegiance they sought. By 1819, these annuities already totaled $152,000 per annum. Particular kinds of presents could also, federal officials hoped, influence Native Americans' behavior: uniforms and medals and chiefs' salaries could advertise the attachment of influential chiefs and captains to the United States, and gifts of livestock and agricultural hardware could help advance the United States' Indian "civilization" policy. The latter program proposed to convert Indians into commercial farmers who would regard land as individual property, a commodity they could exchange for capital or consumer goods, thus making it easier for the federal government to acquire that land.[14]

Gifts would supposedly make Indians more tractable, but Native Americans saw them as symbols of their ongoing relationship with the United States. The 1794 Treaty of Canandaigua promised the Six Nations of Iroquois annual payments of cash and goods in return for their perpetual friendship, and into the twentieth century the Iroquois continued to demand the annual distribution of treaty cloth, which represented their enduring diplomatic relationship with the United States. Two decades after Canandaigua, Iowa Indians informed American officials that they would like to make a land cession in order to procure an annuity, which they may have wanted less for material reasons than to serve as a sign of their "coming more closely under the protection of the United States" and of their friendly relationship with this sovereign. Annuities also represented the recipients' collective unity and identity: an Odawa chief requested at an 1807 conference a gorget inscribed with the declaration that "the Ottawa nation is entitled to eight hundred dollars a year forever by the Treaty of Detroit." This would remind his kinsmen that annuities testified to their national identity. In later decades, chiefs would resist a federal law converting annuities into per capita head-of-household payments, arguing that this would diminish their own authority and their ability to spend funds or resources on behalf of their nation, and also hold back the "civilization" of their people.[15]

Civilizing gifts, along with the education funds that treaty-makers began to supply in the early nineteenth century (beginning with an 1803 grant to the Kaskaskias), would supposedly encourage Native Americans to sell off the hunting territories they no longer needed and assimilate them to American laws and the American market economy. However, Native American leaders proved more than willing to turn the civilization program into an adjunct of their national sovereignty. The school funds that various land-cession treaties granted to the Cherokees, Choctaws, and Shawnees provided those nations' leaders with a unifying political asset under their own control, one that gave them leverage over missionary teachers and some say in the kind of education their children would receive—day schools or boarding schools, technical or academic training. As more Indians acquired an Anglo-American education or became familiar with the values of mainstream American society, they began to adopt additional elements of American "civilization" that supported their sovereignty: national governments and written laws. The Cherokees famously had an elected legislature, court system, and law code by the mid-1820s. The post-Removal Wyandots and Shawnees developed similar institutions in Kansas in the 1840s and 1850s.[16]

In treaty negotiations Indian leaders resisted American commissioners' demands for land but generally agreed to make cessions, which grew steadily larger over time, from 35 million acres during the 1790s to about 100 million acres during the presidency of Andrew Jackson. Within the shrinking bounds of Indian country the United States also obtained permission to construct roadways and government-run trading posts or factories. The federal government saw roads through Indian country as a way to increase its authority and control, as the War Department could use them to move troops in wartime. Arthur St. Clair's military road in western Ohio, for example, contributed to the success of Anthony Wayne's 1794 campaign against the Northwest Indians. Factories, meanwhile, would wean Indian hunters from their dependence on British traders and encourage them to run up debts that the War Department could induce them to discharge with land cessions. Indian leaders, however, mitigated the ill effects of each of these concessions or turned them to advantage. In the Northwest they obtained treaty clauses allowing their people to hunt and fish on ceded lands until game stocks were exhausted, which could take decades in regions far from the white-settlement frontier. Federal roads did not always remain entirely under federal control: the Choctaws and Chickasaws, for instance, retained the right to operate inns and ferries on the Natchez Trace. As for the factories, Native Americans generally treated them more as utilities than engines of debt peonage: the factors sold manufactured goods more cheaply than private traders did, as federal law obliged them to do so, and at many of the trading-houses Indians discharged their debts quickly through the sale of furs and pelts. Many also served as storehouses and distribution points for local Indian nations' annuity goods and cash, so Indian men and women came to associate them with annuities and the diplomatic relationship these symbolized.[17]

With land cession treaties came increasingly elaborate stipulations about territorial boundaries, which American commissioners wished to define accurately. Occasionally federal commissioners would introduce intertribal boundary lines between Indian nations whose lands they did not immediately plan to claim, as in the Treaty of Prairie du Chien (1825), which drew riverine boundaries among the territories of the Ho-Chunk, Menominee, Mesquakie, Ojibwa, Sauk, and Sioux nations. The intent in such cases was to limit interethnic conflicts that might draw in American troops or call into question the United States' authority as a protector and guarantor of peace. In regions where Americans demonstrated a greater appetite for Indian land, Native American chiefs shared federal commissioners' concern with well-marked boundaries and took great care to define or mark their own national borders. At the Fort Harmar conference of 1788–89, Wyandot leaders secured a clause clearly separating their territory from the Shawnees', so that the United States would not take both nations' land in the event of a U.S.-Shawnee war. In the 1790s, Creek chiefs accompanied federal surveyors marking their nation's boundaries, as did Chickasaw leaders in 1807 and Cherokee delegates following a land-cession treaty in 1816. The southeastern Indians understood that one could construe mutually recognized territorial borders as jurisdictional boundaries, one of the features of a sovereign group. The U.S. Supreme Court acknowledged this principle in the 1832 case of *Worcester v. Georgia,* in which the justices ruled that the Cherokees' treaty boundaries constituted a line of autonomy that the U.S. government might cross but the laws of Georgia could not. One might consider the federal protection under which the Cherokees and other Indians fell an abridgement of sovereignty, but Native Americans did not; increasingly they saw it as a shield against discriminatory state laws and a grant of something like coequal status with the states.[18]

That the U.S. government acknowledged Native Americans' boundaries and sovereignty seems a faint blessing when set against the awful reality of Indian Removal, which stripped most of the eastern Indians of their homelands and killed approximately fifteen thousand people by 1850. That Removal left ineffaceable trails of blood and grief across the human landscape of North America is unquestionable. That American Indian sovereignty became one of Removal's casualties seems much harder to argue. The Jackson administration and its successors ultimately carried out several removals, notably of the Cherokees, Creeks, Seminoles, and some of the Potawatomis and Sauks, at gunpoint, but in all cases federal commissioners authorized Removal through treaties signed by Native American leaders and approved by the U.S. Senate. These commissioners employed ample fraud and coercion, to be sure, but since treaties were ultimately negotiated instruments rather than executive dictate, Native American leaders retained a degree of control over their terms. Some, like the New York Oneidas, persuaded the Senate to reject fraudulent Removal agreements. Some, like the Chickasaws, were able to organize their own emigration parties and pay for the costs out of market-rate sales of their eastern lands. About one-third of the Choctaws remained in Mississippi, and the Odawas and Ojibwas, among the most numerous of the Great Lakes Indians, argued and delayed until, in the early 1850s, they finally persuaded the War Department to let them remain in their homelands on small reservations. Those nations who did move, moreover, did not lose their leaders, their corporate identity, or their sense of sovereignty. The Removal agreements they signed did not eliminate the annuities and school funds and other national resources guaranteed by earlier treaties, and they assigned the emigrants new national reserves with defined boundaries. These land grants enjoyed one feature that the eastern Indians' old homelands now lacked, which was their location in territories where no state governments would try to block Native Americans' constitutional governments and laws. Disease, exposure, hunger, and the other vicissitudes of Removal killed thousands of Indians and traumatized thousands more, but they could not kill entire nations and they could not eliminate Natives' sovereignty.[19]

Lewis Cass, territorial governor of Michigan, argued in an 1830 essay that while the U.S. government had long relied on treaties to conduct business with Indians, "a speculative politician has no right to deduce from thence their claim to the attributes of sovereignty." Cass reflected the views of many contemporary Americans, including Andrew Jackson, who made Cass his secretary of war a year later. Cass's assertion ignored the many sovereign attributes that treaties had bestowed on or affirmed for Native Americans: formal assertion of collective identity, recognition as treaty-worthy by a sovereign power, bounded national land claims, and national resources, in the form of annuities and school funds, under the control of Native American leaders. Twentieth-century international law, as expressed by the Montevideo Convention (1933) and the European Union's Badinter Arbitration Committee (1991), would find that these traits made Indian nations similar, if not identical, to independent nation-states. In Cass's own day, American jurists also disagreed with him. Federal courts, the ultimate legal interpreters of American treaties, argued that Native Americans had at least enough autonomy to shield them from state and local laws. In *Worcester v. Georgia,* the Supreme Court declared that American Indians formed separate political communities immune to state law; in *In re Kansas Indians* (1866), the justices ruled that even an Indian nation without collective land holdings remained under the treaty-making authority and protection of the U.S. government; and in *U.S. v. Winans* (1905), the Court backed away from a plenary grant of power it had earlier ascribed to Congress, ruling that Indian treaties were "a grant of rights from" Indians to the United States, not the other way around. It would be several more decades before Native Americans began pressing the U.S. Congress and courts for the restoration of their sovereign assets, such as land claims and fishing rights, that nineteenth-century treaties had once guaranteed, but the treaties themselves had already helped turn Indian nations from leagues of towns or families into bounded territorial states with national leaders and institutions.[20]

Like so much about modern America, this development would have baffled many members of the revolutionary generation. Even if they did not view Native Americans as implacable enemies of their new nation, the founders of the American republic expected Indians to emigrate, die out, or otherwise disappear within a short time, certainly in less than a century. Secretary of War Henry Knox, whose native New England had lost most of its indigenous population in the previous century and a half, wrote in 1789 that if the expansion and growth of white American settlements continued, "In a short period the idea of an Indian this side the Mississippi will only be found in the page of the historian." The secretary of war hoped that the eastern Indians would survive, but as assimilated, commercial farmers and citizens, not as culturally and politically independent peoples.[21]

Inadvertently, Knox, who wanted to furnish Indians with the material technology of "civilized" society, also provided them with the legal "technology" that would help them retain their national identity and survive as Native Americans: treaty-making. What Knox and his white contemporaries saw as inconvenient necessities, Indians viewed as political charters, which allowed Indian nations to retain their autonomy and develop a quasi-sovereign relationship with the U.S. government, analogous to that enjoyed by the states. The credit for this belongs not to Knox or William Henry Harrison or other American officials, however, but to Native American men and women whose ceremonies, speeches, arguments, lawsuits, cultural adaptation, and sheer tenacity turned archaic diplomatic instruments into constitutional documents. In the process, they helped lay the groundwork for modern Native North America, with its 560-plus federally recognized Indian nations and tribal entities and more than 5 million indigenous Americans, a cultural and political mosaic that figured in no eighteenth century European American's vision or planning.[22]

Notes

1. Hannah Arendt, *On Revolution* (New York, 1965), esp. 125–27, 166–67; Leonard Sadosky, *Revolutionary Negotiations: Indians, Empires, and Diplomats in the Founding of America* (Charlottesville, Va., 2009), 200; Eliga Gould, *Among the Powers of the Earth: The American Revolution and the Making of a New World Empire* (Cambridge, Mass., 2012).

2. Colin Calloway, *The American Revolution in Indian Country: Crisis and Diversity in Native American Communities* (New York, 1995), 292–301; Bernard Sheehan, *Seeds of Extinction: Jeffersonian Philanthropy and the American Indian* (Chapel Hill, N.C., 1973).

3. Lorenzo Veracini, *Settler Colonialism: A Theoretical Overview* (New York, 2010), esp. 35–50, 55–57, 64, 77, 93; Mikal Brotnov Eckstrom and Margaret D. Jacobs, "Teaching American History as Settler Colonialism," in *Why You Can't Teach United States History without American Indians,* ed. Susan Sleeper-Smith et al. (Chapel Hill, N.C., 2015), 259–72; Jeffrey Ostler and Nancy Shoemaker, "Settler Colonialism in Early American History: Introduction," *William and Mary Quarterly,* 3rd ser., 76 (2019): 361–68; Bernard Bailyn, *To Begin the World Anew: The Genius and Ambiguities of the American Founders* (New York, 2003), 31–36; Peter Silver, *Our Savage Neighbors: How Indian War Transformed Early America* (New York, 2008), esp. 227–60.

4. Dorothy V. Jones, *License for Empire: Colonialism by Treaty in Early America* (Chicago, 1982); Lauren Benton, *A Search for Sovereignty: Law and Geography in European Empires, 1400–1900* (New York, 2010), 23, 56; Lisa Ford, *Settler Sovereignty: Jurisdiction and Indigenous People in America and Australia, 1788–1836* (Cambridge, Mass., 2010), 28 (1st quotation); John Weaver, *The Great Land Rush and the Making of the Modern World, 1650–1900* (Montreal, 2003), 162–65; Colin Calloway, *Pen and Ink Witchcraft: Treaties and Treaty-Making in American Indian History* (New York, 2013), 5–6. Australian and New Zealand colonists each negotiated only one treaty with the Aborigines and Maoris, and Australia's government disallowed the former. Afrikaaners signed about half a dozen treaties and land-use agreements with Bataung, Ndebele, and Xhosa chiefs. Canadian officials signed seventeen treaties with the Dominion's First Nations peoples.

5. David Andrew Nichols, *Red Gentlemen and White Savages: Indians, Federalists, and the Search for Order on the American Frontier* (Charlottesville, Va., 2008), 28–30, 30 (1st quotation); Andrew Cayton, "'Noble Actors' upon the 'Theater of Honor': Power

and Civility in the Treaty of Greenville," in *Contact Points: American Frontiers from the Mohawk Valley to the Mississippi, 1750–1830,* ed. Andrew Cayton and Fredrika Teute (Chapel Hill, N.C., 1998), 235–69; Robert V. Remini, *Andrew Jackson and His Indian Wars* (New York, 2001), 88 (2nd and 3rd quotations).

6. Francis Paul Prucha, *American Indian Treaties: The History of a Political Anomaly* (Berkeley, Calif., 1994), 154 (quotation); Remini, *Andrew Jackson and His Indian Wars,* 108–29, 163–205; Max Edling, *A Revolution in Favor of Government: Origins of the U.S. Constitution and the Making of the American State* (New York, 2003); Ronald Satz, *American Indian Policy in the Jacksonian Era* (Lincoln, Neb., 1975), 97; Report of the Secretary of War to the President, July 7, 1789, Walter Lowrie and Matthew Clarke, eds., *American State Papers: Class Two, "Indian Affairs,"* 2 vols. (Washington, D.C., 1832), 1:53 (hereafter *ASPIA*). The cost of Removal approached $70 million by 1837, and the program continued until the early 1850s.

7. Benton, *Search for Sovereignty,* 31, 33.

8. Calloway, *Pen and Ink Witchcraft,* 106 (quotation); Treaty of Washington, February 8, 1831, Charles Kappler, ed., *Indian Affairs, Laws, and Treaties,* 7 vols. (Washington, D.C., 1904–71), 2:319–23; Journal of Proceedings of the Treaty with the Menominees, August 30, 1836, Treaty no. 209, Documents Relating to the Negotiation of Ratified and Unratified Treaties with Various Indian Tribes, Documents Relating to Indian Affairs, University of Wisconsin Library, http://uwdc.library.wisc.edu/collections /History/IndianTreatiesMicro; Anthony F. C. Wallace, *The Long Bitter Trail: Andrew Jackson and the Indians* (New York, 1993), 107; Treaty of Washington, November 1, 1837, Kappler, ed., *Indian Affairs,* 2:498–500; Raymond J. DeMallie, "'Touching the Pen': Plains Indian Treaty Councils in Ethnohistorical Perspective," in *Ethnicity on the Great Plains,* ed. Frederick Luebke (Lincoln, Neb., 1980), 38–53.

9. Colin Calloway, *New Worlds for All: Indians, Europeans, and the Remaking of Early America* (Baltimore, 1997), 128–29; Timothy Smith, "Wampum as Primitive Valuables," *Research in Economic Anthropology* 5 (1983): 225–46; Nancy Shoemaker, *A Strange Likeness: Becoming Red and White in Eighteenth-Century North America* (New York, 2004), 64–68; Nichols, *Red Gentlemen and White Savages,* 33–34, 47, 52; Cary Miller, *Ogimaag: Anishinaabeg Leadership, 1760–1845* (Lincoln, Neb., 2010), 103–5; Richard White, *The Middle Ground: Indians, Empires, and Republics in the Great Lakes Region, 1650–1815* (New York, 1991), 446.

10. Journal of the Commission, October 10, 1820, Documents Relating to Ratified Treaty no. 115, Documents Relating to Indian Affairs, University of Wisconsin Library; Hopewell Treaty Journal, January 9, 1786, *ASPIA,* 1:51 (quotations); Joseph M. Hall Jr., *Zamumo's Gifts: Indian-European Exchange in the Colonial Southeast* (Philadelphia, 2009), 111; Cameron Shriver, "Wabash Indians: How Rivers Influenced Eighteenth-Century Miami Community and Territory," paper presented at the Annual Meeting of the American Society for Ethnohistory, New Orleans, September 13, 2013; Miller, *Ogimaag,* 43–44, 109.

11. Journal of the Commission, October 10, 1820, Documents Relating to Ratified Treaty no. 115, Documents Relating to Indian Affairs, University of Wisconsin Library;

James A. Clifton, *The Prairie People: Continuity and Change in Potawatomi Indian Culture, 1665–1965* (Lawrence, Kans., 1977), 224–45, 276–78; William McLoughlin, *Cherokee Renascence in the New Republic* (Princeton, N.J., 1986), 230–31; Greenville Treaty Journal, July 21, 24, 1795, *ASPIA*, 1:69–70, 573; Journal of the Proceedings of the Commissioners at Detroit, August 31, 1815, ibid., 2:20.

12. Nichols, *Red Gentlemen and White Savages*, 35, 39, 50, 101, 139; Robert A. Williams Jr., *Linking Arms Together: American Indian Treaty Visions of Law and Peace, 1600–1800* (New York, 1999), 53–57, 65, 80, 95–97, 95 (quotations); Journal of the Fort Wilkinson Treaty, May 24, 1802; Journal of the Proceedings of the Commissioners at Detroit, August 31, 1815, *ASPIA*, 1:672, 2:20 ("emblematic language").

13. Patricia Galloway, "'The Chief Who Is Your Father': Choctaw and French Views of the Diplomatic Relation," in *Powhatan's Mantle: Indians in the Colonial Southeast,* ed. Peter Wood, Gregory Waselkov, and Thomas Hatley, rev. ed. (1989; Lincoln, Neb., 2006), 345–70; Journal of the Proceedings at Detroit, August 25, 1815, *ASPIA*, 2:19 ("face and heart"); Nichols, *Red Gentlemen and White Savages*, 34, 50, 131, 141; Robert M. Owens, *Mr. Jefferson's Hammer: William Henry Harrison and the Origins of American Indian Policy* (Norman, Okla., 2007), 200–204; Bruce White, "'Give Us a Little Milk': The Social and Cultural Meanings of Gift-Giving in the Lake Superior Fur Trade," *Minnesota History* 48 (1982): 60–71.

14. Nichols, *Red Gentlemen and White Savages*, 122–23, 125, 134, 141; Reginald Horsman, *Expansion and American Indian Policy, 1783–1812* (Norman, Okla., 1992), 38, 41, 45, 59–60; Treaties of New York, August 7, 1790, and Holston, July 2, 1791, Kappler, ed., *Indian Affairs*, 2:25–33; Statement of the Annuities . . . Payable Each Year under Indian Treaties to the Year 1819, *ASPIA*, 2:220.

15. Laurence Hauptman, "Alice Jemison: A Modern 'Mother of the Nation,'" in *Sifters: Native American Women's Lives,* ed. Theda Perdue (New York, 2001), 183; William Clark et al. to the Secretary of War, October 18, 1815, *ASPIA*, 2:10 (quotation); William Hull to Henry Dearborn, November 18, 1807, *Michigan Pioneer and Historical Collections,* 40 vols. (Lansing, Mich., 1876–1929), 40:219–20; Stephen Warren, *The Shawnees and Their Neighbors, 1795–1870* (Urbana, Ill., 2005), 144–45.

16. Nichols, *Red Gentlemen and White Savages*, 193–94; Lori Daggar, "The Mission Complex: Economic Development, 'Civilization,' and Empire in the Early Republic," *Journal of the Early Republic* 36 (2016): 467–91; Treaty of Doak's Stand, October 18, 1820, Kappler, ed., *Indian Affairs*, 2:191–95; Arthur DeRosier, *The Removal of the Choctaw Indians* (Knoxville, Tenn., 1970), 37, 48–52; Warren, *Shawnees and Their Neighbors,* 103, 147–49; Kevin Abing, "A Holy Battleground: Methodist, Baptist, and Quaker Missionaries among Shawnee Indians, 1830–1844," *Kansas History* 21 (1998): 118–37, esp. 124–26; John Ridge to Albert Gallatin, February 27, 1826, Theda Perdue and Michael D. Green, eds., *The Cherokee Removal: A Brief History with Documents,* 2nd ed. (1995; Boston, 2005), 35–44; John P. Bowes, *Exiles and Pioneers: Eastern Indians in the Trans-Mississippi West* (New York, 2007), 180.

17. McLoughlin, *Cherokee Renascence,* 26; Nichols, *Red Gentlemen and White Savages*, 33, 103, 174–75; Satz, *American Indian Policy in the Jacksonian Era,* 97; Jeffrey

Pasley, "Midget on Horseback: American Indians and the History of the American State," *Common-Place* 9:1 (2008), http://commonplace.online/article/midget-on -horseback/; Treaties of Greenville, August 3, 1795, and St. Peters, July 29, 1837, Kappler, ed., *Indian Affairs,* 2:42, 492; David Andrew Nichols, *Peoples of the Inland Sea: Native Americans and Newcomers in the Great Lakes Region, 1600–1870* (Athens, Ohio, 2018), 156–57, 194–95; Treaties of Chickasaw Bluffs, October 24, 1801, and Brownstown, November 25, 1808, Kappler, ed., *Indian Affairs,* 2:55–56, 99–100; Henry Dearborn to Samuel Mitchell, July 9, 1803, Records of the Office of the Secretary of War, Letters Sent, Indian Affairs, microfilm M-15, 1:359–60, National Archives, Washington, D.C. On the factories, see David Andrew Nichols, *Engines of Diplomacy: Indian Trading Factories and the Negotiation of American Empire* (Chapel Hill, N.C., 2016); Treaties of St. Louis, November 3, 1804; Washington, November 14, 1805; and Fort Clark, November 10, 1808, Kappler, ed., *Indian Affairs,* 2:76, 85–86, 95; and Andrew Isenberg, "The Market Revolution in the Borderlands: George Champlin Sibley in Missouri and New Mexico, 1808–1826," *Journal of the Early Republic* 21 (2001): 445–65.

18. Nichols, *Red Gentlemen and White Savages,* 103; Treaties of Prairie du Chien, August 19, 1825; Fort Harmar, January 9, 1789; Coleraine, June 29, 1796; and Chickasaw Council House, September 14, 1816, Kappler, ed., *Indian Affairs,* 2:250–55, 22, 47, 134; Henry Dearborn to Thomas Wright, April 1, 1807, Records of the Office of the Secretary of War, Letters Sent, Indian Affairs, microfilm M-15, 2:298, National Archives; *Worcester v. Georgia,* 31 U.S. (6 Peters), 515, 518, 520, http://supreme.justia .com/cases/federal/us/31/515/case.html. See also Angela Pulley Hudson, *Creek Paths and Federal Roads: Indians, Settlers, and Slaves and the Making of an American South* (Chapel Hill, N.C., 2010), 37–49.

19. Wallace, *The Long Bitter Trail;* John P. Bowes, *Land Too Good for Indians: Northern Indian Removal* (Norman, Okla., 2016), 65–66, 72–76, 129–31, 143–47, 170–73, 200–202; Karim Tiro, *The People of the Standing Stone: The Oneida Nation from the Revolution through the Era of Removal* (Amherst, Mass., 2011), 157–86; Amanda Paige, Fuller Bumpers, and Daniel Littlefield, *Chickasaw Removal* (Ada, Okla., 2010), 57–58, 62–65, 101–2; James M. McClurken, "Ottawa Adaptive Strategies to Indian Removal," *Michigan Historical Review* 12 (1986): 29–55; Clara Sue Kidwell, *Choctaws and Missionaries in Mississippi, 1818–1918* (Norman, Okla., 1997), 159–75; Brenda J. Child, *Holding Our World Together: Ojibwe Women and the Survival of Community* (New York, 2012), 66–78; Warren, *Shawnees and Their Neighbors,* 98–99; Bowes, *Exiles and Pioneers,* 180; Duane Champagne, *Social Order and Political Change: Constitutional Governments among the Cherokee, the Choctaw, the Chickasaw and the Creek* (Stanford, Calif., 1992).

20. "Removal of the Indians," *North American Review,* January 1830, Perdue and Green, eds., *The Cherokee Removal,* 119 (1st quotation); P. Christiaan Klieger, *The Microstates of Europe: Designer Nations in a Post-Modern World* (Lanham, Md., 2013), 17–18; *In re Kansas Indians* (72 US 737), http://caselaw.lp.findlaw.com/scripts/getcase .pl?court=US&vol=72&invol=737; Calloway, *Pen and Ink Witchcraft,* 237–43, 238 (2nd quotation).

21. Report of the Secretary of War to the President, July 7, 1789, *ASPIA,* 1:53. Cf. Jeffrey Ostler, *Surviving Genocide: Native Nations and the United States from the American Revolution to Bleeding Kansas* (New Haven, Conn., 2019), 93–97. On the persistence of New England Indian families and communities in Knox's time, see Daniel Mandell, *Tribe, Race, History: Native Americans in Southern New England, 1780–1880* (Baltimore, 2008).

22. "The American Indian and Alaska Native Population, 2010," http://www .census.gov/prod/cen2010/briefs/c2010br-10.pdf; National Congress of American Indians, "Tribal Nations and the United States: An Introduction," May 2019, 10–11, http:// www.ncai.org/tribalnations/introduction/Tribal_Nations_and_the_United_States _An_Introduction-web-.pdf. The population estimate includes mixed-race Native Americans; the above count of Indian nations includes Alaska Native communities.

6   "Arraying Him against Himself"

*The Jefferson Presidency and the American Future
through the Eyes of Alexander Hamilton*

TODD ESTES

The last years of Alexander Hamilton's life are easy to overlook. Humiliated
and embarrassed by his own political contretemps in the 1800 election, his
party out of power and fading fast, his bitterest political rivals occupying
the two highest seats in government, Hamilton, so the standard narrative
goes, retreated to his law practice and his family, sank into despair and dis-
illusionment about the future, and, lacking influence and power, seemingly
headed inevitably toward his fatal duel with Aaron Burr. It is little wonder
that scholars usually give short shrift to Hamilton's last four years, rushing
through events to get to his death. Even the editors of the *Papers of Alexander
Hamilton* are bluntly dismissive, writing, "His career in national politics had
ended, and he devoted his few remaining years to his family, his law practice,
and his new country estate, the Grange."[1]

The problem with this standard narrative is that it is wrong on nearly all
counts. At the very least, it is overdrawn and incomplete. A close examination of this infrequently studied, cursorily treated period of Hamilton's life
contradicts the portrait that a morose Hamilton withdrew from public life,
was bereft of influence, and took little interest in politics—present or future.
Actually, the situation of being out of power prompted some of Hamilton's
most energized and agonized writing as he was forced to grapple with a
political world markedly changed. While he had every reason, politically and
personally, to be depressed, the years 1800 to 1804 were the extended moment when he reaffirmed his faith in republican empire and tried to make
sense of Jeffersonian democracy. Hamilton reevaluated his own political beliefs as he studied carefully the actions of his great rival in power. And as

he reconsidered, he proposed a strategy for how Federalists could respond to the Jeffersonians and to a president whose actions Hamilton came to understand differently than he expected.

A better understanding of what Hamilton was doing in the post-1800 years helps us better realize the context for two widely misunderstood writings: his 1802 proposal in a letter to James Bayard for a "Christian Constitutional Society" to combat the Jeffersonians and his lengthy newspaper essays from the same period, "The Examination." If we read the Bayard letter as being part of a much larger effort on Hamilton's part—one that grew out of the presidential election contest of 1800–1801 and occupied him frequently during the last four years of his life—we glimpse a critical if little-studied and unappreciated period in Hamilton's life in which he was forced to rethink his own plans and programs, his own sense of the nation and its government, and the future direction of the country in the midst of the Jefferson presidency. His plans for the society were an outgrowth of the themes he expressed in his eighteen-part "The Examination" newspaper essays, published in late 1801 and early 1802. Again, even friendly scholars have also roundly criticized or ignored "The Examination" essays, which responded to Jefferson's first annual message to Congress from December 1801. The editors of *The Papers of Alexander Hamilton* wrote that it "attracted almost no attention from Hamilton's contemporaries, and most scholars have ignored it" too, because the writings were of "inferior" quality to his earlier efforts, such as those he wrote as "Publius" or "Pacificus" or "Camillus"; because Hamilton was much more effective writing *in favor* of programs or policies rather than against; and lastly, they conclude sweepingly, "because Hamilton was no longer a significant force in national politics, his views were of comparatively little interest to either Republicans or Federalists."[2]

In some ways, the critics have a point. In comparison to his justifiably famous writings in favor of the new Constitution, the neutrality policy, and the Jay Treaty, Hamilton's post-1800 work pales. Set in the proper context and examined closely, however, these writings refute the presumption that Hamilton did little more than sulk and retreat in his last years. More importantly, they also show that Hamilton spent those years engaged in an ongoing effort to understand and come to terms with the Jeffersonian presidency and to chart a course forward for the Federalists. These writings are best read in the context of Hamilton's extended project: finding a way to rebuild and reboot the Federalists as a loyal opposition party and then gradually build them back into a majority party that could defeat the Jeffersonians in 1804. Further, his writings offer a window into his larger ruminations on democracy, republicanism, and empire. Hamilton's last years have not only been misunderstood; they have been too little valued in trying to make sense of the intellectual thought of the early republic's best thinkers. Carefully considered, his work during the last years of his life has much to teach us.

The election of 1800 was not Hamilton's finest moment. His anger and resentment and passion for manipulation all got the better of him. Hamilton's role in undermining John Adams prior to the election through his fifty-page attack pamphlet, "Letter from Alexander Hamilton, Concerning the Public Conduct and Character of John Adams, Esq. President of the United States," unquestionably did Hamilton's reputation a great deal of harm—both at the time and since.[3] Even before the 1800 election was settled, Hamilton was already trying to reposition the Federalists for the next contest.

In many ways, he thought, it might actually be in the best long-term interests of the Federalist party if Adams lost to Jefferson. Rather than having Adams returned to office for four more ineffectual years that might further damage the party and the nation, there were reasons why Jefferson might, counterintuitively, prove useful to a resurgence of Federalism on proper principles. First of all, Hamilton believed it possible to secure from Jefferson "assurances on certain points—the maintenance of the present system especially on the cardinal articles of public Credit, a *Navy, Neutrality*" in return for Federalist support in the House. If such a deal could be struck, then the Federalists would be rid of Adams, saved from Burr, and in business with a new president owing his office to the Federalists.[4]

Hamilton thought that Burr's unprincipled ambition made him "the most unfit man in the U.S. for the office of President" and warned, "Let us not be responsible for the evils which in all probability will follow the preference. All calculations that may lead to it must prove fallacious." However, "If Jefferson is President the whole responsibility of bad measures will rest with the Antifederalists," as Hamilton still referred to the Jeffersonian Republicans. But, "If Burr is made so by the Federalists the whole responsibility will rest with them."[5] Federalists would do well by doing right, Hamilton thought.

As Hamilton worked assiduously to secure Jefferson's selection in the House, he suggested that Jefferson as president might not be nearly the threat that Federalists (including Hamilton) had long been arguing he would be in the newspapers. It was simply not true, Hamilton asserted, that Jefferson "is an enemy to the Executive, or that he is for confounding all the powers in the House of Rs." Hamilton noted that when he served together with his rival under Washington, Jefferson was "generally for a large construction of the Executive authority." Furthermore, Jefferson had never advocated the Senate interfering in executive authority. For all these reasons, Hamilton believed Jefferson would not be a party to the weakening of the presidency should he assume the office.[6]

Furthermore, Jefferson was not such a zealot that in pursuing his program he might endanger his popularity. Hamilton observed, "He is as likely as any man I know to temporize—to calculate what will be likely to promote his own reputation and advantage." The result of this temporizing, Hamilton believed, would be "the preservation of systems, though originally opposed, which being once established, could not be overturned without danger to the person who did it." His "true estimate" of a prospective Jefferson presidency concluded that the nation was likely to see brought forth "a temporizing rather than a violent system."[7]

Jefferson's administration was likely to be a disappointment to his hardcore followers who hoped for the kind of radical change of which Hamilton thought Jefferson incapable. The result would be an ineffectual presidency that did no real harm to Hamilton's systems and was likely not to be popular enough with voters to merit reelection.[8]

Accordingly, when Federalists gathered in New York City in April 1801 to nominate candidates for the state assembly, Hamilton used the occasion to adumbrate a posture and ideology of opposition to the Jeffersonians nationwide. Hamilton urged New York Federalists to "harmonize" their politics with their friends in New England, but his address was surprisingly moderate and even charitable toward Jefferson. He was, he told the crowd, "disposed to hope the best from the administration of Mr. Jefferson, yet it was certainly desirable to be able to present such a phalanx as might enable us to support the chief magistrate, if he went right, and sufficient to deter him if he appeared disposed to go wrong." Hamilton hoped that the Federalists in opposition "would form an honorable contrast to the conduct of our opponents under the late administration." Hamilton "was for supporting Mr. Jefferson's administration in every measure not blaringly repugnant to the honor & interest of our country." He closed by calling on his party to "retain their union & their zeal—and not relax in their exertions."⁹

Hamilton's calls for moderation were not new. During the war crisis with France in 1798, he clearly favored strengthening the government, punishing seditious practices, and preparing a provisional army, but he also steered a middle course between Federalist extremists on the one side and Jeffersonian activists on the other. It was Hamilton who, although he supported the Alien and Sedition Acts, urged caution in administering them. "Let us not establish a tyranny," he wrote. "Energy is a very different thing from violence."¹⁰

Throughout the summer and fall of 1801, as his political speeches made clear, Hamilton was both much sought after and a willing participant in the political world. And then he suffered the worst tragedy that can befall a parent: his nineteen-year-old son, Philip, was killed in a duel with a Jeffersonian lawyer in November 1801 defending his father's name. For a time, Hamilton was unable to write about the death of his first-born child. Even as heart-rending letters of condolence poured in from notable friends, a devastated Hamilton was mostly silent. Philip's death was soon followed by another family tragedy that grew out of the first—the mental breakdown of his seventeen-year-old daughter, Angelica, in the face of Philip's death. Very close to her older brother, Angelica was stricken and reduced to a partially lucid, childlike state until her death at age seventy-three. The combination of these tragedies—the way that one death robbed him of two of his beloved children—devastated Hamilton.¹¹

And yet he persisted. Less than a month after his son's death, he took to the pages of the *New-York Evening Post* to launch an eighteen-part series that ran from December 1801 until April 1802. Spurred by his reaction to Jefferson's first annual message of December 8, 1801, and still drenched in grief, Hamilton took up his pen and reflected on the Jefferson presidency. With time, Hamilton was changing his mind. His earlier calls to fellow Federalists to give Jefferson time and to support him when warranted now gave way to disappointment and criticism, tinged with bitterness and sarcasm. "Instead of delivering a *speech* to the House of Congress, at the opening of the present session, the President has thought fit to transmit a *Message*," he hissed acerbically, contrasting unfavorably Jefferson's sending of a message with the live speeches given by Washington and Adams. Then he mocked Jefferson for cravenly pursuing popularity, noting that the new message was likely to win public acclaim since it promised Americans freedom "from the burdens and restraints of government." After all, Hamilton wrote derisively, "Good patriots must, at all events, please the People." Jefferson's pursuit of personal popularity may have secured for him the affections of the people but it harmed the nation. Anyone "anxious for the safety of our Government" ought to be alarmed. The new president's message "makes, or aims at making, a most prodigal sacrifice of constitutional energy, of sound principle, and of public interest, to the popularity of one man."[12]

The first eight numbers of "The Examination" developed criticisms of Jefferson's policies on public credit, foreign affairs, internal revenue, and more. Hamilton detected a pattern of action that tried to destroy the "national spirit and a national character; and to let in the most powerful means of perverting and corrupting both the one and the other. This is more," Hamilton observed, "than the moderate opponents of Mr. Jefferson's elevation ever feared from his administration; much more than the most wrongheaded of his own sect dared hope." Most of all, "it is infinitely more than any one who had read the fair professions in his Inaugural Speech could have suspected." What most aggrieved Hamilton, he claimed, was the way the new administration allegedly turned away from the Constitution produced in Philadelphia in its headlong pursuit of foreign principles: "In vain were the anxious labors of a Washington bestowed. Their works are regarded as nothing better than empty bubbles destined to be blown away by the mere breath of a disciple of *Turgot;* a pupil of *Condorcet.*"[13]

Hamilton had been wrong about Jefferson. Rather than "temporizing" while sustaining the essential structures of Federalist governance, rather than pursuing a moderate, bipartisan course as his inaugural address suggested, Jefferson was already turning the ship of state around. Less than a year into Jefferson's term, Hamilton realized that his sanguine expectations of Jefferson's leadership and his reassurances to fellow Federalists on that score had been deeply erroneous. "The Examination" is filled with anger, frustration, and disappointment. But the series also sets forth a significantly revised plan for how to combat this assault on Federalism. What is too little appreciated in this series is the way in which Hamilton, surprised by his longtime rival, reevaluated his assessment of a Jefferson presidency and then made midcourse corrections and adjusted his political planning once he realized that his initial expectations were mistaken.

Hamilton was not the only Federalist trying to calculate how to combat the Jeffersonians. In February 1802, in the midst of "The Examination" series, Hamilton received a letter from Gouverneur Morris about responding to the repeal of the Judiciary Act. Morris had a bold plan: "Would it not be useful to establish Committees of Correspondence from Baltimore to Boston of which New Yk. to be the Center as being a more favorable Position to collect opinions thro that Tract of Country?" These committees should be appointed "by the People" and should contain merchants who were "moderate men" who might collect petitions in support of resolutions that the repeal was inexpedient, that the Judiciary Act was considered useful to the administration of justice and the stability of the system, and that it was the opinion of "many cool and discerning Men" that a repeal was "fraught with such Danger" that the petitioners hoped to see it stayed.[14]

Hamilton replied one week later, pouring cold water on Morris's committees of correspondence ideas. These suggestions were premature and "suppose a much sounder state of the public mind than at present exists." Hamilton believed that any effort to capture public disapproval of administration measures "would only serve to manifest the direct reverse. Impressions are indeed making but as yet," he warned Morris, "within a very narrow sphere." But Hamilton did not despair. "The time may ere long arrive when the minds of men will be prepared to make an offer to *recover* the Constitution, but the many cannot now be brought to make a stand for its preservation." He told Morris bluntly, "We must wait awhile."[15]

In the meantime, Hamilton was developing a foundation on which to base political opposition to Jefferson. In another letter just a few weeks later, he told Charles Cotesworth Pinckney that grounding Federalist politics in a defense of the Constitution made good political sense. The repeal of the Judiciary Act in particular "demands a systematic and persevering effort *by all Constitutional means* to produce a revocation of the precedent, and to restore the Constitution." The best way to do this, he thought, was to call a meeting of leading Federalists from various states to establish a strategy and plan and set a proper line. Hamilton worried that without a centralized, coordinated effort, the party might be led astray by what he called "incorrect men with very incorrect views" who could promote "*combinations* and *projects* injurious to us as a party, and very detrimental to the Country." Hamilton had clearly found his anchor: the Federalist Party should portray itself as a defender of the Constitution, protesting Jeffersonian usurpations.[16]

Hamilton voiced these same sentiments publicly in "The Examination." He argued that the voice of "true patriotism" would lead Americans to a vigorous "restoration of their VIOLATED CHARTER." Hamilton noted that the people had rejected the appeals of "Demagogues" in creating their Constitution and would soon come around this time too: "They will look around and select from among the throng, the men who have heretofore established a claim to their confidence," and they will scorn "the wretched impostors, who, with honeyed lips and guileful heart, are luring them to destruction!" In the end, the American people would escape the present danger, and "they will once more arrange themselves under the banners of the Constitution," repairing the damage done and guarding against any future assaults.[17]

But how to think about Jefferson's execution of the presidency? In the sixteenth "Examination," he began a long treatment of Jefferson's alleged inconsistencies and deviations from past practices and beliefs:

> The President, as a politician, is in one sense particularly
> unfortunate. He furnishes frequent opportunities of arraying
> him against himself—of combatting his opinions at one period
> by his opinions at another. Without doubt, a wise and good man
> may, on proper grounds relinquish an opinion which he has once
> entertained, and the change may even serve as a proof of candour
> and integrity. But with such a man, especially in matters of high
> public importance, changes of this sort must be rare. The contrary is
> always a mark either of a weak and versatile mind, or of an artificial
> and designing character, which, accommodating its creed, to
> circumstances, takes up or lays down an article of faith, just as may
> suit a present convenience.

Hamilton needed to turn Jefferson into an inconsistent, flip-flopping politician in order to make sense of his actions as president. So much seeming deviation from Jefferson's professed public views could only make sense if one "array[ed] him against himself" and found President Jefferson vastly different from before he held power.[18]

Still angered by the repeal of the Judiciary Act, Hamilton acidly remarked that the new position of the administration must be that "ALL OFFICES ARE HOLDEN OF THE PRESIDENT." Such a doctrine, he noted, was "contrary to every republican idea," but he claimed it was voiced by advocates of the measure: "Had a Federalist uttered the sentiment, the cry of monarchy would have resounded from one extremity of the United States to the other. It would have been loudly proclaimed that the mask was thrown aside, by a glaring attempt to transform the servants of the people into the supple tools of Presidential ambition."[19]

Hamilton surely engaged in hyperbole here, but in many ways, Jefferson actually *had* taken Federalist concepts of governance and put them to Republican uses. He had out-Federalized the Federalists, as Henry Adams and other historians later charged, but not quite in the way that Adams and others believed. Instead, Jefferson left his rivals flummoxed by his use of many tactics of Federalist governance—a strong, active presidency; an unwillingness to allow the Constitution's silence on some matters to prevent taking actions that clearly benefited the nation—deployed in service of Jeffersonianism.[20]

Important recent scholarship offers new ways of understanding Jefferson's presidential leadership. This work also suggests that Hamilton might have been pleased (if perplexed) with aspects of Jefferson's presidency, particularly his advocacy and practice of strong executive leadership and his commitment to deepening the country's sense of nationalism in various ways. Jeremy D. Bailey has argued that Jefferson's conception of executive power was actually quite expansive, somewhat Hamiltonian, but that it was also new in that it was firmly rooted in popular democracy. Bailey delineates three core principles in Jefferson's conception of executive power. First, only the president could unify "the will of the nation and thereby embod[y] it." As the nation's sole nationally elected leader, the president, more than Congress, could truly claim to speak for the national will. Second, to represent that national will, which might emerge rapidly during emergencies or extraordinary situations, the president "must sometimes act outside the law, or even against it, on behalf of the public good." In return, the executive had to appeal to the people for their approval of such singular discretionary actions. Finally, to provide a measure by which the people could judge the executive's actions, presidents should periodically issue "declarations of principle" that articulated the reasons for deviating from past practices even while reaffirming those fundamental practices and values themselves.[21]

Another recent study makes it clear that Jefferson was also a devoted nationalist, a president whose actions not only make little sense without being viewed through the prism of nationalism but whose political career from the

American Revolution forward was grounded in a firm pursuit of such goals. "Nearly everything Jefferson did in public life (and much obliquely in private) he justified in the name of the American nation," writes Brian Steele. Jefferson combined this nationalism with his commitment to popular democracy (for whites) and fused them into a strong and broadly popular political philosophy of governance that he and his fellow party members put into practice after 1801. This recent scholarship on Jefferson has thus helped us better understand why Hamilton might have found things to appreciate in his rival's approach to the presidency.[22]

At least part of what makes "The Examination" less successful than his other famous newspaper series is the real ambivalence Hamilton seems to have felt toward the Jeffersonian project. Just when Hamilton thought he had his rival pinned down, Jefferson was evolving into something wholly unexpected—yet not altogether alien from what Hamilton might have advocated himself. Just as Hamilton railed in frustration against Jefferson's acts of "arraying him against himself," Hamilton surely recognized and resented the ways in which Jefferson's executive actions—on Louisiana, on the judiciary, on public credit and the debt—forced Hamilton to array *his* own past self against his present self. Brian Steele best captures the moment of awakening that surely came to Hamilton as he considered Jefferson's actions and discovered him to be both a nationalist and a believer in executive energy: "Insofar as Jefferson read his election as the nation's recovery of the state, his theory would sanction the kind of energetic state that Hamilton might appreciate even if he could never fully admire the uses to which that state would be put."[23]

Jefferson's presidency provided a moving target, not a fixed position against which to run. This explains Hamilton's belief that more time was needed to study and draw a bead on the opponent before the Federalists took their campaign to the people. Hamilton closed the series in April 1802 with a bitter denunciation of the way the Jeffersonians had ungratefully—and without due acknowledgment—built on the solid foundation of government the Federalists had constructed in their twelve years in power. Jefferson and his followers were claiming credit that did not fully belong to them, all the while attacking their predecessors, men "who have been slandered out of the confidence of their fellow-citizens." Hamilton took some hope, however, that the popularity and public acceptance of the Jefferson Republicans was but a temporary condition: "Let them rest assured that the people will not long continue the dupes of their pernicious sorceries. Already, the cause of truth has derived this advantage from the crude essays of their Chief, that the film has been removed from many an eye."[24]

Hamilton was now ready to turn to the popular politicking that he had rejected as premature just a few months earlier. It was time, Hamilton hinted to James Bayard, to get started "in resisting the follies of an infatuated administration." But a short-term fix was not enough: "We must not content ourselves with a temporary effort to oppose the approach of the evil. We must derive instruction from the experience before us. . . . There must be a systematic & persevering endeavour to establish the fortune of a great empire on foundations much firmer than have yet been devised."[25]

Thus, in mid-April 1802, Hamilton laid out a detailed plan for a "systematic and persevering" action designed to reclaim the nation. To those Federalists who counseled patience until public opinion became more reasoned and turned back toward their party, Hamilton was bluntly dismissive. Nothing was more wrong-headed than trusting to reason. "Men are rather reasoning than reasonable animals," he argued, "for the most part governed by the impulse of passion." The Jeffersonians "well understood" this truth, Hamilton noted, and were turning it on the Federalists with great effect. While they professed to appeal only to man's reason, the Republicans at present "are courting the strongest & most active passion of the human heart—*VANITY!*"[26]

Federalists had been burned in the past by "relying so much on the rectitude & utility of their measures, as to have neglected the cultivation of popular favour by fair & justifiable expedients." The opposition had great advantages electorally "for the plain reason, that the vicious are far more active than the good passions, and that to win the latter to our side we must renounce our principles & our object, & unite in corrupting public opinion till it becomes fit for nothing but mischief." Unless the Federalists could "contrive to take hold of & carry along with us some strong feelings of the mind we shall in vain calculate upon any substantial or durable results." Their side would have a hard time with any approach it took, and it would not be easy for them to give any plan "full effect; especially not without some deviations from what on other occasions we have maintained to be right." In plotting courses and weighing options, "we must consider whether it be possible for us to succeed without in some degree employing the weapons which have been employed against us, & whether the actual state & future prospect of things, be not such as to justify the reciprocal use of them." The time had come, Hamilton believed, for Federalists to turn the arts of mobilizing political passions against their opponents, just as those arts had long been turned against the Federalists.[27]

He then offered Bayard his plan for the creation of "The Christian Constitutional Society." Its objects were to be, first, support of the Christian religion and, second, support of the Constitution. Although promotion of the Christian religion was the initial stated object, Hamilton said nothing more about it. The primary goal was plainly support for the Constitution as he advocated in "The Examination." The "present Constitution is the standard to which we are to cling. Under its banners, *bona fide* must we combat our political foes—rejecting all changes but through the channel itself provides for amendments." This new society would rise through "the diffusion of information," not only in newspapers (which reached a wide audience) but in pamphlets (whose audience was more elite). Hamilton called for the creation of a fund to produce these publications and then disseminate them free of charge. Every place that it was feasible, clubs should be created to meet weekly, read the newspapers, and prepare essays in response. He next called for "a lively correspondence" among the various societies, all the better to aid the election of "fit men" to office. Lastly, he wanted to promote institutions of "a charitable & useful nature in the management of Federalists." What he had in mind were immigrant aid organizations and academies for teaching mechanics in the larger cities. Organization in the cities was critical, Hamilton thought, for they "have been employed by the Jacobins to give an impulse to the country."[28]

Hamilton envisioned a democratic political operation—although one that studiously avoided the use of that word, which was still an imprecation to Hamilton and others. Significantly, the democratic practices he outlined here were nothing new for Hamilton. He had done much the same thing in all the other political campaigns in which he figured large: the ratification debate, the debates over neutrality, the Democratic Societies, and the Jay Treaty. In those instances, he and others used public meetings and especially the public papers to shape and mobilize public opinion, to educate the public on the choices before them, and to train fire on the opposing side and its arguments, seeking to undermine their position even as he burnished his own.[29]

The political arm of the society would function as a rapid response unit: rebutting charges and criticisms promptly and spreading the Federalist message. But he was ready now to mobilize the public in order to combat Jefferson in a different way than he anticipated back in 1801, when he argued that Jefferson would be neither dangerous nor innovative nor very successful and urged Federalists merely to be patient and organize for 1804. Jefferson's political jujitsu puzzled Hamilton for a time—and would again on the Louisiana Purchase in the next year—but he had regained his bearings.

Hamilton's Federalist allies, however, did not seem to agree. James Bayard rejected his society out of hand and showed that he had not grasped, as Hamilton had, the new ways Jefferson was using the presidency. Bayard still thought Federalists could simply mark time until the next election. The "other side" was better at organization, Bayard said, because they had the greater share of "political fanaticks." Better, Bayard told Hamilton, not to be "impatient and our adversaries will soon demonstrate to the world the soundness of our doctrines and the imbecility and folly of their own." Bayard still denied the need to organize or politick to combat Jefferson's supple presidential leadership and governance. Realizations like this were what Hamilton had in mind when he lamented to Rufus King that "among Federalists old errors are not cured. They also continue to dream though not quite so preposterously as their opponents. 'All will be very well (say they) when the power once more gets back in Federal hands. The people convinced by experience of the error will repose a *permanent* confidence in good men.'" Hamilton found such thinking laughable.[30]

In that same June 1802 letter to King, Hamilton elaborated on the danger of Federalist complacency and delivered a stinging rebuke to the Jeffersonian dreams of a national future. He remained worried, he told King, that he could "as yet discover no satisfactory symptoms of a revolution of opinion in the *mass*" of citizens, and doubted any would emerge "until inconveniences are extensively felt or until time has produced a disposition to coquet it with new lovers. Vibrations of power," he wrote, "are of the genius of our Government." Furthermore, the prospects for the nation were "not brilliant. The mass is far from sound. At headquarters a most visionary theory presides." Then he bitterly tore apart the assumptions undergirding Jeffersonianism: "No army, no navy no *active* commerce—national defence, not by arms but by embargoes, prohibition of trade &c.—as little government as possible within—these are the pernicious dreams which as far and as fast as possible will be attempted to be realized."[31]

The folly of such dreams, ungrounded in considerations of both history and present reality, was an old theme for Hamilton. In *The Federalist* number 6, Hamilton attacked the complacent visions of those who extolled "those idle theories which have amused us with promises of an exemption from the imperfections, the weaknesses, and the evils incident to society in every shape," and wondered, "Is it not time to awake from the deceitful dream of a golden age" that assumes all will be secure for a republic in a dangerous world? To Hamilton the "deceitful dreams" of those with their head in the sand during the ratification debate were now being repeated just as innocently—and as dangerously, he thought—in the "pernicious dreams" of the Jeffersonian party.[32]

By the end of 1802, a discouraged Hamilton saw little progress in the national political scene. He sneered at "the triumphant reign of Democracy," and with a mixture of frustration and incredulity he noted that "the follies and vices of the Administration have as yet made no material impression to their disadvantage. On the contrary, I think the malady is rather progressive than upon the decline in our Northern Quarter. The last *lullaby* message, instead of inspiring contempt, attracts praise. Mankind," he observed ruefully, "are forever destined to be the dupes of bold & cunning imposture." Then he turned to the issue of Louisiana and deplored the president's lack of a more vigorous policy. He told Charles Cotesworth Pinckney that Jefferson was reputed to be "very stout" in conversation. But when it came to action, the "great embarrassment must be how to carry on war without taxes. The pretty scheme of substituting economy to taxation will not do here, and a war would be a terrible comment upon the abandonment of the Internal Revenue."[33]

Hamilton's dismay only grew as the Louisiana matter played out. A chagrined but still bitter Hamilton wrote in a lengthy *New-York Evening Post* piece in July that while the purchase would bring glory to the administration, all those "possessed of the least candour and reflection will readily acknowledge that the acquisition has been solely owing to a fortuitous concurrence of unforeseen and unexpected circumstances, and not to any wise or vigorous measures on the part of the American government. . . . Let us then, with all due humility, acknowledge this as another of those signal instances of the kind interpositions of an over-ruling Providence." Hamilton, uncharitably, was simply incapable of granting Jefferson any credit for success. If he could take any solace from events, Hamilton might have seen these developments as further refutation of the view that all the Federalists had to do was sit back and wait out Jefferson, trusting that the president would stumble and lead the country back toward the Federalists. By mid-1803, such an event seemed much less likely than Hamilton had thought a year earlier, and the need for an active campaign of political education grew.[34]

If James Bayard had dismissed Hamilton's proposed society, another of Hamilton's correspondents wrote to him encouragingly in August 1803. Virginia Federalist John Nicholas was dismayed that while Republicans cultivated and supported printers and newspapers, Federalists did so little to help their own press. Furthermore, Federalist papers did not act in concert or as part of a network of papers, sharing and reprinting from each other. Nicholas implored Hamilton to lead. "We look up to you with some degree of confidence & hope, for some general & effectual plan in which we may unite our powers and make at least one Manly and vigorous effort," he told Hamilton. Nicholas was also enamored of the idea of holding meetings to organize an active resistance to the Jefferson administration. Although Hamilton did not reply, such correspondence must have pleased him—both the frank acknowledgment by others of the same things Hamilton had long advocated and the clear message that Federalists in other parts of the union still looked to him for leadership.[35]

In the next year—the last of his life—Hamilton looked both backward and forward and reflected on republicanism, democracy, and empire. He wrote back to Timothy Pickering who had questioned him about his statements at the 1787 Constitutional Convention. Hamilton made it clear in his remarks that he was, both then and at present, a committed republican, and he argued that all of his remarks at the convention and his plan of government were in perfect conformance with republican theory. Furthermore, this letter is significant for showing that Hamilton was comfortable with republican government but not with democracy—at least the name if not the practice.[36]

Even as the Pickering letter drew him back into old debates, his attention in the present was becoming increasingly focused yet again on his old rival Aaron Burr. With Burr shifting his focus from the national stage to

New York, Hamilton took aim at him in a February 1804 speech to a Federalist meeting. In urging Federalists to support John Lansing over Burr for governor, Hamilton denounced Burr for his steady pursuit of "the track of democratic policies . . . either from *principle* or from *calculation*." Federalists should beware. If Burr were a man of "irregular and insatiable ambition; if his plan has been to rise to power on the ladder of Jacobinic principles," it was certain that he would govern in the same way. Burr would be "the most dangerous chief that *Jacobinism* can have. . . . He will reunite under him the popular party and give new force for personal purposes." One of those personal purposes, Hamilton charged, was "a dismemberment of the Union . . . likely to be one of the first fruits of his elevation." Hamilton's explicit linkage of his rival to "democratic" and "Jacobinic" ideas was a key tack for Hamilton's political planning at this time.[37]

It is no surprise, given both their contentious past and the increasingly hostile tone and content of Hamilton's words against Burr, that the honor challenge that ensued culminated in the infamous duel. A key aspect to understanding Hamilton's thinking about the future is a line at the end of the statement he drafted on the eve of his honor dispute with Burr. Mindful of "what men of the world denominate honor, impressed on me (as I thought) a peculiar necessity not to decline the call." Failing to meet the challenge and losing his good name would severely restrict any sort of role Hamilton could play in public life: "The ability to be in future useful, whether in resisting mischief or effecting good, in those crises of our public affairs, which seem likely to happen, would probably be inseparable from a conformity with public prejudice in this particular."[38]

Astoundingly, even on the eve of his duel, with so much on his mind, Hamilton still railed against democracy and disunion and was determined to do all he could to arrest both tendencies, then and in the future. The last letter Hamilton ever wrote, to Theodore Sedgwick on July 10, 1804, stated that he had finally abandoned a longer letter to Sedgwick about national politics but wanted to communicate a much shorter note to "express but one sentiment, which is, that Dismemberment of our Empire will be a clear sacrifice of great positive advantages, without any counterbalancing good; administering no relief to our real Disease; which is DEMOCRACY, the poison of which by a subdivision will only be the more concentered in each part, and consequently the more virulent." Hamilton combined in this brief letter his recent fears of the spread of democratic practices and their danger and his longstanding fear, dating to at least the 1780s, of the dismantling of the union.[39]

It is too neat and tidy to simply draw a straight downward arrow tracing Federalist political fortunes from Hamilton's death in 1804 to 1816 when the party put forward its last presidential candidate. How might Hamilton's leadership have contributed to that project had he survived the duel to remain "in future useful"? We cannot know the answer, of course, but we do know that the Federalist Party, far from careening straight downhill after Jefferson's landslide reelection in 1804, revived itself in Jefferson's second term and remained a viable force for a time. New research shows that Hamilton's party, near death after 1804, made what Philip J. Lampi calls "an amazing electoral comeback" between 1808 and 1816. Furthermore, it did so utilizing many of the same tactics Hamilton had advocated in 1802: the widespread use of print media, the aggressive mobilization of voters to increase turnout and achieve electoral success, and the shrewd manipulation of election rules and methods regarding districting and modes of election. All this activity revived the Federalists for a time, and they provided spirited partisan competition for their Jeffersonian rivals. The key to this success was, according to Lampi, the Federalists' ability to adapt "to the new democratic and partisan environment in which they found themselves."[40]

The activities Lampi credits for the Federalist successes were plainly democratic—at least the ones involving persuasion and mobilization. Furthermore, they were the kinds of tactics that Federalists like Hamilton practiced in the ratification debate of 1787–88 and then in the great party battles of the 1790s, and the ones he advocated again in 1802. In all those cases, Hamilton and his allies took to the newspapers, taverns, and street corners; circulated petitions; lobbied and campaigned door to door; and mobilized support for their positions. These activities were the hallmarks of democratic politics in the early republic. And yet "democracy" was an oath on Hamilton's lips, a "jacobinical" scourge on the nation. How to understand this?

The primary hurdle for Hamilton was linguistic, not conceptual. He wrote and spoke forcefully against "democracy," which remained closely linked in his mind with "jacobinism." But Hamilton not only advocated democratic hallmarks in his Christian Constitutional Society; he had practiced such tactics himself consistently—and successfully—since the ratification debate. Furthermore, Federalists revived in 1808 and beyond when they adopted those same tactics. Federalists and Hamilton might have been bothered by the *name* of democracy but they were certainly comfortable with its practices and tactics.[41]

Thomas Jefferson flummoxed his opposition by being unpredictable, a trait of transformative political leaders. He did not govern in predictable ways, confounding the expectations that Hamilton and others laid out in 1800–1801. Not all Federalists understood this and failed to change their understanding of what Jefferson was doing as president. Hamilton did. It took him awhile to let go of his facile expectations for a drifting, "temporizing" presidency that would end in failure. But Hamilton was shrewd enough to realize what Jefferson was doing and to propose ways for Federalists to restructure their opposition along more effective lines. Hamilton did not have all the answers, and he had not figured out Jefferson fully at the time of his own death. His thinking was fluid, and he was working on a way forward that did not involve disunion or the renunciation of republican principles and that would ground Federalist opposition solidly in the Constitution.[42]

A closer look at the last years of Hamilton's life reveals clearly that he was still sought out for his opinions by others, still consulted by numerous correspondents, still invited to speak at party meetings, still engaged in writing for the newspapers. In short, he was a deeply engaged political partisan, as he had always been. Hamilton might not have been able to help the Federalists against Jefferson in 1804. But in the aftermath, he might have taken the lead, refined his initial efforts, and developed a clear critique of the Jefferson presidency. It is possible, even before Jefferson's disastrous Embargo policy enabled the Federalists' political comeback, that Hamilton could have developed fully the underpinnings of both an intellectual argument against Jeffersonian governance along with the structural means for political mobilization, following some of the lines proposed in his Christian Constitutional Society letter, leaving the Federalists revived and poised for a spirited campaign against James Madison in 1808.

Hamilton envisioned a future American nation that would be *both* a republic *and* a potential empire. And he was comfortable operating in a "democratic" political world of public campaigning, petitioning, electioneering, mobilizing, and mass persuasion, even as his last letter scorned the term itself. At the time of his death, Hamilton anticipated playing an active and "useful" role on behalf of his party and the nation. He had articulated an oppositional strategy against the Jeffersonians. We can never know what he might have done in that future or with what degree of success. But a careful examination of the last years of his life shows a man not despondent or disengaged despite his staggering personal tragedies. The conventional wisdom is wrong. Instead, Hamilton spent his last years as he had spent most of his life: working, planning, writing, scheming, and laying the designs for an American future in which he expected, as always, to play a vital role. And as he did so, his eyes were focused squarely on Thomas Jefferson.

Notes

1. "Introductory Note: Letter from Alexander Hamilton, Concerning the Public Conduct and Character of John Adams, Esq. President of the United States," [October 24, 1800], Harold C. Syrett et al., eds., *The Papers of Alexander Hamilton*, 27 vols. (New York, 1961–87), 25:185 (hereafter *PAH*).

2. "Introductory Note: The Examination Number I," [December 17, 1801], ibid., 25:452–53. While a great many historians and biographers have ignored the series, those who have treated it have been similarly dismissive. See Ron Chernow, *Alexander Hamilton* (New York, 2004), 658. For the letter to Bayard, see April [16–21], 1802, *PAH*, 25:605–10, and the editorial note at 25:607 for a discussion of various scholarly interpretations.

3. The "Letter" itself is in *PAH*, 25:169–236. For background, see the editorial note at 25:169–85.

4. Hamilton to Gouverneur Morris, December 26, 1800, ibid., 25:272–73. Hamilton sent a similar letter to James Ross on December 29, 1800, in which he again mentioned the possibility of "obtain[ing] some assurances" from Jefferson and listed preservation of the system of public credit, the Navy, and neutrality. He then added a fourth: "the preservation in office of our friends except in the great departments." See ibid., 25:280–81. Hamilton also included all four points on which he wanted "assurances" in a January 4, 1801, letter to James McHenry, ibid., 25:292–93.

5. Hamilton to James A. Bayard, December 27, 1800; Hamilton to Oliver Wolcott, December 1800 (n.d.), ibid., 25:275–77, 286–88.

6. Hamilton to James A. Bayard, January 16, 1801, ibid., 25:319–20. For a brilliant and subtle discussion of Hamilton's views of Jefferson across time, see James H. Read, "Alexander Hamilton's View of Thomas Jefferson's Ideology and Character," in *The Many Faces of Alexander Hamilton: The Life and Legacy of America's Most Elusive Founding Father*, ed. Douglas Ambrose and Robert W. T. Martin (New York, 2006), 77–106.

7. *PAH*, 25:320.

8. Ibid., 25:323–24. James Bayard was persuaded to support Jefferson, an action that ultimately tipped the election in his favor. See Bayard to Hamilton, March 8, 1801, ibid., 25:344–46.

9. Hamilton, "Campaign Speech, Second Version," [April 10, 1801], ibid., 25:375–78.

10. Hamilton to Oliver Wolcott Jr., June 29, 1798, ibid., 21:522; Hamilton to Theodore Sedgwick, February 2, 1799, Joanne B. Freeman, ed., *Alexander Hamilton: Writings* (New York, 2001), 913. On Hamilton's moderation in general during this turbulent period, see Aaron N. Coleman, "'A Second Bounaparty?': A Reexamination of Alexander Hamilton during the Franco-American Crisis, 1796–1801," *Journal of the Early Republic* 28 (2008): 183–214. For a variety of important perspectives and discussions, see Stanley Elkins and Eric McKitrick, *The Age of Federalism: The Early American Republic, 1788–1800* (New York, 1993), 114–31; Max Edling, *A Revolution in Favor of Government: Origins of the U.S. Constitution and the Making of the American State* (New York, 2003); Gerald Stourzh, *Alexander Hamilton and the Idea of Republican Government* (Stanford, Calif., 1970); Gilbert L. Lycan, *Alexander Hamilton and American Foreign Policy: A Design for Greatness* (Norman, Okla., 1970); Karl-Friedrich Walling, *Republican Empire: Alexander Hamilton on War and Free Government* (Lawrence, Kans., 1999); John Lamberton Harper, *American Machiavelli: Alexander Hamilton and the Origins of U.S. Foreign Policy* (New York, 2004); Lawrence S. Kaplan, *Alexander Hamilton: Ambivalent Anglophile* (Wilmington, Del., 2002); and, especially, Lance Banning, *The Jeffersonian Persuasion: Evolution of a Party Ideology* (Ithaca, N.Y., 1978), and Drew McCoy, *The Elusive Republic: Political Economy in Jeffersonian America* (Chapel Hill, N.C., 1980).

11. For a heartbreaking sense of the crushing loss Hamilton endured in his eldest son's death, compare his later acknowledgments of his friends' letters of condolence to his own letter to Richard Kidder Meade, August 27, 1782, Freeman, ed., *Alexander Hamilton: Writings,* 118–20, in which he writes with the giddiness of a new parent about the superior features of the then seven-month-old Philip. For the sad demise of Angelica in the aftermath of Philip's death, see Chernow, *Alexander Hamilton,* 655.

12. *PAH,* 25:453–54. See also the detailed editorial note (444–53), which discusses the series and makes an argument about Hamilton's significance and effectiveness, the thesis of which I challenge in this chapter.

13. "Examination" no. IX, [January 18, 1802], ibid., 25:501.

14. Gouverneur Morris to Hamilton, February 22, 1802, ibid., 25:527–29, 528 (quotations).

15. Gouverneur Morris to Hamilton, [February 29, 1802], ibid., 25:544–45.

16. Hamilton to Charles Cotesworth Pinckney, [March 15, 1802], ibid., 25:562–63.

17. "Examination" no. XVII, [March 20, 1802], ibid., 25:576.

18. "Examination" no. XVI, [March 19, 1802], ibid., 25:564.

19. "Examination" no. XVII, [March 20, 1802], ibid., 25:570.

20. But note well the cautionary interpretation in Robert M. S. McDonald, "The (Federalist?) Presidency of Thomas Jefferson," in *A Companion to Thomas Jefferson,* ed. Francis D. Cogliano (Malden, Mass., 2012), 164–83.

21. Jeremy D. Bailey, *Thomas Jefferson and Executive Power* (Cambridge, U.K., 2007), 9–10.

22. Brian Steele, *Thomas Jefferson and American Nationhood* (Cambridge, U.K., 2012), 2.

23. Ibid., 236. For extended discussions and important reassessments of Jefferson's presidency that join Bailey's and Steele's, see McDonald, "The (Federalist?) Presidency of Thomas Jefferson"; Bethel Saler, "An Empire for Liberty, A State for Empire," in *The Revolution of 1800: Democracy, Race, and the New Republic,* ed. James Horn, Jan Ellen Lewis, and Peter S. Onuf (Charlottesville, Va., 2002), 360–82; Read, "Alexander Hamilton's View of Thomas Jefferson's Ideology and Character"; and Peter S. Onuf, *Jefferson's Empire: The Language of American Nationhood* (Charlottesville, Va., 2000). For even more recent assessments of Jeffersonian governance, see the essays in Joanne B. Freeman and Johann N. Neem, eds., *Jeffersonians in Power: The Rhetoric of Opposition Meets the Realities of Governing* (Charlottesville, Va., 2019). For fascinating consider-ations by leading scholars of the treatments of Jefferson, including his presidential years, over time, see the essays in Robert M. S. McDonald, ed., *Thomas Jefferson's Lives: Biographers and the Battle for History* (Charlottesville, Va., 2019). More broadly, see Max D. Edling, *A Hercules in the Cradle: War, Money, and the American State, 1783–1867* (Chicago, 2014).

24. "Examination" no. XVIII, [April 8, 1802], *PAH,* 25:594, 597.

25. Hamilton to James A. Bayard, April 6, 1802, ibid., 25:587.

26. Hamilton to James A. Bayard, April [16–21], 1802, ibid., 25:605.

27. Ibid., 25:606. Hamilton then noted, "I need not tell you that I do not mean to countenance the imitation of things intrinsically unworthy, but only of such as may be denominated irregular, such as in a sound & stable order of things ought not to exist." Even as they descended to play the Republicans' games, Federalists would observe a distinction between "irregular" but temporarily expedient tactics and "unworthy" ones.

28. Ibid., 25:606–9. See also ibid., 25:606–7n2 on Hamilton's use of religious ideas in pursuit of political objects.

29. For details, see Todd Estes, *The Jay Treaty Debate, Public Opinion, and the Evolu-tion of Early American Political Culture* (Amherst, Mass., 2006).

30. James A. Bayard to Hamilton, April 25, 1802; Hamilton to Rufus King, June 3, 1802, *PAH,* 25:613; 26:15–16.

31. Ibid., 26:13–15.

32. Hamilton, Federalist no. 6, Freeman, ed., *Alexander Hamilton: Writings,* 181. I am indebted to Peter S. Onuf, in his comments on an earlier version of my paper, for pointing me to this similarity of thought and language in Hamilton's work.

33. Hamilton to Charles Cotesworth Pinckney, December 29, 1802, *PAH,* 26:71–72.

34. Hamilton, "Purchase of Louisiana," [July 5, 1803], ibid., 26:129–36. See also "For the *Evening Post,*" [February 8, 1803], ibid., 26:82–85.

35. John Nicholas to Hamilton, August 4, 1803, ibid., 26:139–42.

36. Hamilton to Timothy Pickering, September 16, 1803, ibid., 26:147–49.

37. Hamilton, "Speech at a Meeting of Federalists in Albany," [February 10, 1804], ibid., 26:187–90. See also Hamilton to Robert G. Harper, February 19, 1804, ibid., 26:190–93.

38. Hamilton, "Statement on Impending Duel with Aaron Burr," [June 28–July 10, 1804], ibid., 26:280.

39. Hamilton to Theodore Sedgwick, July 10, 1804, ibid., 26:309–11.

40. Philip J. Lampi, "The Federalist Party Resurgence, 1808–1816: Evidence from the New Nation Votes Database," *Journal of the Early Republic* 33 (2013): 255–81, 280, 281 (quotations).

41. See Rachel Hope Cleves, *The Reign of Terror in America: Visions of Violence from Anti-Jacobinism to Antislavery* (New York, 2009), and Seth Cotlar, *Tom Paine's America: The Rise and Fall of Transatlantic Radicalism in the Early Republic* (Charlottesville, Va., 2011).

42. See Robert W. T. Martin, "Reforming Republicanism: Alexander Hamilton's Theory of Republican Citizenship and Press Liberty," in Ambrose and Martin, eds., *The Many Faces of Alexander Hamilton*, 109–33.

7   James Madison and American Nationality

The View from Virginia

DREW R. McCoY

In the spring of 1831, when James Monroe reported from his daughter's home in New York City that he planned to sell his only remaining land in Virginia, his old compatriot James Madison was heartbroken. Despite Madison's close knowledge of Monroe's declining health and dire financial predicament, his friend's decision to sever his last connection to the Old Dominion apparently came as a shock. In truth, Monroe's ties to New York were longstanding and hardly incidental. Almost a half century earlier in 1786, at the same time he and Madison were jointly purchasing land along the upstate Mohawk River frontier, Congressman Monroe had married into a New York mercantile family with both Dutch and New England roots. Now, his youngest daughter, who had made a similar marital connection to Manhattan, was taking in her destitute father. Shortly thereafter, on July 4, 1831, the last member of the Virginia Dynasty died and was interred in New York City. During his final illness, Monroe spoke often of Madison, "his oldest and most valued friend," now sadly beyond any reach of a final reunion.[1] In a bitter touch of posthumous irony, perhaps, Monroe finally returned home decades later, with the holocaust of disunion and civil war looming, when the Virginia state government arranged in 1858 for his remains to be exhumed and sent by barge to Richmond for proper reinterment.[2]

As Madison well knew, Virginia during the 1820s and 1830s was not the most hospitable vantage point from which to contemplate the future of America's republican experiment under the Constitution. During the nineteen years of his retirement, Madison suffered the grievous effects of the same agricultural depression in the Old Dominion that contributed to Monroe's demise. Historian Ralph Ketcham has summarized the conventional wisdom on this matter: "Nothing could have been more disappointing for Madison than the inescapable fact that by the time of his death, he had failed in his lifelong efforts to make Montpelier in particular, and Virginia generally, with or without slavery, a prosperous farmer's paradise." The growth and optimism experienced at Montpelier by several generations of Madisons (including for a time Madison himself)—from the 1750s through the end of the Napoleonic Wars in 1815—were irrevocably gone; "nostalgia replaced hope," Ketcham opines, as young Virginians in droves departed the state in search of opportunity elsewhere in the union. Indeed, James and Dolley Madison's fretting concern about their own younger kin, many of whom had either left for greener agricultural pastures to the South and West or married into mercantile families elsewhere, as well as for the many female descendants of their friend Thomas Jefferson, only "sharpened their sense" of what Ketcham calls "Virginia's decline and social pathology."[3] Jeffersonian Republicanism may have triumphed politically in the Revolution of 1800, but thirty years later, the Virginia Dynasty was gone, and their native state had plunged, as historian Susan Dunn has framed the tragedy, into a sad, even pathetic "dominion of memories."[4]

Nevertheless, as Madison contemplated the American future from Virginia during these years, he remained remarkably upbeat and even optimistic. Unlike his dearest friend Jefferson, he was not generally despondent nor he did retreat into the increasingly narrow and desperate provincialism that marked the Sage of Monticello's final years. Unlike Jefferson, Madison never came to regard New Englanders and New Yorkers in the wake of the Missouri Crisis as essentially un-American foreigners, he never conceived of the University of Virginia as a necessary antidote against the corrupt values that a rising generation of Virginians might imbibe at northern colleges, and he never perceived the neo-Jeffersonianism of Henry Clay or John Quincy Adams as rank apostasy or crypto-Federalism. Differences of temperament as well as principle were surely relevant here, but Madison's later years raise some interesting larger questions about regional identity: What did it mean in his case to be a Virginian? What kind of Virginian was he? And how did his Virginia identity affect or even shape his perceptions of the republic's future?

Madison is best understood as a Virginia nationalist whose regional identity was unmistakable but never full-throated and never the benchmark for his vision of what the American republic should be. During his formative years, he had reconciled himself to his Orange County roots with measured and at times agonizing reluctance. As late as his mid-thirties, when he was simultaneously wrestling with the republican crisis of the Confederation era, he was not at all comfortable or certain that Virginia would or should remain his home. Even so, there can be little doubt that Madison's Virginia background contributed to his larger republican vision for the United States, then and later, and once reconciled to his patrimony as the easiest, perhaps necessary basis for the life in politics that he savored, the protection of his state's interests became a matter of obligation to his constituents as much as his instinctive inclination. But as his retirement years demonstrate, Madison never embraced or made central to his view of the future what we might call Virginia tribalism—that is, an attachment to his state's culture and way of life as a superior mode of republican existence. Slavery alone made that tribalism inconceivable, but in a much broader sense, Madison's enlightened provincialism had always been grounded in a larger understanding of American promise that was in no way dependent on his state's dominance or even priority in the union. In short, Madison stoically analyzed what historians are now prone to exaggerate as Virginia's "decline and social pathology" after 1815 within a cosmopolitan framework that was anything but Virginia-centric. We have tended to frame that outlook in terms of his undying commitment to the union that he had done so much to create and preserve. What is less familiar, perhaps, is the extent to which his unionism disdained the insular Virginia tribalism that posed a looming threat to that union's future.

In their comprehensive survey of the full sweep of Madison's and Jefferson's careers, Andrew Burstein and Nancy Isenberg have emphasized "the 'tribal' identities" of their subjects, who were fundamentally "Virginians first," men whose devotion to land and kinship anchored the culture that defined their outlook and behavior. In their account, Virginia's revolutionary gentry in effect started and led the American Revolution during the early and mid-1770s for their own imperial purposes, grounded in the narrow, even clannish values of their region. Indeed, they were "men of power and influence who relished union but prized their own culture above all else."[5] In Madison's case, however, any such characterization rings hollow. Coming of age simultaneously with the revolutionary movement, young man Madison, on the heels of several years at the College of New Jersey, felt if anything trapped on his father's Orange County plantation, which he ruefully described to a college friend as "an Obscure Corner" of the North American world.[8] Disgusted by the persecution of religious dissenters in his neighborhood, Madison longed, he told his friend, for the "free Air" of Philadelphia and the more bustling, tolerant, cosmopolitan environment of the mid-Atlantic colonies.[7] In the spring and early summer of 1774, when the twenty-three-year-old eldest son of Orange County's wealthiest tobacco planter headed north for a gulp of the fresh air he craved (and heard the shocking news of the closing of Boston Harbor along the way), he extended his journey beyond the familiar Philadelphia-Princeton axis into the colony of New York, traveling as far north as Albany.[8]

Apparently curious to see more of North America than the piedmont Virginia world that had nurtured him, Madison's attraction to the Hudson River Valley proved persistent. His broader continental vision grew apace with the revolutionary movement that absorbed him, and ten years later, in the fall of 1784, with his three-year term in the Confederation Congress at an end, Madison seized the opportunity to broaden his firsthand acquaintance with upstate New York. In what has to be one of the few outdoors adventures of a long life conspicuously lacking in manly adventure, Madison spent the better part of two weeks camping his way through the wilderness, from Albany along the Mohawk River to Fort Stanwix and then eighteen miles further into the heart of Oneida country. Here he saw firsthand the effects of the 1779 Continental Army campaign against Iroquois allies of the British, which had "cleared" the area for American settlers, who were now beginning to appear in larger numbers. Madison's companions on this wilderness adventure included the Marquis de Lafayette, with whom he now formed a lifelong epistolary connection.[9] After the mid-1780s, the two men would not meet face to face again until Lafayette's triumphant return to America in 1824–25—by which time, this once remote region of upstate New York was at the center of an epic market revolution fueled by the construction of the Erie Canal.

Madison returned to Virginia in late 1784—his first trip home in almost four years—eager to invest in the Mohawk country, whose rich land and vast potential he described to his closest correspondents in wildly enthusiastic terms. In long discussions at Mount Vernon, George Washington, who had ordered the 1779 military campaign and then personally inspected the region in 1783, shared Madison's enthusiasm for this New York frontier, which he was eager to invest in himself. With Washington's encouragement, Madison soon found a much younger partner in his speculative ventures: James Monroe, former Continental Army officer and now Madison's replacement as a Virginia delegate to the Confederation Congress meeting in New York. In the end, the two young Virginians could not put together enough cash and credit to do more than make a modest purchase of land lying between what later became the towns of Utica and Rome.[10] But Madison was thinking big, and before his Mohawk fever ran its course, he tried to interest Thomas Jefferson, then the American minister to France, in a much larger scheme to raise European capital that might finance a major joint purchase for the three Virginians. Jefferson deemed the scheme impractical—and it went nowhere—and besides, he clearly had no interest in joining any rush to invest in this northern frontier. Instead, Jefferson took this occasion to renew a very different offer and enticement to his young friend, a plan to have both Madison and Monroe (along with William Short) buy land not outside the state but in the vicinity of Monticello, where together they would form their own special neighborhood of enlightened Virginians. Jefferson had already described to Madison a small parcel of worn but decent land, only two miles from Monticello, where Madison might conduct "a farm of experiment" while supporting "a little table and household"—a bucolic scenario that likewise never came to be.[11]

As Jefferson's offer might imply, Madison's biographers have placed this "Mohawk interlude" in the larger context of a lingering personal crisis. Discussing his future, Madison was explaining to correspondents at this time that he wished "to depend as little as possible on the labor of slaves" and, moreover, that he had no "local partialities" that might prevent him from relocating outside his native state.[12] It seems unlikely that Madison, a bachelor whose engagement to a young New York woman had just fallen through, with no children, was actually considering making his home on the Mohawk frontier. His apparent scheme was instead to make a huge fortune in real estate speculation that would free him from dependence on his father's plantation and allow him to reside in a more suitable place of his choice, perhaps Philadelphia. Madison held on to his Mohawk land until 1796, when he sold it for an impressive profit, though far short of what his imagination had once conjured up. If Madison was imagining a personal future in the mid-1780s separate from his Virginia patrimony, this was one dream that decisively failed.[13]

Other dreams survived. Madison's emergence as a pivotal leader in the restructuring of a federal union that might rescue America's republican revolution from the disorder of the 1780s reflected a larger geopolitical vision of a national future, one that combined landed and commercial expansion in multiple directions which might unite rather than divide what had become a fractured confederation.[14] What may be most striking about Madison's Mohawk interlude in this context is that he was looking northward at all. Virginians of course had traditionally looked west and south, to Kentucky (where Madison's father was heavily invested) and especially to the Ohio River Valley, and during the 1780s this trans-Appalachian West indeed represented to the Virginia gentry a glorious future. Inspired by the leadership and example of General Washington, ambitious plans to build a system of canals that would link this vast hinterland to the Old Dominion became a ruling passion of the time.[15] But Madison's own enthusiasm for such ventures, along with his fervent commitment to protecting American claims to the Mississippi River during the Jay-Gardoqui crisis, constituted pieces of a much broader national vision. In his mind, as in Washington's, there was nothing contradictory or incompatible about defending Virginia's investment in the trans-Appalachian West while also supporting the development of New York's vastly promising interior, in both cases anticipating "improvements" that might forge stronger, necessary bonds of union. Jefferson appears to have seen things at least a bit differently, that is, from a more Virginia-centric, zero-sum perspective; in 1784, he spoke squarely in terms of "a competition" among Virginia, Pennsylvania, and New York for the trade of America's interior in which, he was confident, the Potomac River enjoyed "natural advantages" that were destined to pour into the Old Dominion's lap "the whole commerce of the Western world." He added, however, that the Hudson River, while palpably inferior to the Potomac, was already open to navigation, which only underlined his sense of urgency that Virginians mount the necessary improvements before New York somehow laid artificial claim to this anticipated bonanza.[16]

At the time Jefferson made this assessment, New York was only a marginal player in the confederation. Virginia was still far and away the largest, most populous state in the new union formed under the Constitution, with a population approximately equal to New York and Pennsylvania combined, while post-revolutionary New York, lagging behind even neighboring Connecticut in population, remained, as Alan Taylor has noted, "relatively weak but possessed of immense potential."[17] But Jefferson as well as Madison lived long enough to witness the stunning surge of New York to a position of prominence in the American union, leaping ahead of Virginia in both population and power well before Jefferson's death in 1826, with the construction of the Erie Canal after 1815 providing a dramatic exclamation point to the outcome of the regional competition the Virginian had confidently if a bit nervously described four decades earlier. When Jefferson congratulated New York governor DeWitt Clinton for the triumph of American ingenuity that his canal represented, he characteristically framed matters in terms of the New World demonstrating to Europe its superior genius in undertaking the seemingly impossible. But he also could not avoid quietly contrasting the Empire State's progressive support of such improvements to his own state's lukewarm, tight-fisted approach to his new university and the broader system of education that might avert its lamentable descent into "Gothic barbarism."[18] If Jefferson had once been confident about the Old Dominion's supremacy in the American union, that confidence seemed shattered, and on some level he responded by focusing his frustration and wrath on the federal union itself, which after 1819 especially he regarded as a palpable threat to what remained of Virginia's pastoral form of republicanism. It may go too far to say, as the historian Susan Dunn has bluntly observed, that the once cosmopolitan, enlightened, and far-sighted Jefferson "became, in the years before his death, simply—and militantly—*a Virginian*."[19] But his fear of neo-Federalist conspiracies lurking in faraway places like the heavily commercialized states of New England and New York came to dominate his view of the immediate future.

Like Jefferson, Madison pondered the future from a firm vantage point in the Old Dominion, but his reactions as both a planter and a former statesman struck a very different chord. Following his return to Montpelier in 1817, Madison never again left his native state, even as his mind ranged nimbly across time and space. If a youthful Madison had balked at becoming the planter he was apparently destined to be, old man Madison made agriculture as a science, and farming on his Montpelier plantation as a profession, the central focus and passion of his final years. His correspondence reveals his mastery of the intricate details of his farming operations to the very end of his life; indeed, only months before his death, with his health rapidly failing, he described to his agent in Richmond individual bulls on his farms and their potential marketability.[20] For Madison, agriculture became, at one and the same time, the continuing foundation of his larger republican vision, the focus of intense intellectual study, and the business through which he struggled to support himself and his family. And what is most striking, perhaps, is the equanimity with which he rigorously analyzed the surprises and disappointments of these years, always rejecting the notion that they were peculiar to Virginia and patiently accommodating them to the inevitability of change in both Virginia and the nation.

A year into his retirement, Madison prepared a formal address to his local agricultural society that, once published, connected him through correspondence with like-minded agricultural reformers in distant places like New York and Massachusetts.[21] Madison's address was more philosophical and historical than technical—in that sense reflecting his application of reason and logic to all forms of human experience—but pointed toward recommendations that were more precisely directed at local concerns. Even before the Panic of 1819 wreaked havoc with the state's economy, Virginia had its fair share of problems, according to Madison, from soil exhaustion to poor plowing to "the injudicious and excessive destruction of timber and fire wood."[22] By the early and mid-1820s, Madison's own agricultural misfortunes at Montpelier mirrored a more intense and general malaise that had overtaken the state. A personal nadir of sorts was reached in 1825, when he was sufficiently pressed to request a short-term loan from the Bank of the United States, only to suffer the humiliation of refusal on the grounds that his Virginia land was insufficient and unreliable collateral.[23] Along with others in the state, Madison wanted to know why the Old Dominion was suffering. His analysis, however, pointed in quite different directions from many other voices he heard or was exposed to.

One of Madison's acquaintances from his stint in the Virginia House of Delegates during the mid-1780s was Francis Corbin, with whom he had labored shoulder to shoulder in 1788 to secure their state's ratification of the Constitution. By the late 1810s, Corbin, whose political career had been entirely at the state level, was enveloped in bitter despair about the condition of Virginia and, in the wake of the Missouri Crisis, the future of the union. Corbin's misery—which he elaborated in a series of long, rambling letters to Madison—stemmed primarily from his economic woes; like Madison's, his farms no longer seemed profitable, but unlike Madison, he also had eight sons with uncertain futures to worry about. By 1820, a year before his sudden death in his early sixties, Corbin was ready to give up on both Virginia and the union, even threatening, "as old as I am," to flee northward, away from the canker of slavery, "where my sons, uninfluenced by false pride, might engage in honest pursuits for an honest livelihood."[24] For Corbin, in short, slavery explained his and the Old Dominion's predicament; as he argued stridently to Madison, Virginia's experience demonstrated beyond a doubt the general principle that "Farming and Slavery are incompatible with one another."[25] But Madison was reluctant to agree. Acknowledging that he shared Corbin's categorical condemnation of slavery for its multiple evils, he cited evidence that his friend's despair about the future of Virginia agriculture was overdrawn and unfounded, even in the short run while slavery would continue to exist. And he gently corrected Corbin's apparent belief that moving north might be the answer to his personal woes. Cautioning him not to exaggerate "the cares and vexations" of a Virginia planter, Madison advised his friend to consider the pecuniary distress currently being suffered by fellow Americans, whether invested in "commercial stock" or agriculture, throughout the union. The hard times unleashed by the Panic of 1819 were hardly unique to the Old Dominion—or to slaveholding planters.[26]

Madison's temperamental aversion to despair was clearly at work here, as was the degree to which he had accommodated himself over the years to the slavery that he had once pondered fleeing from.[27] But Madison also displayed in his response to Corbin a more general resistance to what he considered simplistic analyses of a complex situation, and especially to any "scape-goating" of single factors, like slavery, as the source of the commonwealth's current woes. In the years after Corbin's death, Madison confronted a much more prevalent and ominous example of this propensity—a growing chorus of Virginians, young and old, who placed the finger of blame not on slavery but on a power-engrossing federal government and especially its tariff policies. Jefferson drifted steadily into this frame of mind, lashing out at second-generation Jeffersonians for their neo-Federalist apostasy. And much worse soon followed, in Madison's eyes, as advocates of the audaciously spurious doctrine of nullification extended their faulty economic analysis into a political movement that threatened the very foundations of the federal union.

Madison's nuanced analysis of his own and his state's agricultural woes led him to engage and even confront the relevant implications for the republic's future in a strikingly different way. His republican vision had always

been anchored in agriculture, in no small part because, as his friend Jefferson had so eloquently explained in his *Notes on the State of Virginia,* living
from the land conferred on the tiller of the soil the personal independence
on which citizenship must rest.[28] This was a heady conceit because on so
many levels farmers were transparently dependent on any number of things
utterly beyond their control. Weather and nature were unpredictable, and
to a great extent uncontrollable, as Madison consistently emphasized in accounting for his own economic woes during the first phase of his retirement. Flooding rains and protracted droughts repeatedly affected his yields
of both grain and tobacco. Even worse were the ravages of insects, from the
familiar "Hessian fly" to the new invader from the South, now steadily moving northward through America's wheat fields, that Madison dubbed the
"chinch bug."[29] As he reported to a correspondent in neighboring Kentucky
in 1826, he had himself been "particularly unfortunate," having made "only
one favorable crop" of either tobacco or wheat since retiring from public
life to "my farm."[30] Like all those who made their living from the soil, not
just in Virginia, Madison found himself at the mercy of seemingly random
environmental threats that resulted, at a moment's notice, in diminished and
disappointing yields.[31]

But he was also discovering firsthand the full implications for American
farmers of an even more ominous form of dependency—on the foreign, specifically European, demand for their surplus produce, even if and especially
when yields approached their full potential. Madison had wrestled intellectually with this matter for the better part of four decades: specifically, would
foreign demand be sufficient to sustain the industry of America's virtuous,
productive farmers as they increased in numbers and expanded aggressively
across space? He had invested his hopes, and his vision of a sustainable
republic, on the ability of the United States to break down the mercantilist
policies of Old World empires that limited those markets and threatened to
push the United States away from its predominant focus on agriculture.[32]
But during the 1820s, Madison essentially acknowledged the futility of his
republican dream of a world of enlightened free trade. The falling prices
that he and other American farmers now confronted in the post-Napoleonic
era were a sobering reminder of how dependent they were on this foreign
demand, and more specifically on "the regulations of other Countries," especially Great Britain, which regrettably persisted in its shortsighted restric-
tive policies.[33] Madison's fervent support of a federal policy of commercial

coercion throughout his career, culminating in the great Embargo of Jefferson's presidency, had reflected his faith in the intrinsic strength of an agricultural people in contests with older European empires during extraordinary times of crisis. But those policies had enjoyed very limited success, and now Madison appeared to admit that even if they had succeeded, the demand for American agricultural surpluses abroad, especially during times of peace and relative stability, was finite and likely inadequate to sustain the industry of so many Americans on the land.[34] Glutted markets and falling prices, especially as agricultural productivity soared on America's fresh lands in the West, explained Virginia's predicament—not slavery, and certainly not the federal tariff that states'-rights extremists in his commonwealth fingered as the culprit. Madison recognized that the rapid, successful development of the trans-Appalachian frontier, a core element of his republican vision, was compounding the Old Dominion's difficulties, but who could call something "an evil," he mused, "which adds more to the growth and prosperity of the whole than it subtracts from a part of the community."[35]

If states'-rights extremists blamed Virginia's woes on malevolent outsiders bent on corrupting the federal government into subsidizing manufactures, they also sought to insulate the commonwealth against the intrusion of the alien, corrupt values they associated with those outsiders. But Madison acknowledged instead that increased manufacturing in other parts of the union would redound to Virginia's great advantage, both by providing a closer, more dependable market for the state's produce while also providing employment for people who might otherwise move west and compete with Virginia's farmers. Here Madison essentially endorsed the larger "home market" argument articulated by the likes of Henry Clay and John Quincy Adams, even as he remained skittish about their readings of the Constitution. Moreover, Madison anticipated, and fully supported, a transition toward manufacturing in the Old Dominion itself, as labor traditionally employed in agriculture—and here of course he was referring in large part to slave labor—might be gradually shifted into these more profitable pursuits. Perhaps the most striking piece of this Madisonian forecast was his recognition that while Virginia currently lacked both the capital and the "managing habits" required for successful and extensive manufacturing, "these requisites" might be "tempted hither from the Northern States."[36] Madison's Virginia of the future, in short, might draw on and increasingly resemble its sister states to the North.

There are two points worth emphasizing here. First, Madison's more nuanced, less despairing estimate of Virginia's agricultural condition and economic future, especially relative to the rest of the United States, may in fact have been reasonably accurate. As William G. Shade has forcefully argued, careful analysis of the relevant data reveals that the Old Dominion during this broad era was a far cry from the decaying agricultural wasteland described by a despondent Francis Corbin and later endorsed by modern scholars like Susan Dunn, who rely heavily on what Shade considers the highly misleading accounts of "ideologically motivated commentators like Frederick Law Olmsted."[37] Shade acknowledges the devastating downturn beginning in 1819, followed by only a very modest short-term revival, but the recovery that began during the 1830s was sustained, if erratically, for the remainder of the antebellum era—too late for Madison himself, perhaps, but not for a rising generation of fellow Virginians. Shade notes that Virginia farmers always led a somewhat precarious existence, held hostage to the vagaries of nature and a market over which they had little control, but this hardly distinguished them, he emphasizes, from American farmers elsewhere. On the whole, antebellum Virginia had "a balanced and thriving agricultural economy," and Madison's own piedmont region, where slave labor continued to predominate, emerged as "the most agriculturally productive" area of the state, leading the Old Dominion in the mixed-agriculture production of wheat, corn, oats, and white potatoes as well as in the raising of swine and cattle.[38] In this respect, Madison's more balanced, even-tempered perspective on Virginia's "decline" appears anything but naive or Pollyannaish.

Second, in so many ways, Madison's analysis and outlook routinely emphasized what Virginia had in common with other regions, as well as its salutary connections, political and economic, to the rest of the union. He was loyal to his state and always mindful of its interests, but his vision of the future lacked any whiff of a tribalistic commitment to its culture or values as superior or even distinctive, and he never expressed a nostalgic attachment to a pastoral Virginia free from the corruption allegedly overtaking other parts of the union. Outsiders appreciated this dimension of his vision. By the end of his life, Madison had earned the respect and even veneration of many New Englanders, who admired him for considerably more than his emphatic stance against nullification. If John Adams and James Madison had never quite warmed up to each other, the same cannot be said of Adams's son, who closed a letter to Madison in 1834 by referring to "the undeviating and grateful respect for your character and person, which I shall carry with me to the final hour of my life."[39] During the 1830s, John Quincy Adams publicly eulogized both Madison and Monroe as nation-builders in terms he would never have applied to Jefferson.[40] Indeed, when John Quincy's wife, Louisa Catherine, responded to Madison's death in the summer of 1836 by privately filling several pages of her diary with effusive encomiums to a man in whom "was found the *simplicity of mental greatness; yielding a rich harvest of excellent fruit, for the benefit of the Country to which he did honour,*" that "Country" was clearly not Virginia.[41] And twelve years later, when Louisa Catherine rushed to her dying husband in the Capitol building as his final hour neared, she had at her side Mary Cutts, a niece of James and Dolley Madison. Cutts was the daughter of an interregional marriage between Dolley's beloved sister Anna and Richard Cutts, a Jeffersonian merchant and congressman from Massachusetts who had been close to Madison personally as well as politically. Growing up during the 1820s and early 1830s, Mary Cutts had spent much of her youth among her Virginia kin and especially at Montpelier—where a bust of John Quincy Adams was on display in the South Passage—all the while savoring and deepening her New England roots. Indeed, shortly before her death in 1856, when Cutts made an extended visit to New England, she referred to her hosts, the Adams family, as "her true-hearted Yankee friends."[42]

During his final years, Madison celebrated the remarkable growth and prosperity of his country. Writing to Margaret Bayard Smith in 1830, he recalled his third and final journey through upstate New York when, in the summer of 1791, he and Jefferson traveled north from Albany through Saratoga and the Lake George region into Vermont before returning through western Massachusetts. Madison recalled that his assignment had been to record observations "related chiefly to agricultural and Economic objects," adding that reviewing those notes now, almost forty years later, their chief interest lay "in the comparison they may afford of the infant state with the present growth of the settlements through which we passed."[43] Other "infant" settlements had also been appearing at that time north of the Ohio River, in territory that Virginia once laid claim to (and hoped to connect to through its imagined canal system) and in which slavery was prohibited. In 1835, when a group of Ohio citizens invited Madison to join them at an anniversary celebration of those rude, late eighteenth-century beginnings, he expressed regret that his advanced age prevented him from "visiting a highly interesting portion of our Country which would be new to me, and of witnessing the natural, social, and political advantages that are attracting so much admiration." Ohio of course was one of those western states whose agricultural productivity was contributing to Virginia's comparatively strait-ened circumstances—and whose farmers were now taking advantage of the Erie Canal to market their produce through New York. But what Madison saw in this western state was a glowing empirical testament to the resound-ing success of America's republican revolution:

> Taking into view the enterprise which planted the germ of a flourishing State in a savage Wilderness; the rapidity of its growth under the nurturing protection of the Federal Councils; the variety and value of the improvements already spread over it at the age of less than half a Century, and the prospect of an expanding prosperity of which it has sufficient pledges, Ohio, may be justly regarded, with every congratulation, as a monument of the happy agency of the free Institutions which characterize the political system of the United States.[44]

Madison's final perspective on his country's future remained stoically optimistic, even in the face of much that clearly discouraged him. He had no practical answer to the dilemma of slavery, in Virginia and beyond, and he knew it, especially as he came to realize the very alarming possibility that a younger generation of Virginians might embrace the institution as a positive good rather than honor his generation's principled commit-ment to universal natural rights.[45] And the specter of disunion raised by the nullification movement, which had gained such alarming traction not only in South Carolina and eastern Virginia but in his own Orange County neighborhood as well, required him to dig deep into his reservoir of faith. Temporary fits of passion might lead some Virginians to doubt the essential role of the union in securing republican government, he mused, but surely reason would prevail for those who remembered the history of the 1780s and beyond. The palpable benefits of that union were too many, and the consequences of disunion so grimly transparent, for any reasonable man to ignore. Among those grim consequences Madison was quite specific by the 1830s; they included "a southern Confederacy, mutual enmity with the

Northern—the most dreadful animosities and border wars springing from the case of Slaves—rival alliances abroad, standing armies at home to be supported by internal taxes—and Federal Governments with powers of a more consolidating and Monarchical tendency than the greatest jealousy has charged on the existing system."[46] As he told Henry Clay in 1833, if "the gulf" of disunion ever seriously approached, "the deluded" would surely "recoil from its horrors"—especially, he might have added, in Virginia, with its legacy of strong leadership in the dual causes of liberty and union.[47] Only a day before his death, with the late 1780s on his mind as always, Madison recalled with modest pride his own sincere and steadfast "co-operation in promoting such a reconstruction of our political system as would provide for the permanent liberty and happiness of the United States." And the verdict of a half-century's experience under the Constitution was indisputable. "Of the many good fruits it has produced which have well rewarded the efforts and anxieties that led to it," he added, summing up his final years, "no one has been a more rejoicing witness than myself."[48]

Madison's beloved union had been formed through reason, and reason, he was confident, would surely sustain it. Twenty-five years after his death, that prophecy proved horribly wrong, and before the bloodshed and devastation of the Civil War had run its course, Confederate soldiers from Virginia and all over the South were camping on the grounds of Montpelier. It is not hard to infer Madison's likely response to secession. What he might have made of a new union forged through the massive application of military force, rather than enlightened reason, must remain anyone's guess.

Notes

1. Tench Ringgold to Madison, July 7, 1831, James Madison Papers, Library of Congress, Washington, D.C. Other relevant letters include Monroe to Madison, April 11, 1833, and Madison to Monroe, April 21, 1833, ibid.

2. Michael Kammen, *Digging Up the Dead: A History of Notable American Reburials* (Chicago, 2010), 86–91. Virginia governor Henry Wise had an even more ambitious scheme at the time—to exhume the remains of both Jefferson and Madison for reburial alongside Monroe—which fortunately fell through.

3. Ralph Ketcham, *The Madisons at Montpelier: Reflections on the Founding Couple* (Charlottesville, Va., 2009), 37, 164, 160. For a full accounting of the younger Madison kin, see pp. 36–37. Madison's sister Frances and her husband left for Alabama in 1819; shortly before Madison's death in June 1836, he likely received the news that their

twenty-year-old son, James Madison Rose, his youngest nephew, had been killed at the Alamo fighting for the independence of Texas. Ibid., 165.

4. Susan Dunn, *Dominion of Memories: Jefferson, Madison, and the Decline of Virginia* (New York, 2007).

5. Andrew Burstein and Nancy Isenberg, *Madison and Jefferson* (New York, 2010), xvi, 44. As their book progresses, without abandoning their larger interpretive framework, Burstein and Isenberg duly note the ways in which Madison departed subtly from this mold, commenting in their conclusion, for instance, that he "felt less compelled to protect Virginia as a 'culture' distinct from others" (626). In a parallel vein, in a book arguing for the state-oriented provincialism of Virginia's elite throughout the broad revolutionary era, Kevin R. C. Gutzman notes Madison's "divergence from the mainline Virginia position" during his retirement years. See Gutzman, *Virginia's American Revolution: From Dominion to Republic, 1776–1840* (Lanham, Md., 2007), 176.

6. Madison to William Bradford, April 28, 1773, William T. Hutchinson et al., eds., *The Papers of James Madison: First Series,* 17 vols. (Chicago, Charlottesville, 1962–91), 1:84.

7. Madison to Bradford, April 1, 1774, ibid., 1:112–13. For a fuller discussion of Madison's correspondence with Bradford and its context, see Drew R. McCoy, *The Last of the Fathers: James Madison and the Republican Legacy* (Cambridge, U.K., 1989), 226–29.

8. McCoy, *Last of the Fathers,* 229.

9. The most thorough account of Madison's journey is in Irving Brant, *James Madison: The Nationalist, 1780–1787* (Indianapolis, 1948), 324–35. See also Ralph Ketcham, *James Madison: A Biography* (New York, 1971), 154–57.

10. Ketcham, *James Madison,* 147; Brant, *Madison: The Nationalist,* 336–40.

11. Thomas Jefferson to Madison, February 20, 1784, Hutchinson et al., eds., *Papers of Madison,* 7:428. See also Burstein and Isenberg, *Madison and Jefferson,* 114–17. A decade later, Jefferson would purchase land in the vicinity of Monticello for William Short, who is emerging as a figure of substantial interest among present-day historians of the early American republic.

12. Madison to Edmund Randolph, July 26, 1785; Madison to Caleb Wallace, August 23, 1785, Hutchinson et al., eds., *Papers of Madison,* 8:328, 350. For a fuller discussion, see McCoy, *Last of the Fathers,* 229–32.

13. Brant, *Madison: The Nationalist,* 341–42. In a striking if apparently coincidental connection, Madison's Mohawk lands adjoined land purchased at roughly the same time by his fellow congressman (and signer of the Declaration of Independence) William Floyd, whose daughter Madison had been briefly engaged to marry. Unlike Madison, Floyd spent summers in upstate New York improving and developing his land before moving there permanently in 1803 at the advanced age of sixty-nine. A slave-owning farmer from Long Island, Floyd brought slaves with him to his upstate frontier home, where those not emancipated appear in the 1810 and 1820 census reports as slaves. When Floyd died near Rome, New York, in 1821, he apparently remained the largest slaveholder in Oneida County. See Jan DeAmicis, "Slavery in Oneida County, New York," *Afro-Americans in New York Life and History* 27 (2003): 69–134.

14. For elaboration, see Drew R. McCoy, "James Madison and Visions of American Nationality in the Confederation Period: A Regional Perspective," in *Beyond Confederation: Origins of the Constitution and American National Identity,* ed. Richard Beeman, Stephen Botein, and Edward C. Carter III (Chapel Hill, N.C., 1987), 226–58.

15. For elaboration and context, see John Lauritz Larson, *Internal Improvement: National Public Works and the Promise of Popular Government in the Early United States* (Chapel Hill, N.C., 2001), 10–18.

16. Jefferson to Washington, March 15, 1784, cited in Dunn, *Dominion of Memories,* 91–92. In his response, Washington agreed that, once the British vacated the forts at Oswego and Niagara, "the Yorkers will delay no time to remove every obstacle in the way" of their own route to the West. Washington to Jefferson, March 29, 1784, Julian P. Boyd et al., eds., *The Papers of Thomas Jefferson,* 44 vols. to date (Princeton, N.J., 1950–), 7:50.

17. Alan Taylor, *The Divided Ground: Indians, Settlers, and the Northern Borderland of the American Revolution* (New York, 2006), 152. Led by Governor George Clinton, New York was fighting aggressively during the 1780s to protect that potential against both the Iroquois and other rivals to its vast inland frontier, including the New England states and the federal Congress. For an excellent overview of the career of Clinton's nephew DeWitt Clinton, and the rise to prominence of their state, see especially Evan Cornog, *The Birth of Empire: DeWitt Clinton and the American Experience, 1769–1828* (New York, 1998).

18. Jefferson to DeWitt Clinton, March 19, 1822, Jefferson Papers, Library of Congress. See also Jefferson to Clinton, April 14, 1817; December 12, 1822, ibid. Madison's great praise of the Erie Canal is nicely caught in Madison to Richard Riker and Others, May 31, 1826, Madison Papers, Library of Congress.

19. Dunn, *Dominion of Memories,* 70.

20. Madison to Bernard Peyton, April 16, 1836, Madison Papers, Library of Congress.

21. See, for instance, Richard Peters to Madison, July 30, 1818; Madison to Samuel Wyllys Pomeroy, ca. February 29, 1820; George W. Featherstonhaugh to Madison, March 1, 1820; Jethro Wood to Madison, March 2, 1820; Madison to Featherstonhaugh, March 7, 1820, April 5, 1821; Madison to Pomeroy, July 21, 1821; William Plumer to Madison, November 6, 1821; Benjamin Waterhouse to Madison, December 12, 1822; Madison to Waterhouse, December 27, 1822; Stephen Van Rensselaer to Madison, February 4, 1823; Madison to Van Rensselaer, February 11, 1823, David B. Mattern et al., eds., *The Papers of James Madison: Retirement Series,* 3 vols. to date (Charlottesville, Va., 2009–), 1:320–21, 2:18–19, 24, 30, 33, 294, 367, 418, 612–13, 621, 643, 647.

22. "Address to the Agricultural Society of Albemarle," May 12, 1818, ibid., 1:282, 260–85.

23. Madison to Nicholas Biddle, April 16, 1825; Biddle to Madison, April 26, 1825; Madison to Biddle, May 2, 1825, Madison Papers, Library of Congress.

24. Francis Corbin to Madison, November 13, 1820, Mattern et al., eds., *Papers of Madison: Retirement Series,* 2:144.

25. Francis Corbin to Madison, September 24, 1818, ibid., 1:357.

26. Madison to Francis Corbin, November 26, 1820, ibid., 2:160–61. For a more detailed and thorough analysis of the Corbin correspondence, see McCoy, *Last of the Fathers,* 222–26.

27. For elaboration on Madison's accommodation of slavery during his later years, see McCoy, *Last of the Fathers,* chaps. 6–7.

28. For elaboration, see Drew R. McCoy, *The Elusive Republic: Political Economy in Jeffersonian America* (Chapel Hill, N.C., 1980).

29. Madison to Richard Rush, July 22, 1823, Madison Papers, Library of Congress. See also, among many letters elaborating the scourge of drought and insects, Madison to George Graham, March 27, 1824; Madison to James M. Hite, April 23, 1825; Madison to Robert H. Rose, July 27, 1826, ibid.

30. Madison to Hubbard Taylor, July 29, 1826, ibid.

31. For a larger, relevant assessment of this resonant Jeffersonian myth about the independence of American farmers, see the early chapters of Patricia Nelson Limerick, *Legacy of Conquest: The Unbroken Past of the American West* (New York, 1987).

32. For elaboration, see McCoy, *Elusive Republic,* esp. chap. 3, and McCoy, *Last of the Fathers,* chap. 5.

33. Madison to James M. Hite, April 23, 1825, Madison Papers, Library of Congress.

34. Madison to Churchill C. Cambreleng, March 8, 1827, ibid.

35. Madison to Thomas R. Dew, February 23, 1833, ibid.

36. Madison to James Maury, April 5, 1828, ibid. See also Madison to Henry Clay, April 2, June 1833, ibid. Also relevant is "Private Notes of Conversations with Mr. Madison," November 1827, Burton Harrison Papers, ser. 3, box 6, Library of Congress, and, more generally, McCoy, *Last of the Fathers,* chap. 5. See also Madison to Thomas P. Jones, November 1827, Madison Papers, Library of Congress, in which Madison thanked Jones for a copy of his address before the Franklin Institute, in which "the facts and remarks on the employment of slaves, in Manufactories, make it particularly interesting to the Southern sections of the Union, and encourage the hopes of a success in the experiments on foot, which may produce a rapid multiplication of them."

37. William G. Shade, *Democratizing the Old Dominion: Virginia and the Second Party System, 1824–1861* (Charlottesville, Va., 1996), 33.

38. Ibid., 33, and, more generally, chap. 1 ("Notes on the State of Virginia"), 17–49.

39. John Quincy Adams to Madison, August 18, 1834, letterbook copy, Adams Papers, Massachusetts Historical Society, Boston.

40. See the relevant discussion in Ketcham, *Madisons at Montpelier,* 138–40. The two eulogies, delivered and initially published separately, in 1831 and 1836 respectively, were published together in one volume following Adams's death; see John Quincy Adams, *The Lives of James Madison and James Monroe, Fourth and Fifth Presidents of the United States* (Boston, 1850).

41. Judith S. Graham et al., eds., *Diary and Autobiographical Writings of Louisa Catherine Adams,* 2 vols. (Cambridge, Mass., 2013), 2:711–12.

42. Catherine Allgor, ed., *The Queen of America: Mary Cutts's Life of Dolley Madison* (Charlottesville, Va., 2012), 79, 77–81. This multiauthored volume contains detailed information about the Cutts-Madison family connections. The reference to a bust of John Quincy Adams at Montpelier is from John H. B. Latrobe to Charles Carroll Harper, August 4, 1832, reprinted in John E. Semmes, *John H. B. Latrobe and His Times, 1803–1891* (Baltimore, 1917), 239–45.

43. Madison to Margaret Bayard Smith, September 21, 1830, Madison Papers, Library of Congress.

44. Madison to A. G. Gano and Others, March 25, 1835, ibid.

45. McCoy, *Last of the Fathers,* 295–308.

46. Madison to Andrew Stevenson, February 10, 1833, Madison Papers, Library of Congress. See also Madison to Daniel Drake, January 12, 1835, ibid.

47. Madison to Henry Clay, April 2, 1833, ibid.

48. Madison to George Tucker, June 27, 1836, ibid.

8   Mastery over Slaves, Sovereignty over Slavery

James Monroe, Virginia, and the Missouri Crisis

JOHN CRAIG HAMMOND

As he prepared to assume the presidency in 1817, James Monroe knew that he would preside over a union marked by deep ideological, partisan, sectional, and regional divisions: divisions that had riven the union since its inception, divisions that the recently ended War of 1812 had manifestly exposed and exacerbated. Accordingly, when Monroe laid out his main goal for the presidency in a letter to his son-in-law and trusted confidant George Hay, he expressed his "wish to bring about a union of the whole population of our country in support of our republican govt." Three months after his inauguration, Monroe undertook what would become the first of three national tours. Monroe's first tour began as an inspection of the coastal defenses, shipyards, and frontier forts that Congress and his predecessor, James Madison, had adopted in the aftermath of the War of 1812. It quickly evolved into an effort to promote sectional harmony and quell lingering partisan discord. Monroe's tour, which included frequent receptions and speeches throughout the mid-Atlantic states and into New England, provided powerful symbols of sectional and partisan reconciliation. Virginia's Old Republicans expressed reservations about Monroe's efforts at sectional and partisan reconciliation in Thomas Ritchie's *Richmond Enquirer,* but Monroe and the press in the northern states judged the tour a resounding success, an homage to the harmonizing effects of union and republican principles. Even the stalwart newspaper of Massachusetts Federalism, the Boston *Columbian Centinel,* allowed that Monroe's presidency heralded "an era of good feelings."[1]

The "Era of Good Feelings" proved short-lived, and Monroe's worst fears concerning sectional conflict would almost be realized in a few short years.

As the Fifteenth Congress neared the end of its second session in February 1819, it took up a statehood bill for the Missouri Territory. New York Republican James Tallmadge proposed amending the bill to prohibit the further introduction of slaves into Missouri and to require the emancipation of all slaves born there at the age of twenty-five as a condition of statehood. In effect, Tallmadge proposed imposing a gradual abolition plan on Missouri similar to those that had nearly eradicated slavery from the northern states over the previous thirty years. After a few days of furious debate, the House passed the Missouri statehood bill with the restrictions on slavery; the Senate rejected the measure, and Congress adjourned with the issue of Missouri statehood and the future of slavery's expansion unresolved. In the summer and fall of 1820, an unprecedented public consensus emerged in the North that Congress should not only place restrictions on slavery in Missouri but should also prohibit slavery "in all new states and territories hereafter admitted to the Union." In January 1820, Congress took up the overlapping issues of slavery in Missouri, slavery in the remainder of the Louisiana Purchase, and slavery in any territories that the United States might acquire in the future, namely Spanish Florida and Texas. After nearly three months of heated debate and frantic behind-the-scenes negotiations, James Monroe signed into law what became known as the Missouri Compromise. Under its terms, Missouri was admitted without restrictions on slavery, Congress prohibited slavery in the remainder of the Louisiana Purchase north of the 36–30 latitude, an effort to prohibit slavery in Texas in the event of American annexation was defeated, and Congress said nothing about slavery in Florida. With that, Monroe and a phalanx of southern planter-politicians defeated what would have become the most comprehensive restrictions on slavery's expansion in the union's history.[2]

In the midst of the Missouri Crisis, Monroe and his closest confidants resigned themselves to slavery's permanence in Virginia and the southern states. Monroe and many other Virginia planter-politicians expressed remorse, regret, and disgust at the revolutionary generation's failure to rid Virginia of the curse of slavery; they also accepted that it had become a permanent feature of Virginian and southern life. The four decades since independence had taught Monroe and the Virginia planter class that slavery would be removed from Virginia on providential terms and in providential time. Until then, Monroe and the southern planter class had to devote themselves to managing properly an institution beset by internal and external enemies and perpetually on the verge of exploding in rebellion. With the revolutionary hopes of gradual emancipation dashed, and fearing that Virginia's dangerously large concentration of slaves invited British invasion and slave rebellion, Monroe and his confidants determined that slavery's continued expansion had become a necessity, the means by which southern planters and statesmen could best manage the institution for the benefit of whites and blacks alike. If the Missouri Crisis convinced Monroe that slavery had become a permanent feature of southern life, it also convinced him that the southern planter class could alone legislate on slavery, not only within states such as Virginia but also in the outer reaches of an expanding union.

With these considerations in mind, when the Missouri Crisis came to a head in the winter of 1819–20, Monroe's paramount concern was to halt the continuing decline of Virginia's tidewater and piedmont gentry—the somewhat amorphous group of planters, politicians, and professionals who believed that their birth, talent, and distinction marked them off as the rightful governing class of Virginia, the other southern states, and the union. Monroe also committed himself to defending against perceived northern efforts to undermine the gentry's sovereignty over slavery as an institution, and their mastery over slaves as persons. For Monroe and the gentry class, maintaining sovereignty over slavery entailed maintaining control of the institution—politically, legally, and in policy terms—not only in the southern states but also in all federal territories, including any territories that the United States might acquire in the future. Planter sovereignty over slavery was inseparable from their ability to exercise mastery over the lives of black people as slaves. If sovereignty over the institution of slavery was lost, Monroe and the Virginia gentry believed that it was only a matter of time before the planter classes lost their mastery over black people as well. If northerners exercised sovereignty over slavery, even in far-off western territories, "universal emancipation" or "have[ing] our throats cut" by slaves incited to rebel would soon enough be forced on white Virginians. Driven by these fears, over the course of the Missouri Crisis, Monroe's commitment to the union became conditional, dependent on the union's ability to prop up—rather than undermine—the planter class and the institution of slavery that underwrote their power both at home and in the union. As Monroe explained at the height of the crisis, he sought the "best course for our union" so long as it was "also that of the southern states." Although Monroe and the gentry frequently squabbled among themselves over the means by which they would defeat northern restrictionists, they remained determined to use state power—whether at the local, state, or federal level—to maintain their sovereignty over slavery and their mastery of slaves.[3]

As the Missouri Crisis wore on in the winter of 1819–20, Monroe convinced himself that the political conflict over slavery's expansion derived from a scheme concocted by New England Federalists in a desperate bid either to rule over the union or to destroy it. The Missouri Crisis reanimated Monroe's longstanding fear that malicious northern politicians would exploit southern vulnerability on slavery for their own political advantage. Northern voters, sincere opponents of slavery, allegedly stood as easy marks for conniving politicians such as Rufus King, who would readily destroy Virginia or the union to elevate himself to the presidency. Animated by this understanding of the Missouri Crisis's sectional politics, Monroe committed himself to vetoing any restrictions on slavery, even in the federal territories. Monroe made it clear to his closest Virginia confidants that "my object has invariably been to defeat the whole measure" of restrictions on slavery's expansion.[4] Rather than working to address northern restrictionists' concerns that slavery was on the verge of uncontrollable expansion or to forging an equitable compromise, Monroe instead worked to secure what he believed to be the best interests of Virginia's slaveholders, which he frequently conflated with the best interests of the union. As threats of disunion escalated, however, Monroe determined that the Missouri Compromise as passed by Congress—which included restrictions on slavery in the remainder of the Louisiana Purchase—was the least bad alternative for Virginia.

Monroe then turned to the Virginia gentry to gain their consent to his signing the Compromise into law. But in working to gain their consent, Monroe mainly managed to deepen both his fears and the fears of the Virginia gentry that any effort to address the growing problem of slavery's expansion simply aided the efforts of New England Federalists and closet monarchists to destroy slavery and the gentry so that they could rule over the union. He also confirmed the Virginia gentry's conviction that any federal action to restrain slavery's expansion—no matter how mild and no matter how clearly constitutional—amounted to an existential threat to the planter class's mastery over slaves as persons and sovereignty over slavery as an institution. In the course of the Missouri Crisis, Monroe and the Virginia gentry formulated an understanding of the federal government's relationship with slavery and planters that rendered illegitimate any present or future northern efforts to use the powers of the federal government to take some kind of meaningful action against slavery's expansion. With that, they all but insured that the United States could never peacefully address the problem of slavery—let alone arrest its continued growth and expansion—short of disunion and civil war.

Although historians have focused their studies on the overly broad question of slavery in the United States or the narrow issue of sectional political strength, contemporaries understood the Missouri Crisis as a conflict over the future of slavery's expansion in an American union with designs on the core of the North American continent. In the half decade following the War of 1812, northerners and southerners, easterners and westerners, all recognized that conquest, expansion, and the consolidation of the American union in its western and southern borderlands had entered a new phase. In the period immediately surrounding the Missouri Crisis, the United States was involved in heated negotiations with Spain over the acquisition of Florida and Texas, which southern politicians had long insisted was included in the Louisiana Purchase but unjustly denied to the United States by Spain. Secretary of State John Quincy Adams's aggressive negotiations with Britain had won for the United States joint occupation of the Oregon Country and an American outlet on the Pacific. Since the close of the War of 1812, six western territories had either received or applied for statehood. At the same time, in the decade leading up to the Missouri Crisis, the well-being of Virginia slavery became powerfully tied to its continued expansion in the West. Between 1810 and 1820, over 120,000 slaves—the bulk of them hailing from the Chesapeake—were either sold into the new domestic slave trade that fed the emerging cotton kingdom's nearly insatiable appetite for slave labor or were forced west with migrating slaveholders. "The rage for the western country" ran deep among white Virginians in the immediate aftermath of the war. In the decade leading up to the Missouri controversy, the West became a vast outlet for Virginia's "excess" slave population and served as a welcoming place for the sons of Virginia's gentry to make and remake themselves as a new planter class. For Virginia planters and statesmen, in the aftermath of the War of 1812, the growth and expansion of slavery in the West became powerfully tied to the well-being of slavery at home.[5]

In the year preceding the Missouri Crisis, northern Republicans floated various proposals to limit slavery's expansion in the present and future territories of the United States. In April 1818, New Hampshire Republican Arthur Livermore proposed amending the Constitution to prohibit slavery "in any State hereafter admitted to the Union." In November 1818, thirty-three northern representatives voted against admitting Illinois to statehood because its constitution contained insufficient safeguards against slavery. In January 1819, Pennsylvanian John Sergeant proposed that Congress enact a "general ordinance, whereby the fundamental principles of civil and religious liberty shall be guaranteed to the inhabitants of the Territories exterior to the limits of the United States, and made the basis of all Governments hereafter to be established in the Union." Issued in the midst of negotiations with Spain over Florida and Texas, Sergeant's proposed "general ordinance" would have served as a new Northwest Ordinance for the remainder of the Louisiana Purchase and in any territories that the United States might acquire from Spain in the future. For northern restrictionists, then, the Missouri Crisis was part of a larger effort to block or limit slavery's expansion not just in Missouri but also in the remainder of the Louisiana Purchase, in the expected future acquisitions of Spanish Florida and Texas, and in any other territory that might be acquired by the United States in the future. As Pennsylvania Republican Jonathan Roberts remarked during the Missouri Crisis, the real question before Congress was "whether freedom or slavery is to be the lot of the regions beyond the Mississippi." Northern congressmen understood restrictions on Missouri as part of a larger project to end forever slavery's expansion in a union that was seeking to shore up its western and southern borderlands through the rapid acquisition and incorporation of new territory. They were backed by a growing chorus of northern voters and politicians who demanded that in addressing the question of slavery in Missouri, Congress also prohibit the "further extension of slavery in all states and territories hereafter admitted to the Union."[6]

The unique circumstance of the Missouri Crisis—Missouri had applied for statehood, leaving it in an ill-defined position between territory and state—allowed southern politicians to make a distinction between the immediate question of Missouri statehood and the separate questions involving slavery's expansion elsewhere. According to southern congressmen opposed to restrictions, forcing Missouri to adopt a plan of gradual abolition as a condition of statehood violated the principles of state equality and state sovereignty. It also clashed with the doctrine of equal footing, which held that states admitted to the union entered with the same rights as the original thirteen states. Thus, incoming states possessed the sovereign right to determine whether to permit or exclude slavery; just as Virginia reserved the right to maintain or abolish slavery, so did Missouri once it had met the constitutional and legal requirements for statehood. Southern politicians also alleged that the imposition of conditions on Missouri statehood came dangerously close to justifying some kind of federally imposed plan of gradual emancipation for the states where slavery already existed. If Congress could force a plan of gradual abolition on Missouri, why couldn't it do the same to Maryland or Virginia? So went southern reasoning. Efforts to restrict slavery in Missouri were "a most flagrant insult to state rights and sovereignty in general. If Congress are permitted to prescribe rules to the young state of Missouri, with impunity, who can tell how long it will be ere the sovereignty of Virginia will be assailed by the same daring hand?" Restrictions on slavery in Missouri heralded a loss of sovereignty over slavery in Virginia.[7]

With southern politicians united in their belief that restrictions on slavery in Missouri were both unconstitutional and bad policy on slavery, northern restrictionists had no hope of gaining enough southern defections to get a Missouri bill with restrictions through the Senate. A handful of northern congressmen—most importantly the four southern-born senators from Indiana and Illinois—agreed that restrictions on Missouri violated the principles of sovereignty, equality, and equal footing. Those four consistently defeated Missouri restrictions in the Senate, and the possibility of adding to their ranks in the House bolstered southern hopes that Missouri could be admitted without restrictions. As for northern congressmen, public pressure continued to force even those who favored compromise to insist on restrictions as a condition of statehood. In private, however, they increasingly conceded that "Congress have left the favourable time pass. They should have prohibited slavery when the Territorial government was formed" at the time of the Louisiana Purchase in 1804. The most restrictionists could hope for was "to admit Missouri without restriction" but "prevent the further introduction of slavery in the territories."[8]

By early February 1820, a majority of northern congressmen accepted that they stood little chance of getting a Missouri bill with restrictions through Congress. At the same time, the majority of southern congressmen, though opposed to the policy of prohibiting slavery in the remainder of the Louisiana Purchase, raised no objections to the measure's constitutionality. By mid-February, a compromise admitting Missouri without restrictions but prohibiting slavery in the bulk of the Louisiana Purchase was in reach. As the final details were worked out and voted on, a group of northern congressmen in both the House and Senate tried to add to the Compromise a provision blocking slavery's expansion into Texas, should the United States acquire it. But with the House and Senate on the verge of settling the issues of slavery in Missouri and slavery in the remainder of the Louisiana Purchase, the restriction on slavery in Texas went down to defeat. As passed, the Missouri Compromise admitted Missouri without restrictions, prohibited slavery north of the 36–30 line, and said nothing about slavery in any future territory acquired by the United States.[9]

Since 1818, a group of northern restrictionists—all of them Republicans and members of Monroe's party—had sought to halt slavery's expansion forever. In addition, public opinion in the North overwhelmingly favored the exclusion of slavery from "all new states and territories hereafter admitted to the Union." Nonetheless, a sufficient number of northern congressmen stood willing to exchange slavery in Missouri for the exclusion of the institution elsewhere. And while the southern extremists who identified with Virginia's Old Republicans decried the prohibition of slavery north of 36–30, most southern politicians understood that the Missouri Compromise granted overwhelmingly favorable terms to southern slaveholders. Northern restrictionists had sought to forever halt slavery's territorial expansion; southern politicians had whittled that down to a ban on slavery, during the territorial phase, in lands that seemed at best ill-suited for slavery. When word that a compromise had been reached arrived in Charleston, South Carolina, the *City Gazette* concluded that while the Missouri Crisis was a "trying time in Congress," the "trial has passed, and we look now only for harmony and conciliation on all sides." In their private correspondence, southern congressmen also expressed contentment with the Missouri Compromise. Alabama senator John Walker deemed the compromise "a wise and necessary measure—and has saved the Republic." Walker's correspondent, native Virginian and recently retired Alabama senator Charles Tait, "preferred a full & intire victory." Falling short of that, Tait recommended that the "President & the Southern Senators will take care for the future how Treaties are formed with the Indian Tribes west & north of the proposed state of Missouri. If they so choose the point the compromise surrendered by the South may become mostly nominal." Properly executed Indian policy could turn the region north of 36–30 into an Indian reservation. North Carolina senator Montfort Stokes accepted the 36–30 line as a "prudent and proper concession." By February 1820, then, a majority of congressmen—including a majority of congressmen from slave states—were willing to accept a Missouri Compromise that excluded slavery north of 36–30. As February turned into March, James Monroe stood as the sole remaining obstacle to the Missouri Compromise becoming law.[10]

Historians have badly misunderstood Monroe's role in forging what would become the Missouri Compromise. Until mid-February 1820, Monroe steadfastly opposed any compromise that would place any restrictions on slavery, including restrictions in federal territories. Monroe only reversed course when he became convinced that fates far worse than a ban on slavery in the upper Great Plains awaited Virginia and the South if the Missouri Crisis went unresolved any longer. Monroe reluctantly supported the Compromise, and only then because he believed it was the least bad outcome for Virginia and the slaveholding states of the South. On the surface, Monroe's actions during the crisis seem inconsistent: adamantly opposed to any restrictions on slavery's expansion, he eventually supported the ban on slavery north of the 36–30 line. Historians typically take Monroe's late support for the line as demonstration of his commitment to union and compromise. But Monroe's actions during the Missouri Crisis were driven by his underlying concern for maintaining the planter class's sovereignty over slavery as an institution, mastery over the lives of slaves, and Virginia's preeminent place in the union. Monroe signed the Compromise into law in March 1820 because he feared that allowing the Missouri Crisis to continue promised a host of calamities far worse than a ban on slavery north of the 36–30 line. Specifically, Monroe envisioned two scenarios playing out. Monroe feared that northern politicians were on the verge of passing a more general ban on slavery's expansion in all states and territories. Then, if the crisis remained unresolved because of Monroe's refusal to sign a general ban into law, northern politicians would use the issue to win the presidency for either Rufus King or DeWitt Clinton. The second option was disunion. Monroe indicated his willingness to allow the New England states to secede and form their own separate confederacy, which would then allegedly crown King and Clinton president and heir apparent. However, Monroe feared that Pennsylvania would join the northeastern confederacy. With that, Monroe fully expected that the southwestern states and territories would form their own separate confederacy, leaving Virginia in an enfeebled confederacy with the Atlantic slave states, vulnerable to foreign invasion and slave rebellion.

James Monroe's actions during the Missouri Crisis were driven primarily by his concerns for protecting the Virginia gentry and their control over slavery. Indeed, Monroe's personal life and professional career were inseparable from the protection of slavery. Monroe inherited a single slave in 1775. By 1820, he owned at least seventy-five slaves, and those slaves underwrote the financial well-being of Monroe's large, extended family. In 1814, Monroe purchased his ne'er-do-well brother's slaves to keep them from going to creditors. Two years later, Monroe loaned "some slaves" to his brother after purchasing a 325-acre estate for him in Albemarle. In the midst of the Missouri Compromise, he took an active part in selling slaves and his landholdings. He also was active in managing the working lives of slaves scattered across his family's numerous properties. In 1828, Monroe sold all of the slaves from his Albemarle estate to a Florida planter for $5,000, which he used to cover a note on money borrowed from John Jacob Astor during the War of 1812. Although Monroe might have deprecated slavery's existence and continuation in Virginia, like so many slaveholders he was financially dependent on his slaves, while his holdings in land and slaves solidified his family's social status.[11]

Prior to serving as president, Monroe frequently found himself fending off internal and external attacks on the gentry's sovereignty over slavery as an institution and mastery of slaves as persons. As a member of the Virginia legislature and the state ratifying convention in 1788, he voted against ratification, identifying with Antifederalist planters who opposed ceding any authority over Virginia to the federal government. While serving as governor in the early 1800s, Monroe took the lead in suppressing Gabriel's Rebellion in 1800 and the Virginia rebellion scares of 1802. These rebellions spurred Monroe to take action to prevent further ones. As governor, Monroe worked with President Thomas Jefferson to create a colony external to the limits of the United States where free blacks and slaves suspected of plotting "conspiracy, insurgency, Treason, and rebellion" would be permanently banished. Gabriel's Rebellion turned Monroe into an early and enthusiastic advocate of colonization—not to facilitate emancipation but to protect slavery by forcibly exiling free blacks and potentially rebellious slaves. During the War of 1812, Monroe served as both secretary of state and war. During the war he was tasked with fending off British raids in the Chesapeake that resulted in the flight of approximately 3,400 slaves to British forces (Monroe suspected that 6,000–8,000 slaves had fled). After the war, Monroe personally oversaw delegations seeking the return of escaped slaves or British compensation for planter losses, noting that "the owners ought to see that the govt. has done all that it could to recover them." He also spread tales that Chesapeake slaves had been sold into Caribbean slavery, hoping that it would discourage slave flight. Like other Virginia planters, Monroe feared that Britain would again invade the Chesapeake and use former slaves to incite flight and rebellion among those still held in bondage. As president, Monroe sought to defend Chesapeake planters by securing funding for forts, including Virginia's "Fortress Monroe."[12]

The Missouri Crisis pushed Monroe and the Virginia planter class to accept a position they had long been moving toward: slavery in Virginia and the United States as a permanent institution. Although Monroe remained publicly silent throughout the Missouri Crisis, he expressed his positions on slavery, restriction, and expansion through a series of essays penned by his son-in-law George Hay. Hay wrote the essays, published under the pen name "An American," with Monroe's support. Slavery "will most probably continue to exist through all succeeding time," explained Hay. "The difficulty" of emancipation "is insurmountable: and to my apprehension, it is perfectly clear that there is no plan that can be adopted which will not produce a wider waste or ruin," he claimed in another essay. "Rely upon it, as an unquestionable truth, that it is not at this moment in the power of human wisdom to devise a plan for the gradual abolition of slavery which does not require for its completion a degree of virtue, philanthropy, and moderation, among both whites and blacks, which it would be folly to anticipate." Continuing, Hay insisted that "there is, indeed, no plan that can be devised, which will not bring, even upon those intended to be relieved, incalculable suffering." The "difficulties attending this subject are insuperable," he concluded. But the difficulties of emancipation—no matter how gradual or how far off in the future—were in a sense immaterial to Hay. Slavery "was *expressly* sanctioned by the old, and recognized without censure by the new, testament." Any attempt to limit slavery's expansion with an eye toward its gradual abolition was "a plain, palpable reversal of the decree of the Almighty." In sum, "slavery has always existed," and "it will most probably continue to exist through all succeeding time." Monroe's support for Hay's essays was unqualified: "Your papers have certainly been well received & produced a great effect," wrote Monroe, who then added, "You have sustained the cause of the South & West."[13]

Monroe's close confidant Virginia senator Philip Barbour shared Hay's conviction of slavery's permanence. And just as Monroe worked with Hay to formulate his essays, Monroe worked with Barbour on putting together Barbour's main speech opposing restrictions on slavery's expansion. In that speech, Barbour lamented that "sad reality" had taught him the problem of slavery "is incurable by human means." Whether slavery was good or evil, Barbour did not know. That was a question best left to preachers. Questions of good and evil aside, "It is sufficient for us, as statesmen, to know that it has existed from the earliest ages of the world, and that to us has been assigned such a portion as, in reference to their number and various considerations resulting from a change of their condition, no remedy, even plausible, has been suggested, though wisdom and benevolence united have increasingly brooded over the subject." The revolutionary hope that somehow, someday, a protean moment would appear and usher in a period of peaceful, gradual emancipation in Virginia no longer animated Monroe or his closest Virginia allies. Instead, time and experience had demonstrated that no earthly power was capable of abolishing slavery without making the situation worse for both blacks and whites.[14]

Having resigned themselves to slavery's permanence, Hay, Barbour, Monroe, and the broader planter class now sought to provide for "the proper and effectual management of slaves" to mitigate against the dangers inherent in holding so many people in slavery. Doing so required unrestricted access to the trans-Mississippi West. As Barbour noted at the height of the Missouri Crisis, "the real question is, what disposition shall we make of those slaves" in the existing slave states? "Shall they be perpetually confined on this side of the Mississippi, or shall we spread them over a much larger surface by permitting them to be carried beyond that river?" Only by maintaining unfettered access to the vast regions "beyond the river" could the Virginia gentry effectively manage slavery at home. To allow Congress to restrict expansion in the West amounted to ceding sovereignty over slavery's future and mastery over the lives of slaves in Virginia to the federal government. Indeed, as one slaveholder remarked, prohibiting expansion was tantamount to "a declaration that slavery does not exist within the United States; but if it does, that Congress may abolish it, or confine it to narrow limits." As Hay explained, if northern states were permitted to prohibit expansion, then "the states south of the Ohio and east of the Mississippi are to have a line drawn around them, and they are to hold their right, their safety, and their character, at the mercy of every fanatic, who chooses to preach about humanity." The "danger of insurrection" could be mitigated only by slavery's continued expansion. Furthermore, Hay counseled, "If I were an inhabitant of Pennsylvania, or of a more northern region, I would entreat my country-men never to open their lips on the subject of slavery. I would entreat them to leave it in the hands of those alone who have an interest in it." Questions involving slavery's expansion had to be left to planters alone. To allow north-erners any say on the matter would be to cede sovereignty over slavery as an institution and mastery over the lives of black people. To "mitigate this irremediable evil," Virginia slaveholders had to be permitted to "dis-perse" slaves "throughout the country."[15]

Monroe, Hay, and Barbour heartily endorsed the theory of "diffusion," the belief that slavery's expansion would "diffuse" the Atlantic slave states' enslaved black population. According to Monroe and other expan-sionists, to permit slaves "to spread over an extensive country" in the West would diffuse Virginia's dangerously large population of slaves, which by 1819 they were likening to a powder keg ready to explode. By lessening the number of slaves in Virginia, diffusion would decrease the likelihood of a massive slave rebellion while discouraging future British invasions of the Chesapeake. Diffusion also promised to "ameliorate"—a favorite term of the expansionists—the condition of slaves. With fewer slaves to care for, whether in the Atlantic or the western states, planters would supposedly bet-ter provide for their slaves (who largely provided for themselves, in any case). Not only was diffusion and amelioration the most humane course of action the federal government could take with regards to slaves, they believed; it also promised to lessen the likelihood of slave rebellion as slaves who labored under better material conditions would allegedly be more content with their lot. Contra the arguments of historians William W. Freehling and Lacy K. Ford, for most Virginia planters, expansion and diffusion would not serve as a means by which gradual emancipation could be effected in the Old Dominion or in western states with smaller slave populations. As Virginia jurist Spencer Roane wrote, the "evil" that was slavery was "irredeemable." Instead, constant expansion and diffusion would allow for the "proper and effectual management" of Virginia's ever-growing enslaved population. Not only would such measures benefit slaves; they would also save Virginia from invasion and rebellion.[16]

James Monroe shared the sentiments of Hay and Barbour. In a letter to Hay, Monroe reflected on the circumstances that had led Virginia planters to endorse the prohibition of slavery in the Northwest Ordinance of 1787. In the 1780s, Virginia's planter politicians "were all inclined to extend the right of perfect freedom" to the trans-Appalachian West, "as suddenly as we could," in order to limit "domestic slavery as much as we could." Support for prohibiting slavery's expansion in the Northwest in the 1780s "was a generous sentiment which grew out of the revolutionary struggle." Virginia's planter politicians could afford these generous sentiments in the 1780s because "we had then no experience of the dangers menacing us from domestic slavery, & went the full length with our northern brethren." Ignorant of slavery's enormous dangers, they supported arguably the most important prohibition on slavery's expansion in American history. But "we have since had experience" with both the impossibility of gradual emancipation and the dangers inherent in keeping nearly half of the state's population in slavery, dangers that Monroe witnessed firsthand as governor and as secretary of war and state. Virginians such as Monroe had to be given full power to safeguard against those dangers. All that Monroe asked of the North was "that they will show some regard for our peculiar situation": massively overpopulated with slaves and subjected to constant threats of internal rebellion and external invasion. Preserving mastery over slaves and sovereignty over slavery in Virginia necessitated that Virginia and the southern states alone control slavery's expansion both within and without the limits of the United States. By properly managing the geography of slavery and the concentration of slaves, and by maintaining absolute sovereignty over slavery as an institution, Monroe and southern planters could put off indefinitely the conflagration that threatened to consume every slave society.[17]

Monroe's concerns for protecting slavery also shaped his understanding of the past, present, and future of sectional politics in the union. By December 1819, Monroe had convinced himself that the congressional effort to restrict slavery in Missouri was part of a larger conspiracy, hatched by Federalists, either to rule over the union or to destroy it. As Monroe understood matters, the origins of the Missouri Crisis stretched all the way back to the "same spirit which prevailed in 1786" and resulted in the Jay-Gardoqui Treaty. The

Jay-Gardoqui Treaty of 1786 ceded American navigation rights on the Mississippi River to Spain, and at the time southern politicians alleged that it originated in a New England plot to dominate the union by denying the South access to the West. According to Monroe, the same "dormant spirit" of New England sectional chauvinism now drove Federalist actions during the Missouri Crisis. Monroe alleged that the New England and New York Federalists who had seized on the Missouri Crisis had no interest in the well-being of slaves, the future of slavery's expansion, or the union. Instead, they had "seized on a popular topic"—slavery expansion—"which gives them the command of the best affections of their constituents." Enjoying popular backing at home for the first time since the War of 1812, the Federalists now sought to "dismember the Union" unless they could rule over it.[18] With this understanding of the sectional politics of the Missouri Crisis, Monroe redoubled his commitment to halting efforts to force restrictions on Missouri slavery as a condition of statehood.[19]

Monroe worked extensively behind the scenes with leading southern politicians to formulate some kind of strategy to defeat restrictions in Congress. Sometime in late January he met in private with South Carolina representative Henry Pinckney, where they discussed the efficacy of Hay's essays. They also decided that publication of the Virginia Ratification Convention of 1788's journals would hinder their cause, as it revealed that the founders agreed that Congress did indeed possess the authority to restrict slavery in the federal territories. He also met with James Barbour to plot strategy on the effectiveness of holding Maine statehood hostage to Missouri. He and Barbour corresponded on the best arguments for the latter to make in the Senate for admission without restriction. Finally, Monroe had at least one meeting with the southern members of his cabinet where they discussed strategies for defeating restrictions in Congress. Although James Monroe might have been president of an immense, diverse, and divided union, during the Missouri Crisis he acted more like the Virginia gentry's ambassador to the federal government, charged with protecting the interests of Virginia slaveholders by defeating any bill that included restrictions on slavery.[20]

Monroe's position on restrictions shifted abruptly as the regional and sectional dynamics of disunion, along with the sectional politics of the crisis, began to change in mid-February 1820. By then, Monroe feared that King and Clinton had struck a deal that would bring Pennsylvania and Maryland into their northeastern confederacy, whose boundaries would extend to "the Potomac" and "Allegheny Mountains." A division of the union at the Potomac would have effectively created a separate southern confederacy. In and of itself, the creation of a northeastern confederacy left Monroe unbothered. But its theoretical creation promised to generate an even more difficult set of problems for the Atlantic slave states. Monroe and his closest confidants expected that the creation of a separate northeastern confederacy would quickly lead to disunion between the slave states of the Atlantic Coast and the slave states of the interior and the Mississippi Valley. As Monroe explained to one of his many Virginian correspondents, "How long could we calculate on preserving our union with the west," if Pennsylvania, New York, and Maryland left for union with the Northeast? With "one sectional division being made," and "with so many ambitious men rising in the West," Monroe expected that it would only be a matter of time before the western slave states, led by men such as Andrew Jackson and Henry Clay, formed their own separate union.[21]

The formation of separate southeastern and southwestern confederacies promised to worsen Virginia's problems. With Virginia and the Atlantic slave states isolated from the West, Virginia would continue its economic decline and Virginia's dangerously large slave population would only continue to increase. Worse still, a Virginia isolated with the Atlantic slave states would become ever more susceptible to British invasion and slave rebellion. In an alternative scenario, Monroe also feared that if the question was not settled in the present session of Congress, the northern compromisers who worked with the South would either be compelled to vote for a ban on slavery's future expansion everywhere or they would be replaced. At the same time, northern restrictionists would use the issue of slavery to elevate Rufus King or Dewitt Clinton to the presidency. In the next session, northern restrictionists would vote to prohibit slavery in all states and territories, and King or Clinton would sign the bill into law. While Monroe remained adamantly opposed to signing into law any compromise that restricted slavery in the West, by February 1820 he had convinced himself that he had to sign the Missouri Compromise to spare Virginia from a worse fate: disunion and the isolation of Virginia in a feeble confederacy with the Atlantic slave states, or a Rufus King presidency and a restrictionist Congress that would forever halt slavery's expansion. Monroe had to sign not to save the union but to save Virginia's union with an expanding Southwest. With Monroe now committed to signing the compromise forged by Congress into law, one obstacle remained: the Virginia gentry.[22]

The tidewater and piedmont planters who had fashioned themselves the Old Republicans during Jefferson's second term took a particularly strong interest in the Missouri Crisis. The crisis allowed Monroe and the gentry to make sense of the past, present, and future of the gentry class. Crystalizing fears that their sovereignty over slavery and their mastery over African Americans stood under relentless attack from internal and external enemies, they girded themselves to withstand the present crisis and to prepare for future assaults.

These Virginia gentry had faced periodic economic and political crises since the 1760s. The three decades preceding the Missouri Crisis had seen their political standing and influence diminish both in Virginia and in the United States, despite the election of three successive Virginians to the presidency. The diversification of Virginia's economy and the rapid growth of a white population lacking substantive financial, political, or social ties to the old gentry resulted in a steady decline in the gentry's influence over state politics. To maintain their political power, they resorted to securing an inordinately large share of seats for the tidewater and piedmont in the state assembly, and in the 1810s they were already facing calls for a redistribution of assembly seats. The gentry feared that an increasingly national economy, an expanding federal union, and a federal government that chartered banks, built canals, and established protective tariffs would diminish their influence even more. Farmers with access to bank credit and canals had little need for planter loans and docks.[23]

In the immediate aftermath of the War of 1812, the Old Republicans fought against the rechartering of the Bank of the United States and federal funding for internal improvements such as canals and roads. According to the Old Republicans, banks and canals threatened "consolidation" of the federal government, which would inevitably feed the growth of federal power and the attenuation of the gentry's wealth and influence. Monroe's growing reputation as a nationalist and his efforts to create what he called an "amalgamation" of parties added to the gentry's worries that their influence and power over the union would continue to decline. Finally, the Panic of 1819 threatened economic ruin to members of the planter class, who had long borrowed carelessly against their land and slaves. The general direction of economic and political life both in Virginia and in the United States after 1815 proved especially demoralizing to the Virginia gentry, who believed that they alone embodied the principles of true republicanism, and that they alone remained true to "the revered patriots of 1776."[24]

For the gentry, the Missouri Crisis amounted to the latest in a long-running series of assaults on their personal mastery over slaves and their political sovereignty over slavery as an institution. "The Florida business—the Missouri debate which is to be got up next winter with improved scenery—& the tariff bill" were "worse than any of the grievances we resisted when colonies," lamented would-be college professor and Jefferson protégé Francis Walker Gilmer. For members of the gentry such as Gilmer, Monroe, Barbour, and Hays, the purpose of government—whether at the local, state, or federal level—was to empower the gentry who then ruled over others. Consolidation—whether by the British Empire in the 1770s or by the federal government in 1820—undermined their power at home and in the union. They also feared that it undercut their mastery of others, particularly their slaves and lesser whites. For the gentry, the Missouri Crisis was simply the inevitable outcome of "consolidation," the byword for the alleged efforts of once-discredited Federalists to rule over the union by destroying the wealth, standing, and influence of the gentry.[25]

Francis Walker Gilmer exemplified the gentry's linkage of their perilous hold on power with the Missouri Crisis and consolidation, sovereignty over slavery, and mastery of slaves. For Walker, whose family's fortunes had declined precipitously over the previous decade, the Bank of the United States and the Missouri Crisis were simply the means by which Virginians were "to be taxed to support the Yankees & make [Rufus] King President or have our throats cut" by slaves incited to rebel. The gentry's sovereignty over slavery would be lost with a King presidency—the true goal of restrictionists. With sovereignty lost, mastery would soon go too. The gentry could submit to a King presidency and forced emancipation, or New Englanders would encourage slaves to rebel. These sentiments deepened the gentry's conviction that the Missouri Crisis had nothing to do with the enslavement of blacks; it was simply a scheme concocted by "sniveling, sanctimonious" Yankees to enslave the Virginia gentry. Hay insisted that "the whole affair" was simply "a base and hypocritical scheme to get power under the mask of humanity," a sentiment with which Monroe agreed. As Gilmer framed matters in the aftermath of the Missouri Compromise, "We are from this day forth, tributary to northern shoe makers," and "potato[,] pumpkin, and Ruta-bega men." Rather than ruling themselves, their slaves, and the union, Virginia's gentry would henceforth be ruled by northern shoemakers and farmers. If the gentry resisted, black slaves would be inspired to rebel.[26]

Taking these concerns one step further, Monroe's personal physician and close confidant Dr. Charles Everett warned that the moment "Virginia principles" on slavery and state rights "cease to govern this union we shall be delivered" over to a fate "worse than Federalism"—"universal emancipation." Virginia native and former Alabama senator Charles Tait expressed similar concerns that the growing attacks on slavery and republicanism heralded doom. "With the avowles in discussion and the *temper of the times* it is impossible not to connect this question with the momentous one of Emancipation of our Slaves," warned Tait. Moving from sovereignty over slavery as an institution to mastery over African Americans as persons, Tait tied threats of emancipation not only to "the right of property" but to "our social repose" and "our safety." Excluding slavery from Missouri and halting its expansion elsewhere would allow blacks to dictate the terms of interaction with whites—southern whites' "social repose." It also threatened rebellion or black reprisals. Pulling together these sentiments, the *Richmond Enquirer* warned against any compromise: "If we yield now, beware—they will ride us forever." The masters and rightful rulers of Virginia and the union would become slaves of New England Federalists and their black minions.[27]

These understandings of slavery, expansion, and the politics of the Missouri Crisis shaped the reactions of both Monroe and the Virginia gentry to the Missouri Compromise. By February 1820, Monroe had convinced himself that he had to sign the Compromise into law to save Virginia and slavery from a far worse fate. Thus, when word reached Richmond that Congress had struck a compromise and that Monroe was prepared to sign the bill into law, the gentry nearly revolted against Monroe. Although neither the Virginia gentry nor the Virginia assembly had any authority over the matter, Monroe nonetheless felt compelled to gain their consent before he signed the Compromise into law. Making matters worse for Monroe, the Republican caucus that was expected to nominate Monroe for the presidency in the upcoming election of 1820 was set to meet just as Richmond received word that Monroe would sign into law the Compromise. Monroe's supporters had to adjourn the caucus meeting out of fears that the Old Republicans would deny Monroe the nomination, as the Old Republicans made clear that they would nominate someone else if Monroe went through with it.[28]

Over the next three months, Monroe, Barbour, and Hay corresponded extensively with major and minor members of the gentry—including Jefferson and Madison—to explain why Monroe felt compelled to sign the Compromise into law. Monroe published a testy letter in the *Richmond Enquirer* sketching out the series of alarming scenarios that might transpire if he vetoed the Compromise bill and the Missouri Crisis remained unresolved. The choices facing the gentry were stark: they could support Monroe and the Compromise, or Rufus King would become president of the United States. "Mr Kings doctrines avowed immediate emancipation," cautioned Monroe, as he directly linked the Missouri Crisis to sovereignty over slavery and mastery over slaves. Monroe would preserve the gentry's sovereignty over slavery and their mastery over slaves as persons. In a personal letter to Charles Everett, Monroe defended his lifelong commitment to protecting the interests of Virginia's planter class, stretching back to his service in the Confederation Congress in 1786. Defending his signing of the Compromise into law, Monroe added, "If I did my duty then & have done my duty" now, Virginia "ought to be the last State who would entertain any doubt as to the future." Monroe's and Hay's campaign worked. Madison effectively gave Monroe his blessing to sign the Compromise on the grounds that a prohibition on slavery west of Missouri made no difference to the ability of Virginians to control slavery at the state and federal level. Monroe signed the Missouri Compromise into law on March 6, 1820.[29]

Monroe's determination to win gentry support for his signing of the Compromise only deepened their shared belief that the Missouri Crisis was really about sectional political power and the enslavement of white Virginians, rather than a sincere effort to limit slavery's expansion. It also pulled together their fears concerning the past, present, and future of sectional politics in the union. Parties might temporarily quell sectional conflicts, but planter-politicians must always be on guard against cunning hypocrites such as Rufus King, who—though caring little for the well-being of slaves—always stood ready to exploit the slavery issue in their mania to subjugate the planters who were the true guardians of republican government. The politics of slavery and sectionalism—fraught with difficulties from the

214/ John Craig Hammond

union's inception in the 1770s—became ever more explosive and difficult as Monroe validated the planter class's conviction that there never was and that there never could be a legitimate effort to restrict slavery's expansion. All such efforts originated in "the Spirit of 1786," an effort by designing Federalists to destroy the Virginia gentry, the only group in the United States who stood between the republicanism of the Constitution and the monarchism of the Federalists.

In seeking the Virginia gentry's approval of his signing the Missouri Compromise bills into law, Monroe not only stoked the worst fears of the Virginia gentry; he also legitimated their increasingly radical positions on the relationship between the federal government and slavery. "Mr Kings doctrines" might not have "avowed immediate emancipation." But halting slavery's expansion forever would have forced the slave states to grapple with the long-term feasibility of their slave societies. Instead, Monroe and the Virginia gentry walked away from the Missouri Crisis convinced of slavery's permanence and the necessity of indefinite expansion. They also insisted that the interests of the union in restricting slavery's expansion had to yield to the particular needs of the Virginia gentry and the broader class of slaveholders who reigned across the South. Thus, federal coercion on slavery of any kind—even the mildest of coercions, barring slavery from unsettled territory—had become strictly off-limits in the future. In both the short- and long-term, Monroe and the Virginia gentry all but assured that the federal government could never take any kind of meaningful action to restrict slavery's growth and expansion. And given their own deep personal, financial, ideological, and political dependence on the enslavement of others, it was difficult to imagine how Monroe and other slaveholders would voluntarily end slavery on their own. Southern whites would never abolish slavery on their own, and they would do everything within their power to resist outside efforts, or the efforts of slaves, to do the same. It is difficult to dispute historian Annette Gordon-Reed's conclusion that "the problem of American slavery could only have been solved in the way that it ultimately was solved: through bloody conflict and strife." Only a massive and prolonged invasion of the kind that happened during the U.S. Civil War could allow slaves and their white antislavery allies to destroy planters' sovereignty over slavery as an institution and mastery of the lives of slaves.[30]

James Monroe and many of the founders had hoped that time and expansion would bridge the sectional differences that had threatened the union since its inception. The Missouri Crisis, however, demonstrated to contemporaries that time and expansion had only served to deepen and exacerbate sectional conflicts. The Missouri Compromise offered a temporary solution to the configuration of slavery in the union's past, present, and future. Ultimately, though, the Missouri Compromise failed to address bigger, more intractable issues that would ultimately lead to Civil War. What was the place of slavery in an extended union intent on conquering a continent? Where could Virginia and southern slaveholders exercise their sovereignty over slavery as an institution and their mastery over black people? In 1860, a new set of northern restrictionists answered those questions by electing Abraham Lincoln and a Republican Congress committed to halting forever slavery's expansion. In response, southern slaveholders broke apart the union to preserve their sovereignty over slavery as an institution and their personal mastery over slaves as persons.

Notes

Portions of this chapter appeared previously in John Craig Hammond, "President, Planter, Politician: James Monroe, the Missouri Crisis, and the Politics of Slavery," *Journal of American History* 105 (March 2019): 843–67, and are reprinted with the permission of the *Journal of American History*, Oxford University Press, and the Organization of American Historians.

1. James Monroe to George Hay, August 5, 1817, Daniel Preston and M. C. De-Long, eds., *A Documentary History of the Presidential Tours of James Monroe, 1817, 1818, 1819* (Westport, Conn., 2003), 424; Noble E. Cunningham Jr., *The Presidency of James Monroe* (Lawrence, Kans., 1996), 30–40; *Columbian Centinel* (Boston), July 12, 1817. Historians once agreed that an outpouring of nationalism followed the War of 1812. However, Alan Taylor, "Dual Nationalisms: Legacies of the War of 1812," in *What So Proudly We Hailed: Essays on the Contemporary Meaning of the War of 1812*, ed. Pietro S. Nivola and Peter J. Kastor (Washington, D.C., 2012), 67–96, and Taylor, *The Internal Enemy: Slavery and War in Virginia, 1772–1832* (New York, 2013), 395–98, show that nationalism was confined mainly to the North and West, and that the primary effect of the war in Virginia was to deepen the gentry's conviction that the union had strayed from Virginia's true republican principles, had failed to protect slavery during the war and would likely continue to do so in the future, and no longer served Virginia's interests.

2. For the most recent literature on the Missouri Crisis, see John Craig Hammond, "President, Planter, Politician: James Monroe, the Missouri Crisis, and the Politics of Slavery," *Journal of American History* 105 (2019): 843–67; John R. Van Atta, *Wolf by the Ears: The Missouri Crisis, 1819–1821* (Baltimore, 2015); Michael J.

McManus, "President James Monroe's Domestic Policies, 1817–1825: 'To Advance the Best Interests of Our Union,'" in *A Companion to James Madison and James Monroe,* ed. Stuart Leibiger (New York, 2013), 438–55; Martin Ohman, "A Convergence of Crisis: The Expansion of Slavery, Geopolitical Realignment, and Economic Depression in the Post-Napoleonic World," *Diplomatic History* 37 (2013): 419–45; Matthew Mason, "The Maine and Missouri Crisis: Competing Priorities and Northern Slavery Politics in the Early Republic," *Journal of the Early Republic* 33 (2013): 675–700; John Craig Hammond, "'Uncontrollable Necessity': The Local Politics, Geo-Politics, and Sectional Politics of Slavery Expansion," in *Contesting Slavery: The Politics of Freedom and Bondage in the New American Nation,* ed. John Craig Hammond and Matthew Mason (Charlottesville, Va., 2011), 138–60; George William Van Cleve, *A Slaveholders' Union: Slavery, Politics, and the Constitution in the Early American Republic* (Chicago, 2010), 211–23; Lacy K. Ford, *"Deliver Us from Evil": The Slavery Question in the Old South* (New York, 2009), 112–40; John Craig Hammond, *Slavery, Freedom, and Expansion in the Early American West* (Charlottesville, Va., 2007); Robert Pierce Forbes, *The Missouri Compromise and Its Aftermath: Slavery and the Meaning of America* (Chapel Hill, N.C., 2007); and Matthew Mason, *Slavery and Politics in the Early American Republic* (Chapel Hill, N.C., 2006).

3. Charles Everett to Monroe, February 20, 22, 1820, James Monroe Papers, New York Public Library (hereafter JMP, NYPL); James Monroe to Philip Barbour, February 3, 1820, Philip Barbour Papers, New York Public Library. An inordinate amount of historiography focuses on either praising or criticizing Monroe's involvement—or, as some contend, lack of involvement—in forging the Missouri Compromise. Rather than focusing on Monroe's statesmanship during the Missouri Crisis, this chapter instead examines how Monroe's identity as a Virginia planter influenced his understanding of the crisis and his actions in shaping its outcome and consequences. For divergent evaluations of Monroe's role in the Missouri Crisis and Compromise, see, for example, Glover Moore, *The Missouri Controversy, 1819–1821* (Lexington, Ky., 1953); Harry Ammon, *James Monroe: The Quest for National Identity* (New York, 1971); Cunningham, *Presidency of James Monroe;* Forbes, *Missouri Compromise;* McManus, "James Monroe's Domestic Policies"; and Hammond, "President, Planter, Politician."

4. Monroe to Charles Everett, February 11, 1820, James Monroe Papers in Virginia Repositories, University of Virginia Microfilm Publications (Charlottesville, Va., 1969).

5. William Doswell to Thomas W. Claybrooke, June 17, 1817, Claybrooke-Doswell Families, Letters, 1804–1833, Personal Papers Collection, Library of Virginia, Richmond. For expansion between 1815 and 1819, see John Craig Hammond, "Slavery, Settlement, and Empire: The Expansion and Growth of Slavery in the Interior of the North American Continent, 1770–1820," *Journal of the Early Republic* 32 (2012): 175–206; Adam Rothman, *Slave Country: American Expansion and the Origins of the Deep South* (Cambridge, Mass., 2005); Van Cleve, *Slaveholders' Union,* 228–31; and Ohman, "A Convergence of Crisis." For the ideological connections among black slavery, white republicanism, and expansion, see Peter S. Onuf, "The Empire of Liberty:

Land of the Free and Home of the Slave," in *The World of the Revolutionary American Republic: Land, Labor, and the Conflict for a Continent,* ed. Andrew Shankman (New York, 2014), 316–51. For the ideological, economic, and political importance of the domestic slave trade to Upper South planters, see Calvin Schermerhorn, *The Business of Slavery and the Rise of American Capitalism, 1815–1860* (New Haven, Conn., 2015), and Edward Baptist, *The Half Has Never Been Told: Slavery and the Making of American Capitalism* (New York, 2014).

6. *Annals of Congress,* 15th Cong., 1st sess., 1675–76; 15th Cong., 2nd sess., 305–11; 16th Cong., 1st sess., 336; Hammond, *Slavery, Freedom, and Expansion.* For the use of "the fundamental principles of civil and religious liberty" as a euphemism for excluding slavery, see the speech of John Taylor of New York, *Annals of Congress,* 16th Cong., 1st sess., 966. For calls to prohibit slavery in "all states and territories hereafter admitted to the Union," see, for example, "To the Editors of the American," *American and Commercial Daily Advertiser* (Baltimore), January 3, 1820; "From the Rhode Island American," *Niles' Weekly Register* (Baltimore, Md.), December 20, 1819; "From a Philadelphia Paper," *Niles' Weekly Register,* December 11, 1819; "Resolutions of the New Jersey Legislature," *Niles' Weekly Register,* January 22, 1820; "Meeting at Camden," *Washington Whig* (Bridgeton, N.J.), December 20, 1819; "Resolutions of the House of Assembly of New York," *Niles' Weekly Register,* February 5, 1820; "Resolutions of the New Hampshire Legislature," *Niles' Weekly Register,* July 8, 1820; "Extension of Negro Slavery," *Niles' Weekly Register,* November 27, 1819; "Slavery," *Connecticut Courant* (Hartford), December 7, 1819; "Town Meeting," *Liberty Hall and Cincinnati Gazette,* December 21, 1819; "Meeting at Keene, New Hampshire," *Concord Observer* (N.H.), December 20, 1819; "Meeting of the Citizens of Cherry-Valley and Its Vicinity," *Cherry Valley* (N.Y.) *Gazette,* January 4, 1820; *Journal of the Senate of the State of Ohio, Being the First Session of the Eighteenth General Assembly, Begun and Held in the Town of Columbus, in the County of Franklin, Monday, December 6, 1819: and in the Eighteenth Year of Said State* (Columbus, 1820), 145–47, 154, 169; *Journal of the House of Representatives of the State of Ohio, Being the First Session of the Eighteenth General Assembly, Begun and Held in the Town of Columbus, in the County of Franklin, Monday, December 6, 1819: and in the Eighteenth Year of Said State* (Columbus, 1819), 166, 176, 198–99; and United States, *Senate Journal,* 16th Cong., 1st sess., 82, 114, 118, 131, 136. For connections between the Missouri Crisis and southern interests in Florida and Texas, see, for example, Charles Tait to John Walker, November 19, 1819, Walker Family Papers, Alabama Department of Archives and History, Montgomery; William Short to Thomas Jefferson, December 1, 1819, Jefferson Papers, Library of Congress, Washington, D.C. (hereafter LOC); "Missouri Question—Continued," *Argus of Western America* (Frankfurt, Ky.), March 9, 1820; "Missouri Question," *American Providence* (Providence, R.I.), March 24, 1820; and "Extension of Slavery," *Intelligencer* (Bellows Falls, Vt.), March 20, 1820.

7. "Missouri," *Richmond Enquirer,* May 14, 1819. For the southern position on Missouri restrictions, see Van Cleve, *Slaveholders' Union,* and Hammond, *Slavery, Freedom, and Expansion.*

8. William Trimble to Ethan Allen Brown, January 29, 1820, Ethan Allen Brown Papers, Ohio Historical Society, Columbus. For the votes and divisions that beset Congress during the Missouri Crisis, see McManus, "James Monroe's Domestic Policies."

9. For the votes on slavery west of Louisiana and Arkansas, see *Annals of Congress,* 16th Cong., 1st sess., 424, 426–28, 469, 1587–88. In addition to the proposals to prohibit slavery in Texas, Samuel Foot of Connecticut proposed that Congress require all territories and incoming states to exclude slavery as a condition of statehood. See *Annals of Congress,* 16th Cong., 1st sess., 1171–72. The best account of the deals, pressures, and politics that went into the making of the Compromise is McManus, "James Monroe's Domestic Policies."

10. Hammond, *Slavery, Freedom, and Expansion,* 161; "The Question Settled," *City Gazette* (Charleston, S.C.), March 10, 1820; John Walker to Charles Tait, April 17, 1820, Tait Family Papers, Alabama Department of Archives and History; Charles Tait to John Walker, May 20, 1820, Walker Family Papers, Alabama Department of Archives and History; Montfort Stokes to John Branch, February 27, 1820, Slaves and Slavery Collection, Missouri Historical Society, St. Louis.

11. For Monroe's extensive land and slaveholdings, see Gerard W. Gawalt, "James Monroe, Presidential Planter," *Virginia Magazine of History and Biography* 101 (1993): 251–72. For Monroe and his brother, see James Monroe to (nephew) James Monroe, May 9, 1814; November 26, 1816, James Monroe Papers, Special Collections Research Center, Swem Library, College of William and Mary, Williamsburg, Virginia. For Monroe's personal involvement in managing his holdings in slaves and the laboring lives of slaves that he had given as a gift to his daughter Eliza and son-in-law George Hay, see George Hay to Monroe, December 24, 1819; Monroe to James Madison, November 24, 1819, James Monroe Papers, LOC; and Monroe to Hay, December 17, 1820, James Monroe Collection, James Monroe Museum, Fredericksburg, Va. For the 1828 sale of his slaves, see James Monroe to James Madison, March 28, 1828, James Monroe Papers, LOC.

12. Monroe to Jefferson, February 13, 1802, Thomas Jefferson Papers, Manuscript Division, LOC; *American State Papers: Documents, Legislative and Executive, of the Congress of the United States, from the First Session of the First to the Second Session of the Tenth Congress, Inclusive, Commencing March 3, 1789, and Ending March 3, 1809* (Washington, D.C., 1834), class X, *Miscellaneous,* 464–65; Monroe to Madison, April 22, 1815, James Madison Papers, Manuscript Division, LOC; Van Cleve, *Slaveholders' Union,* 152–66; Pauline Maier, *Ratification: The People Debate the Constitution, 1787–1788* (New York, 2010), 42, 235–36; Taylor, *Internal Enemy,* 351–65.

13. "An American," *Richmond Enquirer,* November 23, 30, 1819; January 1, 18, 1820; Monroe to George Hay, January 10, 1820, JMP, NYPL. For the Hay-Monroe correspondence on the "American" essays, see Monroe to Hay, December 20, 1819, James Monroe Collection, Virginia Historical Society (hereafter JMC, VHS); Hay to Monroe, December 24, 1819, James Monroe Papers, LOC; Monroe to Hay, January 10, 1819, JMP, NYPL; and Monroe to Hay, January 1820, JMC, VHS. For the new emphasis on the permanence of southern slavery and the necessity of properly managing it

through continued expansion, see, in addition to the essays of "An American," "Cato," *National Intelligencer* (Washington, D.C.), December 4, 1819; "Limner," *National Intelligencer,* November 3, 1819; *National Intelligencer,* January 29, 1820; and "From the National Intelligencer" and "State of Missouri," *Richmond Enquirer,* February 25, 1819. Hay's authorship of the "An American" essays was well-known in Washington. See Louisa Catherine Johnson Adams to John Adams, December 18, 1819 [December 11–21], Adams Family Papers, Massachusetts Historical Society, Boston.

14. *Annals of Congress,* 16th Cong., 1st sess., 332, 335. For the revolutionary generation's struggles with slavery in Virginia, see Eva Sheppard Wolf, *Race and Liberty in the New Nation: Emancipation in Virginia from the Revolution to Nat Turner's Rebellion* (Baton Rouge, La., 2006).

15. *Annals of Congress,* 15th Cong., 2nd sess., 1189; 16th Cong., 2nd sess., 1344; "An American," *Richmond Enquirer,* January 13, 18, 1820; Spencer Roane to James Monroe, February 16, 1820, JMP, NYPL.

16. Monroe to George Hay, December 20, 1819, JMC, VHS; "An American," *Richmond Enquirer,* November 23, 30, 1819; January 1, 1820; Spencer Roane to Monroe, February 16, 1820, JMP, NYPL. For diffusion as a means toward gradual abolition, see William W. Freehling, *The Road to Disunion: Secessionists at Bay, 1776–1854* (New York, 1991), and Ford, *"Deliver Us from Evil."* For a more critical analysis of amelioration that focuses on how planters in the broader Americas used amelioration to preserve slavery, see Christa Dierksheide, *Amelioration and Empire: Progress and Slavery in the Americas* (Charlottesville, Va., 2014).

17. Monroe to George Hay, December 27, 1819, James Monroe Collection, James Monroe Museum.

18. Monroe to George Hay, December 20, 1819, JMC, VHS; Monroe to Charles Everett, February 11, 1820, James Monroe Papers in Virginia Repositories.

19. There was no plot to put Clinton or King in the presidency or for disunion. However, Clinton, King, and other northerners argued to their colleagues in private that the North had to act as a party or voting bloc on important issues such as tariffs, internal improvements, and slavery's expansion. King also expressed concerns that the union had been dominated by southern interests since its inception. In short, Federalists and Clintonians sought to exploit the Missouri Crisis for their own political gain, but there was no plot to subvert the union or to make King or Clinton president, even if both would have welcomed election to the presidency. My reading on the situation is that the initial effort to restrict slavery was a genuine move by northern Republicans to halt slavery's expansion forever, something they had attempted to do off and on since April 1818. Federalists—who tended to vote *against* the Tallmadge Amendments when they were first introduced in February 1819—only later sought to exploit the Missouri Crisis to turn what remained of the Federalist Party into a sectional party that could command popular majorities and win elections in the North. The Federalists such as King who sought to exploit genuine northern support for restriction badly overestimated northern Republican willingness to ally with former Federalists on anything other than slavery restrictions. In addition, the Federalists displayed their typical

incompetence at putting together a political coalition behind the scenes, lending an air of implausibility to the Virginians' charge of an eastern plot. By February 1820, King's antics had worn out even reliable, principled restrictionists such as Jonathan Roberts of Pennsylvania, who eventually voted to admit Missouri without restrictions. Too many historians have too uncritically accepted the Virginians' allegations that the Missouri Crisis was at root a political power play by Federalists. While Federalists sought to exploit the crisis for their own gain, northern Republicans primarily sought to bring an end to slavery's expansion in the union. Furthermore, historians have incorrectly alleged that the political ambitions of northern restrictionists somehow sullied the purity of northern efforts to restrict slavery's expansion, as if principle and political advancement were mutually exclusive.

20. Monroe to George Hay, January [?], 1820, JMC, VHS; Monroe to Barbour, February 3, 1820, Barbour Papers, New York Public Library.

21. "Extract of a Letter from a Gentleman in Washington to His friend in Richmond," *Richmond Enquirer*, February 17, 1820. Although we recoil at the idea of disunion and secession in the twenty-first century, nations falling apart was a common occurrence in the Americas from the 1770s through the mid-nineteenth century. The United States nearly fell apart into a series of regional confederacies in the 1780s; in 1815, a group of New Englanders gave serious consideration to creating a separate New England confederacy allied with Great Britain. The states of the former Spanish Empire also faced a continuing series of secession crises. The states of Central America and Texas seceded from Mexico, and through the 1860s, the Yucatan Peninsula frequently rebelled against Mexico as it sought independence from Mexico City. The independent states of South America were also constantly falling apart: Gran Columbia originally included Venezuela, Ecuador, Panama, Colombia, and parts of present-day Peru, Guyana, and Brazil. See Steven Hahn, *A Nation without Borders: The United States and Its World in an Age of Civil Wars, 1830–1910* (New York, 2016). The attachment to the union by Monroe and many of his contemporaries was practical and pragmatic far more than it was sentimental. For contemporary understandings of union, see, for example, Max M. Edling, "Peace Pact and Nation: An International Interpretation of the Constitution of the United States," *Past and Present* 240 (2018): 267–303.

22. "Extract of a Letter from a Gentleman in Washington to His Friend in Richmond," *Richmond Enquirer*, February 17, 1820. Monroe repeated the substance of these arguments in Monroe to Madison, February 19, 1820, James Madison Papers, LOC; Monroe to George Hay, February 10, 1820, Monroe Papers, New York Public Library; Monroe to [Spencer Roane?], February 14, 1820, James Monroe Collection, Pierpont Morgan Library, New York; Monroe to Charles Everett, February 11, 1820, James Monroe Papers in Virginia Repositories; and Monroe to Unknown, February 15, 1820, James Monroe Collection, James Monroe Museum. Senator James Barbour made more or less the same set of arguments in Barbour to Roane, February 13, 1820, Miscellaneous Collection, W. L. Clements Library, University of Michigan, Ann Arbor. On February 13, 1820, Monroe convened a secret meeting with leading southern politicians where they seem to have agreed that they had to accept the 36–30 line as

the least worst alternative. See Hammond, "President, Planter, Politician." Monroe's concerns about the situation turning against Virginia and the South seem to have been provoked by a letter that he received from former Pennsylvania senator Abner Lacock warning that Pennsylvania's congressional delegation was seriously considering joining a separate northeastern confederacy; see LaCock to Monroe, January 30, 1820, James Monroe Papers, LOC.

23. For recent work on challenges to gentry power within Virginia and the union, see William G. Shade, *Democratizing the Old Dominion: Virginia and the Second Party System, 1824–1861* (Charlottesville, Va., 1996); Woody Holton. *Forced Founders: Indians, Debtors, Slaves, and the Making of the American Revolution in Virginia* (Chapel Hill, N.C., 1999); Susan Dunn, *Dominion of Memories: Jefferson, Madison, and the Decline of Virginia* (New York, 2007); Kevin R. C. Gutzman, *Virginia's American Revolution: From Dominion to Republic, 1776–1840* (Lanham, Md., 2007); and Andrew Burstein and Nancy Isenberg, *Madison and Jefferson* (New York, 2010).

24. Spencer Roane to Monroe, February 16, 1820, JMP, NYPL.

25. Francis Walker Gilmer to Peter Minor, August 3, 1820, Correspondence of Francis Walker Gilmer, 1784–1826, Special Collections Department, University of Virginia Library, Charlottesville.

26. Francis Walker Gilmer to Peter Minor, February 22, 1820; March 25, 1821, Correspondence of Francis Walker Gilmer; "To the Editor, Letters from St, Louis," *Richmond Enquirer,* May 21, 1819; George Hay to Monroe, February 17, 1820, James Monroe Papers, LOC. For the decline of the Gilmer family, see Gutzman, *Virginia's American Revolution,* 179–81.

27. Charles Everett to Monroe, February 20, 22, 1820, JMP, NYPL; Charles Tait to Thomas W. Cobb, February 29, 1820, Walker Family Papers, Alabama Department of Archives and History; *Richmond Enquirer,* February 10, 1820.

28. For the gentry's criticism of Monroe and their initial disbelief that he would sign the Compromise into law, see, for example, Burrill Bassett to Monroe, February 7, 1820, James Monroe Collection, James Monroe Museum; "Missouri Resolutions," *Richmond Enquirer,* February 10, 1820; George Hay to Eliza Hay, February 12, 1820, James Monroe Papers, LOC; Thomas M. Bayley to Monroe, February 15, 1820, JMP, NYPL; and John Tyler to Spencer Roane, February 14, 1820, Gilder Lehrman Institute, GLC, 03670, New-York Historical Society.

29. "Extract of a Letter from a Gentleman in Washington to His Friend in Richmond," *Richmond Enquirer,* February 17, 1820; Monroe to Madison, February 19, 1820, James Madison Papers, LOC; Monroe to Charles Everett, February 11, 1820, James Monroe Papers in Virginia Repositories. For Monroe's, Hay's, and Barbour's efforts to convince the gentry that he had to sign the Compromise into law, not to save the union but to save Virginia, see, for example, Philip Barbour to Spencer Roane, February 13, 1820, Miscellaneous Collection, W. L. Clements Library; Hay to Monroe, February 16, 17, 1820, James Monroe Papers, LOC; Monroe to Madison, February 19, 1820, James Madison Papers, LOC; and Roane to Monroe, February 16, 1820, JMP, NYPL. For the *Richmond Enquirer's* grudging acknowledgment of the necessity of signing the

Compromise into law, see "Missouri Question—Compromise, &c.," *Richmond Enquirer,* February 17, 1820. For Madison's acceptance of signing the Compromise, see Madison to Monroe, February 23, 1820, James Madison Papers, LOC.

30. Annette Gordon-Reed, "Thomas Jefferson and St. George Tucker: The Making of Revolutionary Slaveholders," in *Jefferson, Lincoln, and Wilson: The American Dilemma of Race and Democracy,* ed. John Milton Cooper Jr. and Thomas J. Knock (Charlottesville, Va., 2010), 15–33, 16 (quotation).

9   Antiquarian America

Isaiah Thomas and the New Nation's Future

PETER S. ONUF

On July 14, 1776, Isaiah Thomas, printer and editor of the *Massachusetts Spy*, read the Declaration of Independence aloud to an excited crowd of patriots in his new hometown of Worcester. This was the first reading of the Declaration in the new commonwealth of Massachusetts, where the Revolution began nearly fifteen months earlier in violent confrontations between the townsmen of Lexington and Concord and King George's troops. Thomas had been a key operative in the Sons of Liberty in Boston before the British occupation of the Massachusetts capital forced him to flee inland with his press in January 1776.[1] It was only fitting that the young printer, now twenty-seven years old, should give voice to a document drafted by the Second Continental Congress in Philadelphia in the name of the American people. The medium was the message: Worcester patriots and their counterparts in communities across the continent were galvanized by their own bold words, coming back to them in the Declaration's eloquent cadences. What they heard was familiar or "self-evident," not new or revolutionary. But the way Thomas's auditors heard themselves, the chorus of voices channeled through print and spoken by the printer, changed everything in their small world. The people of Worcester declared themselves to be Americans, a new people now seeking recognition from the "powers of the earth."[2]

Isaiah Thomas was the right man at the right time and place, the modest mouthpiece for many voices, including his own. The same could be said for the famous Virginia patriot Thomas Jefferson, whose authorship of the Declaration was not widely known until the party battles of 1790s, when many "Americans" questioned whether they did in fact (or feeling) constitute a single people—and Jefferson and his Republican followers suspected that

Anglophile High Federalists in New England were plotting a counterrevolutionary return to British rule.[3] The "self-effacing" Jefferson did not claim "originality of principle or sentiment" in drafting the Declaration. "There was but one opinion on this side of the water," he famously wrote Henry Lee in 1825, a little more than a year before he died: "All Americans thought alike on these subjects" *before* Congress issued the document. The goal was "to place before mankind the common sense of the subject," he concluded, with a nod to Thomas Paine's sensationally popular pamphlet of January 1776.[4]

Strictly speaking, of course, Congress was the Declaration's author. Congressmen collectively edited and authorized publication of the draftsman's original text. Although these changes were distressing to Jefferson, he was philosophically committed to denying authorship.[5] Monarchs issued commands from on high, speaking with their own original authority; republican leaders were public servants, speaking for—and with the authority of—the people. Thomas Jefferson and Isaiah Thomas were both actors in an ensemble production. As they declared independence, they recognized their dependence on each other.

Jefferson's modesty may now be hard to credit. Intensely self-conscious of his role in the revolutionary drama, Jefferson's entire career pivoted on the nation-making moment he scripted for his countrymen. Yet the Virginian understood not only that the nation, or what was already being called "public opinion," made the moment possible, but that printers and print technology enabled the extraordinarily rapid circulation of the text.[6] If we customarily exalt the founders as apostles of the Enlightenment, Jefferson and his enlightened colleagues celebrated the "useful knowledge" and ingenious inventions of artisans, manufacturers, and "scientists." Isaiah Thomas basked in the refracted celebrity of Benjamin Franklin, the great printer-patriot. Print constituted the critical link between patriot elites and a mobilized people, making citizens equal in the imagined community of the virtual republic. Yet print texts were "real," material products of printers' presses, impressions on paper that left their imprint on the minds of readers. And the Enlightenment cult of the artisan effected a leveling-up of printers and other skilled workers to a dynamic, mediating—rather than merely "middling"—status in revolutionary American society equivalent and complementary to the role assumed by the people's representatives in their new governments.

Jefferson thought that Philadelphian David Rittenhouse, the mechanical genius who fabricated an orrery (or model of the solar system), should not waste his God-given talents on public service. "No body can conceive that nature ever intended to throw away a Newton upon the occupations of a crown," Jefferson told his friend in 1778. "There is an order of geniusses above" the "obligation" that every other good citizen owed his country. He also would have exempted Franklin, another benefactor of the people. Of course, Rittenhouse and Franklin both dedicated their lives to the common cause.[7] The foundational principle of citizen equality was no mere abstraction. It led would-be aristocrats of Jefferson's class to descend from their high horses and open their eyes to the contributions skilled artisans, farmers (the "chosen people of God"), and other productive workers made to promote the public good; it inspired ordinary folk to rise up, both to overthrow Britain's despotic rule and to improve themselves in a new world of limitless opportunity.[8] Here was the common ground where the two patriots, Thomas Jefferson of Virginia, a skilled worker in words, and printer-publisher Isaiah Thomas of Massachusetts, could meet. The moment in July 1776 when they embraced a new American identity shaped the subsequent course of their lives.

The genteel Jefferson became the great democratic foe of old regime aristocracy and its American avatars, while the upwardly mobile Thomas "elevated himself from a humble station in life to a sphere of extensive usefulness."[9] After amassing a fortune as a publisher and bookseller, he founded the American Antiquarian Society (AAS) in 1812, connecting him with learned and accomplished men across the expanding union—including Jefferson.[10] Jefferson never ceased to be a gentleman, and it is doubtful Thomas ever persuaded anyone capable of judging such things that he really was one. But both men were committed to the democratic revolution they helped initiate. As party leader and president, Jefferson sought to keep the "Spirit of 1776" alive in a vigilant and engaged citizenry; as an antiquarian, Thomas sought to collect and preserve the evidence of what the American people had achieved in their Revolution so that successive generations could chart their way forward. As they looked anxiously to the future, both men sought to guarantee that Americans would remember they were the makers of their own history.

This essay focuses on Isaiah Thomas's distinctive conception of American antiquarianism. In retrospect, "antiquarian" appears to be a curious, somewhat antiquated cognate for "historical." Thomas and his coadjutors chose the term for what they saw as compelling reasons, however, emphasizing their commitment to the most precise and exacting standards in their ambitious national project of collecting everything that was relevant—and everything *was* relevant—to reconstructing and illuminating the American people's unfolding history. In his declining years and after his death, New Englanders focused more narrowly on the texts and relics of their own past, and Thomas's antiquarianism was drained of its progressive, expansive, and democratic connotations. What had made his antiquarianism distinctive was absorbed into historical study or found a new home in the archaeology of "ancient America." But his vast and seemingly indiscriminate collection of printed materials, manuscripts, and material objects (or "curiosities") survived and expanded, keeping alive a sometimes flickering memory of what Thomas wanted us to remember.

Antiquarianism was a well-established field of study in early modern Europe. Antiquaries constituted a cosmopolitan community of the leisured and learned, lay and clerical, devoted to the systematic collection of artifacts and texts that would enable them to reconstruct and revive the classical civilizations of Greece and Rome. By the late seventeenth and eighteenth centuries, national societies began to focus on local antiquities as well, connecting the ancient world to successor regimes on the Roman imperial periphery, thus laying the deep foundations of new national histories.

The invention of printing loomed large as antiquaries contemplated the emergence of their own contemporary worlds and harvested antiquities closer to home. Scholars rigorously analyzed early print sources, devoting as much critical attention to their provenance as their content.[11] The scientific study of typography created opportunities for gifted practitioners to contribute highly specialized knowledge of craft traditions to the antiquarian enterprise. A few printers thus found their way into the aristocratic purlieus of the English Antiquarian Society.[12] Before the founding of Thomas's American Antiquarian Society, Americans with an aristocratic passion for antiquities apparently had nothing to collect and no society to join. Nostalgic, postprovincial creoles could only look "homeward," to the "Old World," for a meaningful past, tracing their genealogies to the places their ancestors had left behind. Yet if, as Benedict Anderson suggests, displaced creole elites took the lead in rejecting metropolitan "tyranny" and imagining new national identities, they also would be eager producers and consumers of new narratives and modes of historical understanding.[13]

This was the opening that the Son of Liberty and cultural national-ist Isaiah Thomas seized. Fashioning himself as a new kind of antiquary, he invited fellow patriots to enlist in his society and embrace their new identity, individually and collectively. In America, printers would not merely be useful adjuncts to the learned, classically educated gentlemen who domi-nated European antiquarian societies. They would take the lead, making the history of their craft central to the antiquarian enterprise. Thomas's anti-quarians would reconstruct their country's history in new ways, appropriate to its unprecedented circumstances. Beginning with the history of print in America, they would focus on home ground, investigating both the im-print of European settlement and the still legible traces of the lost civiliza-tions of their "ancient" indigenous predecessors. The American Revolution marked the culmination of an enlightened age, when a self-declared people rejected the traditional assumption that they were defined by their status as subjects of rule, proclaiming instead their fealty to the self-evident ideas of Jefferson's Declaration. Printers like Isaiah Thomas were possessors and pur-veyors of "useful knowledge" about the ways knowledge was produced and reproduced. Benjamin Franklin called Thomas the "American Baskerville," identifying his younger colleague with the great English typographer John Baskerville of Birmingham.[14] Thomas's mastery of his craft and its history gave him a uniquely illuminating perspective on how these nation-making ideas were translated into action and how British subjects became Ameri-can citizens.

Contemporary historians endorse Thomas's claims for the importance of printers in the "print public sphere" for the American Revolution, though the ideological interpretation—and the position of elite (that is, privileged) thinkers and writers—still holds sway a half-century after its paradigmatic formulation.[15] Jefferson is idolized; Thomas is barely remembered. The En-lightenment cult of the mechanic proved evanescent and the figure of the artisan-antiquarian anomalous. Franklin and Thomas proudly identified themselves as printers, but both left the business behind as they embarked on public careers. Likewise, the printing business itself changed in funda-mental ways, as the traditional organization of labor in the print shop gave way to an increasingly elaborate division and degradation of labor. Ambi-tious young men of humble origins were inspired by Benjamin Franklin, an enduring cultural hero, but they could not follow in his footsteps. It is no accident that Jürgen Habermas defined his "public sphere" as "bourgeois," for that is precisely what master printers became, with newspaper editor, publisher, and bookseller Isaiah Thomas providing a conspicuous case in point.[16] The artisan receded from the forefront of the national imaginary, and notwithstanding Thomas's heroic efforts and enormous expenditure, the antiquary never figured in a prominent way. Scurrilous newspaper editors who fomented—and benefited from—partisan political polarization were wayward, unworthy successors to courageous printer-patriots of revolutionary times; antiquaries could not escape their transatlantic caricature.

Shortly after Thomas founded his new society in 1812, Sir Walter Scott offered readers a memorable portrait of *The Antiquary*.[17] Jonathan Oldbuck, the titular character (though not the hero) of Scott's popular novel, is a classic British (in this case Scottish) eccentric, obsessed with useless knowledge about worthless old things and given to groundless speculations: he is the living, laughable embodiment of the old regime. The portrait is hardly accurate, but it does evoke the enduring connections between family genealogy and local history that characterized British antiquarianism. Thomas was not immune to the social appeal of European learned societies, and the proliferation of their American counterparts played a key role in fostering and fulfilling elite aspirations for ambitious, self-made men. But Thomas was no Oldbuck, nor was he a would-be great man in the mold of town founder William Cooper.[18] Thomas did not harbor any nostalgia for the provincial old regime, identifying instead with the printer-patriots who played such a crucial role in its destruction and now lay a claim to a place in the new national pantheon through the practice of antiquarianism.

Thomas could think of himself as an antiquary because his mastery of his craft and its history would have justified his pretensions in the Old World, despite his humble origins. In any case, there was no established class of antiquaries in America to question his credentials. But Thomas could not pretend to be a historian. The break with Britain inspired a cohort of learned gentlemen—men of letters, *not* of print—to assume the role of "historian" in order to chronicle the heroic achievements of the revolutionary generation.[19] Surveying the grand sweep of history with philosophic condescension, they identified the Revolution with the "westward course of empire" and traced the progress of civilization through successive stages.[20] Thomas saw things differently. The printer-antiquarian was less concerned with conjectures about the origins and development of human society across the millennia than with the mechanisms that spurred mass mobilization at a particular moment in far-flung places across the continent. Philosophers and theologians might dwell on the logic of history or the benign dispensations of Providence, but the ideas that immediately mattered were already "self-evident" to the ordinary, "common" people who made the American Revolution.

The apparently conflicting perspectives and methodologies of the historian and the antiquarian proved complementary in the era of revolutionary regime change and nation-making. Thomas Jefferson's conception of history, derived from the provincial lawyer-statesman's civic humanism and his immersion in the moral philosophy of the Scottish Enlightenment, made him receptive to the appeal of Isaiah Thomas's American antiquarianism.[21] Antiquaries cultivated the kind of local knowledge in particular places that was conspicuously lacking in newly settled, highly mobile settler societies—and that inspired lonely, learned men like Jefferson to seek membership in the transatlantic "republic of letters." But Jefferson was also a provincial patriot who displayed characteristically antiquarian impulses as he systematically collected books, manuscripts, curiosities, and data about the peoples, climate, and natural resources of his new world and offered the fruits of his scholarly labors to the cognoscenti of the enlightened world in his *Notes on the State of Virginia*. Yet if Jefferson knew Virginia, he knew very little about the *American* "people" that he and his congressional colleagues "invented" or "imagined" into existence at Philadelphia in 1776. This was the practical business of popular political mobilization, of persuading real people to commit themselves to the common cause and then sustaining those commitments.

The useful knowledge of printer-patriots was critical to the democratic project, as they translated philosophical principles into the people's commonsense vernacular and grounded them in lived experience. As an antiquarian, Thomas sought to collect and preserve the evidence of these nation-making transactions. His antiquarianism can be seen in the broader context of western nation-making, as aristocratic antiquaries elsewhere formed societies to recover and celebrate neglected folk histories.[22] Yet Thomas's idiosyncratic antiquarian project was the only one that was *not* patronized and populated by an aristocratic elite. In memorializing and sustaining the process of popular political mobilization in which he had played such a conspicuous role, the successful man of business made a bid for a more exalted social status and an enduring place in the nation's memory. But his antiquarianism was distinctively democratic, irresistibly drawing him back to his humble origins. He and his fellow antiquaries would enable Americans to know and tell their own history, so recognizing themselves as a people who had claimed—and would continue to claim—the fundamental human right to determine their own destiny.

Isaiah Thomas established his credentials as an antiquary with the publication of his masterpiece, *The History of Printing in America,* in 1810.[23] An encyclopedic study of printers and the production of printed material in North and South America from first settlement until the Declaration of Independence, Thomas's two-volume work anticipated the ambitious scope and exalted purposes of the society he founded two years later. In the *History,* Thomas described his own early career in the third person, emphasizing his humble origins and establishing his identity as a proud member of the craft community.[24] New England printers figured disproportionately in his group portrait, and later correspondents offered corrections and additions about the craft in more distant locations.[25] But Thomas was at pains to offer balanced and complete accounts of all the printers he could identify anywhere, whatever their political inclinations and wherever their subsequent careers took them. The community of printers transcended its individual members. Printers were bound to each other both by a traditional sense of guild solidarity and by their consciousness of the press's power in an enlightened age.

By ending his story in 1776, Thomas underscored the central importance of printers and print in the progress of Western civilization and the coming of the American Revolution. Yet the *History* was also an exercise in nostalgia, an antiquarian effort to capture a fast-receding moment before the evidence for a proper history disappeared. How could the printers' story be told as the floodtide of evanescent and ephemeral print material that transformed the revolutionary landscape—handbills, newspapers, and pamphlets—receded from view? Collection and preservation of this precious legacy were urgent, patriotic imperatives. As an editor, publisher, and bookseller, Thomas developed an extensive network of correspondents and collected a vast inventory of printed material through purchase and exchange. His overstocked warehouses and bulging personal library enabled him to write his *History* and subsequently constituted the core of the Antiquarian Society's collection. As he anticipated the ultimate liquidation of his library in the series of wills he drafted from 1792 (on the eve of his forty-third birthday) up to his death in 1831, he also hoped to promote library-building and the antiquarian impulse by donating books to worthy institutions and individuals.[26]

Thomas's compulsive collecting defied the market calculations that animated his business career. For the antiquarian patriot, the materials he sought to preserve were priceless, and he correctly anticipated their extraordinary value for future generations. It was our duty, Thomas told his fellow antiquaries, "to bestow on posterity that, which they cannot give to us, but which they may enlarge and improve, and transmit to those, who shall succeed them." He conceived of this intergenerational transaction as something like "paying a debt we owe to our forefathers," or in more personal terms, what the elderly Thomas owed to his younger self.[27] The paradoxical problem was that there was no present-day market for relics of the recent past that in the future would be cherished as "antiquities." For the time being, much of what Thomas collected was worthless.[28] But his band of antiquarian patriots would preserve his and their collections until the time when future generations recognized their value. Their nostalgic laments were a prayer for future remembrance. "Generation has followed generation, and scarce any efforts have been made to rescue from oblivion the comparatively recent antiquities of America," antiquary Isaac Goodwin told the society in 1820: "The memorials of our fathers, the origin of our institutions, are scarcely remembered."[29]

In *The History of Printing*, Thomas struck the modest, self-effacing pose that he would assume as the founder of the AAS. He claimed he undertook this ambitious project at the behest "of some of my friends." Thomas and fellow patriots had long hoped "that some person distinguished for literature" would render "this service to the republic of letters." No classically educated man of letters rose to the occasion. As a master printer, however, Thomas claimed "a knowledge of many interesting facts" unknown to those not initiated into the mysteries of the craft.[30] With an antiquary's expertise, he could provide solid evidence for the philosophical historian's hypotheses. In the spirit of the collaboration he sought to promote in the AAS, he called on the eminently learned Princeton professor Reverend Samuel Miller to frame the history Thomas proceeded to reconstruct in such authoritative detail over the course of his two volumes. In long excerpts from Miller's *Brief Retrospect of the Eighteenth Century*, Thomas disappeared from his own preface, allowing his distinguished interlocutor—and future AAS member—to argue eloquently for the preeminent power of the press in the revolutionary transformation of the modern world.[31] The truth of such claims was self-evident to the master printer. But Miller helped Thomas build a bridge between antiquarian workers in the field of facts and learned men who constructed grand narratives.

Printing made the world smaller. "The art of printing has multiplied records beyond former example," Miller told Thomas's readers, and "increased intercourse between distant countries."[32] At the same time, the flow of information transformed social and political relations. At first newspapers served as "as a medium of communication *to* the public," making the will of the sovereign known to his subjects. But public prints progressively assumed a much "more extensive . . . office." Even as they amplified and diffused the sovereign's voice, newspapers became "the vehicles of discussion," enabling the voices of the people to be heard. Situated at the nexus of the Crown's authority and public opinion, printers became editorial interlocutors, representing one to the other. Long before any overt challenge to the legitimacy of royal rule in the American provinces occurred, the circulation of information began to subvert the hierarchical assumptions of the imperial old regime. When the press became "free," Miller wrote, "the principles of government, the interests of nations, the spirit and tendency of public measures, and the public and private characters of individuals are all arraigned, tried, and decided" in what contemporaries were beginning to call the "court" of public opinion.[33] The effect was to put rulers and ruled on the same level. But the causes of this great transformation defied easy explanation. As they became aware of its extraordinary power, what exactly did contemporaries mean by the "press"?

Samuel Miller's answer in his *Brief Retrospect* was the one favored by learned scholars then and now, the Enlightenment—that epochal demystification of the old regime by a forward-looking, enlightened elite. His discussion of "political journals" was only one chapter—and the only one in which ordinary "people" figured in a significant way—in an encyclopedic (and hardly brief, three-volume) account of how the cognoscenti unlocked nature's secrets, revived classical learning, communicated with each, and organized in learned societies. The progress of print technology was presented, in passing, as an irresistible (and still somewhat mysterious) force. Newspapers, Miller concluded, "have become immense moral and political engines" of incalculable power.[34] Thomas's fact-filled volumes humanized Miller's abstraction, populating the press with printers and emphasizing the "useful knowledge" that propelled technical innovation. Miller's prefatory paean to the Enlightenment served as a grace note to Thomas's exposition, offering a measure of the printers' collective achievement.

European antiquaries devoted great effort to investigating the early history of print in a spirited, ongoing debate about which country could claim credit for its invention. Obsessed with the rare and valuable books, or incunabula, of the fifteenth century, they neglected more recent developments in the trade. In America, Isaac Goodwin observed in an address to the AAS after Thomas's death, "the press had been performing wonders which almost staggered credulity" and "might well have [been] attributed to magic."[35] Thomas and his fellow antiquaries took their bearings from their own country's recent and ongoing history. Their Old World counterparts might have little interest in American history, but antiquarian methods could be applied in the New World to remarkable effect. "The early part of the history of the United States, is not, like that of most other nations," Thomas noted, "blended with fable." The course of American history could "be traced with the clearness and certainty of authentic history." Here was the genius of Thomas's antiquarianism: its practitioners would not lose themselves in a vain search for origins but would instead track the people's progress to their Revolution—and beyond. Colonists "made records of events as they passed, and they, from the first, adopted effectual methods to transmit the knowledge of them to their posterity."[36] Americans did not need Miller's Enlightenment to find their way back through their history and on into the future. To the contrary, the "authentic history" of the American people would light the way forward for peoples everywhere.

Thomas's *History* exemplified the antiquarian enterprise, showing how his own community of master-craftsmen mobilized Americans in their fight for their independence. "We are able to convey to posterity, a correct account of the manner in which we have grown up to be an independent people," Thomas wrote, "and can delineate the progress of the useful and polite arts among us, with a degree of certainty which cannot be attained by the nations of the old world."[37] Yet the American story could only be properly told if antiquaries mobilized to collect, compare, and analyze the abundant evidence that lay so close at hand—or underfoot; even the printed materials that flowed from patriot presses might prove ephemeral. Classical learning was not a requirement, and could be a liability, for the American antiquary. As Thomas's career indicated, what was most needed was the determination to collect, preserve, and accurately record everything relevant to the lived experience of prior generations. But understanding the past on its own terms was not an end in itself, as the desiccated image of the antiquary suggested it was in Europe. The antiquary was a genuine flesh-and-blood patriot, dedicated to keeping the past alive for future generations.

In the typographical imagination, Benjamin Franklin assumed an exalted role in communicating the nation-making message. "Whatever he printed, he impressed on his own mind," printer John Russell told Isaiah Thomas and other members of the Faustus Society when they convened in Boston in 1808. "When a book came from his press, FRANKLIN was as well taught as his author." Printing and reading made an almost physical impression that spread through the people with the circulation of texts. Russell proceeded to laud Thomas, "the next in rank" to Franklin, "and who, we are happy to observe, yet lives to advance still further the interests of our profession, and the improvement of science."[38] But Thomas did not set himself above his brethren. The future antiquarian understood that ordinary printers gave the "mighty machine" of the press its dynamic, living force. He memorialized his fellow printers in his *History of Printing in America,* honoring each with a biography. In 1812, two years later, he invited fellow patriots in Worcester and across the continent to think of themselves as antiquarians as they joined him in keeping the memories of all previous generations of Americans alive.

Thomas's *History of Printing in America* was the product of prodigious antiquarian research. His collection of printers' biographies depended on the typographical expertise he brought to bear on his extraordinary collection of printed materials from their presses and his own. There was no other collection like it, and if Thomas had not been a collector, those materials would have been "scattered" to the wind.[39] Collecting worked a sort of magic, making the ephemeral permanent, preserving the past for the future. The printer's acute awareness of how easily the things he produced could be consumed and discarded made their preservation urgently imperative. It was the paradox of the publishing business: in theory, the multiplication of texts should have eliminated the "danger of the total loss of any work," but experience taught Thomas "that of thousands of editions of printed books, not a copy of them is now to be found; and if, of others, there may remain here and there a copy among rubbish, they are of no use, for no one knows where to search for them."⁴⁰ The unsold books in his warehouses testified mutely to their worthlessness: no longer worth buying, they were not worth keeping.

The AAS was founded at a moment of existential peril for the fragile federal union as it embarked on a second war for national independence against the mother country in 1812. Libraries of historical societies and other cultural institutions in Boston and other seaport cities were particularly vulnerable to the depredations of British invaders, with the threat of fire looming largest for Thomas. Worcester's isolated, "inland situation" promised to preserve the society's collections from "the ravages of an enemy" as well as "the ravages of time," but the more insidious threat was the forgetfulness of the American people. At some time in the future, Thomas feared, "a decline may be the state of our country."⁴¹ Increasingly virulent partisan divisions in New England, culminating in the Hartford Convention in late 1814, suggested that the crisis of the union might come sooner than later.

The antiquarian paradox in America was that the accelerating pace of expansion and development threatened "all things," including the ongoing flood of printed material, with obsolescence and destruction. "In a course of years," things that were now worthless would be rare and valuable, or "antique." The extraordinary idea that "modern productions" should be collected because of their *future* status as antiquities would have baffled Old World antiquarians. But it underscored the central importance of historical memory in a modern republic, and the material evidence that sustained it. "The ingratitude of republicks is proverbial," Isaac Goodwin lectured his fellow antiquaries in 1820, and no other people "more justly merit this reproach than Americans." Imagining themselves a "new" people, Americans were constantly on the move, forgetting where they came from: "The virtues of the primitive founders of our republick, the projectors of our most valued institutions are forgotten, and their names are seldom mentioned."⁴² Heedless of the past, they would be unable to see their way forward; casualties of their own wastefulness, they would consign themselves to "oblivion."⁴³ Virtue itself would soon become the sort of curiosity aristocratic antiquaries in the Old World kept in their private cabinets.

Republics, the French philosopher Montesquieu taught, depended on the virtue of self-governing citizens prepared to sacrifice everything for their countrymen.⁴⁴ Citizens must recognize each other as fellow citizens. They were, as Jefferson put it in the Declaration, "created equal." This acknowledgment of common origins—from the creator and through the successive generations who cultivated the common country—was the foundation, or grounding, of patriotic attachments in "nature's nation." But Americans did not *know* they were Americans until they opened their eyes, recognized themselves in each other, and proclaimed the "self-evident" ideas that justified their bid for independence. Patriotism was predicated on the enlightenment that enabled Americans to overcome the isolation, alienation, and mistrust fostered by the vast distances separating them—and the despotic rule of a distant metropolis. Far from being the tribal reflex of a mindless mob, or what Samuel Johnson in 1775 famously called the "last refuge" of the opportunistic "scoundrel," patriotism for American revolutionaries constituted the epochal triumph of enlightened reason over blind prejudice.[45]

Citizenship in America was a state of mind and feeling. It became manifest in the mass mobilization of the latent potential—the ambitions and aspirations—of ordinary folk like the young printer Isaiah Thomas. There was nothing miraculous or providential about this awakening. Thomas knew that vigilant, engaged, and virtuous citizens could not be taken for granted. Of course, a chorus of moral philosophers agreed, the potential—those self-evident ideas—had always been there. But, as Thomas and Miller emphasized, they had lain dormant until activated by printer-patriots during the imperial crisis. The printer and the man of letters understood that there was no such thing as an "American mind" that the introduction of new, universal, abstract ideas suddenly, radically transformed. To the contrary, printers changed their world by flooding it with print, creating a dynamic new print environment—or "sphere"—that made it possible for a diverse, far-flung population of Anglo-American creole provincials to shed the demeaning descriptors and see themselves simply as Americans, capable of thinking and acting as a single people.

What print had done could be undone by its evanescence, degradation, and disappearance. Post-revolutionary Americans, in their "national vanity," were all too prone to take themselves—and their patriotism—for granted, imagining (if they bothered thinking at all) that they would rise up to save the republic if it should ever again face an existential crisis. This complacency was predicated on a naive conception of self-sovereignty and self-sufficiency, a libertarian origins myth that vies with founder-worship for primacy in the American national imaginary. Thomas and his fellow antiquaries prized liberty and they did not hesitate to acknowledge the achievements of both "primitive" and latter-day "founders." But they condemned both the "individual vanity" and false patriotism of the isolated lover of liberty who failed to acknowledge his obligations to his fellow citizens and the servility of would-be subjects who worshiped at the altar of great men, past and present.[46]

What was vitally important for antiquarian patriots was to sustain a vital sense of attachment among Americans across the great spaces of the continent and through time, across generations. This is what future antiquary Thomas Jefferson had in mind when he proclaimed that every generation was like an "independant nation" with respect to both predecessors and successors. Republics were unlike monarchies, where past generations exercised a tyrannical sway over those who followed: intergenerational relations—like international relations among republics—were peaceful and reciprocally beneficial. Grateful to those who came before, the living generation would internalize its obligation of "usufruct" or stewardship for its successors.[47] It was incumbent on the living to preserve and not waste the people's estate. Republican gratitude reflected awareness of these debts and obligations. To know themselves as a people, Americans had to locate themselves in the succession of generations.

An enlightened people needed the kind of evidence that antiquaries were best equipped to collect and preserve. Americans needed to know their own "authentic history" and so avoid the seductive allure of the flattering, fabulous, mythic narratives that had propped up despotic regimes throughout mankind's history.[48] Forgetfulness was the enemy, and preservation of a great, comprehensive collection of print sources and artifacts would keep the memory of prior generations alive. Patriotic antiquaries modeled the citizen engagement that alone could preserve the republic. Antiquarian scholarship dispelled mysteries, collapsing the gulf between generations and thus enabling the present generation to keep faith with those who came before. "It is the truth we seek," Unitarian minister and book collector William Bentley wrote, and "the truth, wherever we dig, we would find." The antiquary "can sit down" with our ancestors, embracing their humanity, "tho' at first they may seem to speak a strange language." He saw "the Patriarch in his grey hairs, & in the charms of his countenance, whether he be found in the habiliments of antient or modern times," writing his history and so connecting the generations "with the simplicity of a child."[49] It was precisely because antiquaries recognized that their ancestors were in some sense foreigners, speaking a "strange language," that they could serve as intergenerational interlocutors.

The virtue that sustained republics was manifest in the citizen's willingness to sacrifice himself for his country. Republican self-sacrifice presupposed powerful attachments with fellow citizens, within and across generations. In stark contrast, Montesquieu taught, monarchical regimes governed by force and fear, isolating subjects from each other and preempting attachments that threatened their rule.[50] Defenders of "legitimate" authority thus fostered ignorance and impotence, teaching servile subjects that their godlike rule was traceable to a hallowed past, time out of mind. But a free press taught Americans to think for themselves and so "to discriminate between liberty and licentiousness," Thomas wrote in his *History of Printing:* "This freedom of the press was the first, and one of the greatest agents in producing our national independence."[51] The circulation of information dispelled darkness, enabling enlightened citizens to see beyond themselves and look to a future of their own making. They would see through the mystifications that buttressed royal authority, including the so-called histories written by fawning courtiers. As revolutionaries mobilized in defense of their liberties, scales fell from their eyes. Republican iconoclasts obliterated the symbols of monarchical rule in the built environment as well as in the texts that proclaimed their independence. In doing so, however, Americans did not repudiate their history. They instead cleared the way for a deeper, more inclusive, and enlightened historical self-understanding that royal rule had suppressed and obscured.

The paradoxical genius of American antiquarianism was to conceive of succeeding generations in a way that simultaneously distinguished and conflated past, present, and future. The collections Thomas and his coadjutors assembled in Worcester constituted the site of this cross-temporal nexus. "Our library and Museum will continually increase," Thomas told his friend Bentley, "for every benevolent Antiquarian will reflect that with this National Institution he may most safely deposit for the benefit of present and future generations, the treasure he has collected."[52] The subjects of a monarch, like slaves of a master, lived in an eternal present: nothing ever changed, and there was nothing to learn from, or leave to, history. But republican citizens were acutely aware of the need to keep the memory of the fathers alive, lest they betray the promises they had made to posterity.

Self-conscious founder-fathers might envision a linear progress across generations that would exempt the new United States from the cycle of decline and fall that explained the inevitable decline and fall of classical republics. But the lessons of ancient history, powerfully reinforced by the intimate experience of the life cycle, could not be easily repressed. It was imperative therefore that citizens of every succeeding generation recognize their responsibility to keep the past alive, conscious that it could only live *within* them. The "sacred fire of liberty" was not a public spectacle but rather a state of mind, or "spirit," that animated each citizen.[53] Citizens could exult in their collective power, agreeing with Jefferson that their new republic had "the strongest government on earth," because it was grounded in their consent.[54] Yet this civic subjectivity constituted a daunting, anxiety-inducing psychological burden: patriotic Americans asked much more of themselves—and, perhaps more importantly, of each other—than King George III had ever demanded. The constantly changing past *should* always be present in the minds of republican citizens. "The state of society, which we behold," Reverend William Jenks reminded the AAS at the first anniversary of its founding, "has resulted from the accumulated labours of many generations." Acknowledging those labors meant assuming a responsibility to the future. "The man who thinks little of his ancestors, will be careless of his posterity."[55]

A free press enabled enterprising Americans to share innovations and discoveries with one another and so spur the progress of enlightenment. For Thomas, technological development was the necessary concomitant of man's natural sociability: a "natural disposition to invent" and then to "reveal the products of his ingenuity" was "implanted" in man by an "allwise Creator." Inventions only became meaningful, or "useful," in a social context, where they contributed to people's happiness and well-being. Inventive man followed the lead of the "allwise Creator" in desiring "to communicate his discoveries to his contemporaries and to posterity." This sociable imperative was mirrored in the "insatiable curiosity" of grateful beneficiaries who sought "to become acquainted with the origin and history of every discovery made by his fellow men."[56] An enlightened citizenry thus would look backward as well as forward, for pathways of progress ran *through* the past *toward* a better future. To "collect and preserve," as antiquarians enjoined, was to honor and perpetuate the divinely implanted impulse to create and communicate. Despotic regimes suppressed curiosity and cultivated ignorance, proclaiming their own exclusive access to the mind of an inscrutable god; republicans preached the transparency that enabled enlightened citizens to act collectively on behalf of their common humanity. In the "book of nature," God's intelligent design was legible to all who would open their eyes.[57]

Patriotism and piety were inextricably linked in the antiquarian ethos. A large percentage of Thomas's recruits were ministers of the gospel, men of letters who also preached the Word—and who saw no contradiction between reason and revelation.[58] Their faith was catholic and inclusive, not national or sectarian. For New England preachers, this meant eschewing—or at least muting—the typological tendency to equate America with Israel and thus assert their region's primacy in the unfolding national narrative.[59] Americans were not a "chosen people," arbitrarily immunized against the misfortunes of all others. They were "exceptional" only to the extent—and as long as—they were conscious of their role in shaping their own ongoing history.

The antiquarian appeal to a "remote and distant posterity" was a kind of prayer that future generations would sustain the historical consciousness of an enlightened age and cherish the memory of those who labored to preserve the legacy of the past.[60] In William Jenks's exalted language, the "Antiquary" returned from "excursions" into the past "laden with invaluable spoils of time to swell the treasures of science and art."[61] "It is a labour of great interest to the present age," Worcester lawyer Samuel Burnside confidently asserted, "but will be more so to posterity."[62] It was an article of faith for antiquarians that grateful future generations would recognize the incalculable "benefits" they received from the society's collections, "more and more accumulating in the progression of the ages."[63] If they failed to do so, the republic itself would be doomed to fail, for the vital connections between and across generations could not then be sustained.

Antiquarians could not know that their prayers would be answered. The "great interest" Burnside discerned in 1817 was belied by the apparent worthlessness of much of what antiquarian collectors saved from oblivion. Too often, William Bentley complained, "Antiquaries have been judged as our Ancestors have been. They have been denied to be gold, because they have been coined" in a strange currency, "and because they have not the same inscriptions as current money."[64] Few of their countrymen shared the antiquarians' interest in "remote and distant" times, past or future. Some suspected the motives of elite neighbors who affirmed their high status by joining learned societies; most were simply indifferent, particularly in frontier regions where Indian antiquities were most abundant and most at risk.[65] But popular indifference was precisely what made collecting and preserving antiquities so imperative for Thomas and his associates. American antiquarians collected with a patriotic purpose, offering the people a portrait of themselves, their ancestors, and their "ancient" predecessors that would make them conscious of the history they were making.

The American antiquarian bore only the faintest resemblance to his classically learned European namesake. Every enlightened citizen was a prospective donor to the AAS's collections. "It is an association founded in individual patriotism, and fostered by national supplies of generosity," Isaac Goodwin proclaimed when the first Antiquarian Hall was completed in 1820. The movement was from "individual" to "national," from Thomas's original inspiration to a rapidly expanding membership and reciprocal flow of antiquities from the far corners of the union to the society's new building in Worcester. Just as the circulation of printed materials united the rebellious colonies in 1776, the ongoing process of collecting and preserving "every thing American, every thing illustrative of the ancient history of this continent" would sustain the patriotic spirit and so "redeem our country from any further imputation of ungrateful neglect."[66]

Thomas's small band of antiquaries fashioned themselves as a patriotic vanguard, taking the lead in a continent-wide mobilization to counter powerful centrifugal tendencies that threatened to tear the country apart. To do so, they had to purge antiquarianism of its Old World associations. Given the stereotypical image of the antiquary, some prospective members doubted their qualifications; others cited the paucity of antiquities, as they were conventionally defined, in their neighborhoods. The famously irascible John Randolph of Roanoke struck both notes when he accepted an offer of membership: he felt it "incumbent" on him to let the AAS know that "I possess not one qualification, which I have been led to annex to the character of an antiquary," and that he resided "in a country utterly destitute on any object of antiquarian research."[67] Many prospective members asked for clarification of the society's objects, which Thomas and his colleagues provided in occasional publications during the early years. The recruitment of Jefferson and other prominent figures was reassuring: their acceptance letters—unlike Randolph's—enthusiastically endorsed the AAS's patriotic agenda.[68]

Thomas did not see membership as merely honorific. The success of the antiquarian enterprise depended on the active engagement of patriotic

Americans. Well-situated members campaigned to persuade state legislatures to deposit official documents in the society library; editors, publishers, and authors were urged to donate their work (and so guarantee its preservation); citizens were pressed to make private collections of books, manuscripts, and antiquities of all sorts available to present and future generations. All of the resulting activity would generate a dynamic, disinterested system of correspondence, a democratic "republic of antiquities" that would exploit networks of communication and exchange for the higher patriotic purpose of binding the union together. Isaiah Thomas would thus mobilize antiquarian allies to keep the memory of an earlier, nation-making mobilization alive, conserving and refreshing the transgenerational historical consciousness that constituted the republic's soul.

American antiquarianism was in many ways deeply conservative. Thomas's antiquarian researches memorialized a glorious time when printer-patriots played a critical role—perhaps *the* critical role—in promoting the progress of the popular political enlightenment and preparing the way for the American Revolution. He founded the American Antiquarian Society at a moment when the very existence of the new republic—much less its continuing progress—seemed to hang in perilous balance. The union's near collapse spurred a renewal of national feeling. Patriots across the continent, fearing for the future, reaffirmed their fealty to the republican creed; by cherishing and preserving the fathers' precious legacy, they would redeem the republic.

It was a fortuitous—and evanescent—moment for recruiting members to a new *national* organization located in a region forced to come to terms with its suddenly diminished, peripheral status in an expanding union.[69] The eclipse of High Federalist opposition to the Jeffersonian Republican ascendancy signaled an end to the vicious partisan warfare of the French Revolutionary and Napoleonic era, when geopolitical instability strained the bonds of union to the breaking point. It was an "Era of Good Feelings," culminating in President James Monroe's enthusiastic reception in Boston, the epicenter of Federalist disaffection. Thomas and his associates would model a disinterested patriotic leadership in the postwar world, exploiting their region's cultural capital as well as a rich store of antiquities available for its collecting. But their organization would not be "local," like the Massachusetts Historical Society and similar institutions; it would be "American," dedicating its members to a broader, more inclusive project of collection and preservation.

American antiquarianism therefore can be seen in historical context as a distinctive expression of patriotic sentiment and national feeling. Antiquarians affirmed their commitment to the republican experiment—and to the revolutionary founders' faith in the future—at a time when the bonds of union seemed to be fraying and partisan and sectional sentiments were in ascendancy. For the self-identified "printer" and patriot Isaiah Thomas, this first great crisis of the American federal union had a powerful political dimension. As he disengaged from the print trade, he could not help but see that the figure of the printer-patriot—his image of his younger self—was increasingly archaic, a time-bound antiquity. Over the course of his business career, the master artisan was superseded by an emerging division of labor, with publisher-capitalists, booksellers, editors, and deskilled journeymen taking his place. The printer-patriot epitomized the model citizen in the people's republic; the specialized workers who replaced him—like the machine-driven workers in Adam Smith's pin factory—were no longer masters, no longer fully autonomous or independent, perhaps no longer capable of bearing the responsibilities of citizenship.

In the new print regime, newspaper editors came closest to exercising the kind of cultural authority Thomas imputed to printer-patriots of the revolutionary era. Yet it was all too painfully clear that they were no longer disinterested agents of popular enlightenment or conduits for the expression and consolidation of "public opinion." Editors were tools of new masters, hacks who relied on the patronage of political parties and lucrative government printing contracts. Significantly, Thomas's *History of Printing in America* focused on the development of his trade *before* independence. Following generations would have to tell their own story—if they had a story worth telling. Samuel Miller offered a devastating account of the degradation of the press in 1790s: it was much too "free" for its own, or the republic's, good. Thomas felt compelled to offer a mild dissent to this indictment, reprinted in the preface of his own *History* in a defensive footnote. Despite the acknowledged "rage of party spirit," Thomas insisted, "there are among the men who conduct the public journals of America, many, whose literary acquirements are not inferior to those of their predecessors."[70]

Being lectured at by Miller may have been discomfiting to Thomas for personal reasons. There were echoes here of the kind of condescension from the socially superior man of letters that may have offended the proud artisan. Miller also called into question the very possibility that printers could ever again assume the exalted place they had once occupied. For the most part, Thomas maintained cordial, if somewhat distant relations with active printers, instead cultivating his network of longtime, often retired veterans of the trade. But he did disclose his most cherished hopes for the future to posthumous readers of the many successive versions of his last will and testament. Right up to—but not including—his last will, he promised to endow an academy for poor but worthy young apprentices to the trade in Boston. Properly educated, a rising generation of editors might redeem the tainted profession.[71]

Thomas's identification with the future beneficiaries of his largesse is conspicuous: they would not have to experience his struggle for livelihood, literacy, and the skills of the trade. The young printers he imagined into existence in the sacred precincts of his will would be new, improved versions of himself, assuring him that he would achieve a kind of immortality, both as exemplar and benefactor. But financial reverses, amplified by the dislocations of war and the nationwide financial crisis of 1819, forced Thomas to reconsider the objects of his philanthropy. Perhaps the failures of his apprentices and partners in the trade to replicate his own success, or even to make a decent living, made him realize the barely concealed vanity of his project; certainly, the setbacks experienced by his namesake son and successor, Isaiah Thomas Jr., before his early death hit even closer to home. Thomas would not be able to sponsor a new generation of printers to carry on a trade that he had long since abandoned—and that no longer resembled the one he had once known. If he were to leave his imprint on posterity, it would be by preserving what he and his fellow craftsmen had produced, not by reproducing himself.

The aging antiquarian cherished and sought to perpetuate the memory of his younger self. In successive wills, Thomas thus invested a progressively larger portion of his sizable fortune in the Antiquarian Society in order to secure a permanent, posthumous home for the vast collections he amassed over the course of his life.[72] Thomas's wills testify eloquently to his solicitude for the things he collected. The donation books he maintained for the AAS (one for books, the other for various "curiosities") chronicle the ongoing transfer of his private collections to the society's library and cabinet. Before the erection of Antiquarian Hall, this meant moving items from one shelf to another in Thomas's home.[73] Of course, notable gifts from other antiquarians sustained the vitally important sense that the AAS was a collective enterprise, manifesting shared patriotic commitments.[74] But the disproportionate flow of donations from Thomas to the society (or from the private Thomas to his public counterpart) suggests the ongoing importance of the process of collecting, donating, and preserving for his understanding of himself as an antiquarian patriot. The fate of the republic hinged on the future of collections that documented its ongoing history, antiquarians insisted, and the society Thomas founded and funded was the only truly national institution dedicated to this exalted purpose. His gifts to the AAS offered a model of good citizenship that fellow antiquarians might emulate but could never match.

Many members of the founding generation shared the old printer's anxieties. If the union collapsed and the republic failed, they would be forgotten, for what they founded would no longer exist. Jefferson feared that partisan historians would willfully misrepresent the past and therefore betray the Revolution's future promise.[75] The deeper fear for American antiquarians was that the original, uncorrupted primary sources for constructing the young nation's "authentic history" would themselves be obliterated: their collections constituted the vital signs of the republic's ongoing civic health. For old men like Thomas and Jefferson, the approach of death exacerbated anxieties about the state of the union. Would the memories they sought to preserve in their private libraries and collections survive them? Would the United States (or the American Antiquarian Society) still exist when they were gone? Would they be remembered?

Thomas was chronically anxious about the Antiquarian Society's financial situation. During his lifetime, his generous gifts—in kind and in cash—kept the organization afloat, and in a single extraordinary year, 1820, he underwrote the huge costs of erecting Antiquarian Hall and publishing the first volume of the society's *Transactions*.[76] Thomas's generosity reflected the failure of fellow antiquarians to share his financial burden—and undoubtedly discouraged them from doing so. No equivalent learned society was so conspicuously associated with a single patron or with collections he privately amassed. Thomas undoubtedly reveled in the gratitude members of the AAS routinely, even ritualistically, expressed. Yet he also understood that his resources were limited—particularly in the aftermath of the 1819 panic—and thus bemoaned the absence of prosperous coadjutors.

The AAS fashioned itself, or rather aspired to be, a national institution, but it necessarily depended—like all equivalent, privately endowed cultural institutions—on the support of prosperous local patrons. Thomas made much of the society's location in Worcester as a safe, central inland location but recognized the need to cultivate connections and hold regular meetings in Boston, the regional metropolis. Worcester did not abound in deep-pocketed philanthropists with a taste for antiquities. Resources were scarce in Thomas's neighborhood, and so were antiquaries with his highly specialized interests. Thomas longed for learned neighbors.[77] By identifying, cultivating, and certifying a select group of local luminaries as "antiquarians," Thomas's society could help him overcome that sense of isolation; an ambitious national—and international—recruitment campaign could create a far-flung community of antiquaries who shared the old printer's passions. But an expanding membership generated little revenue, even when the AAS began to collect membership dues or "taxes."[78] The patriotic impulses of members were instead channeled into donating antiquities and freely sharing the products of their intellectual labors. As long as he lived, Thomas would continue to bear the financial burden by himself.

After 1820, Thomas shared his concerns about the AAS's future with friends in the council, its governing body, resulting in a series of wide-ranging proposals, all depending on further investment he was unable or unwilling to make. Membership expansion, particularly overseas, promised to raise the society's profile and—in the fullness of time—might recruit more generous members. Thomas could also take heart from the proliferation of learned societies, many of which were eager to foster cordial relationships with the AAS. With publication of the *Transactions,* the society finally had something to exchange: such publications were the currency of the realm in the associational world. Excited to see the fruits of their antiquarian labors in print, members directed a steady stream of submissions to Worcester. But the costs of the first volume, and particularly of its high-quality engravings, were daunting to Thomas. For the next several years, he promised the successor volume's imminent publication but struggled in vain to devise an economical scheme for its publication.[79]

With the burst of activity in 1820, Thomas and his fellow antiquarians must have felt that their time had come. But rising expectations preceded the disappointment and demoralization that marred Thomas's final years. The AAS's expanding collections, like its expanding membership, raised further problems. How could distant citizens in the antiquarians' republic be mobilized to fulfill its mission? How could the invaluable resources accumulating in Worcester be made accessible and useful? The ever-expanding library and cabinet demanded a librarian; the fruits of antiquarians' research demanded publication. It was all more than Thomas thought he could afford. As he approached his death, the society itself seemed somewhat antiquated. "Materials are already on hand sufficient for one or more volumes," AAS member Jacob Porter told readers of the *American Journal of Science* a decade after publication of the first volume of the *Transactions* and two years before Thomas's death. Unfortunately, the "want of funds" frustrated potential contributors, while visitors to Antiquarian Hall lamented the continuing absence of "a catalogue of the library and cabinet." Needless to say, Porter concluded, "it would also greatly increase the usefulness of the institution if a librarian and cabinet keeper were appointed, with an adequate salary, to attend regularly at the institution."[80]

In the final versions of his will, Thomas abandoned his young printers and left the bulk of his estate to the Antiquarian Society. But he did so with misgivings. He had no reason to believe that a new, energetic, and sufficiently generous generation of antiquarians would rise up in Worcester and take the place the founder had once filled. Thomas instead harked back to the society's beginnings, when the commonwealth of Massachusetts granted his band of antiquaries a charter of incorporation and the promise of perpetuity. "As it is possible, on account of the Members living remote from each other, and the inconvenience of assembling any considerable number of them together," he wrote in his November 1820 will, "then in that case I give the same in all its parts in trust to the Commonwealth of Massachusetts," with the hope that the commonwealth would hold the AAS's property in trust for "the first other American Antiquarian Society, which shall petition to them and obtain a Charter of incorporation; or to such other new Institution bearing the same name, and established for the same purposes as the present Society, which may obtain the privilege of incorporation in any other of the United States."[81] At the very moment when Antiquarian Hall, "a splendid memorial of individual generosity—the highest evidence of the patriotism and publick spirit of its munificent founder," opened in Worcester, Thomas prepared for the society's dissolution, removal, and rebirth.[82] If Thomas's wealthy neighbors failed to recognize the AAS's great value and keep it alive, another group of patriots could take its name and assume the burdens of stewardship, finding a home for its collections elsewhere—in some great city or, better still, in an inland metropolis, closer to the nation's heart.

Surely there must be patriotic philanthropists somewhere who would want to preserve this great national institution? Or were today's antiquarians, like yesterday's printer-patriots, a disappearing race, curiosities no longer worth collecting? Perhaps the antiquarians Thomas left behind in Antiquarian Hall, the house he built for them in Worcester, were mere phantoms of his imagination, like the generation of young printers he imagined housing in the house he never built in Boston.

The American Antiquarian Society's most successful and enduring outreach into the expanding frontier of the rising American Empire was in the Ohio Valley where the sons and daughters of New England helped spearhead settlement. This is where enterprising and curious men of letters were astonished by the surviving monuments and artifacts of "ancient America." Archaeologist Caleb Atwater and his colleagues made meticulous surveys and drawings of sites, monuments (including the famous mounds at Marietta), and objects. They were convinced that they were encountering the artifacts of a lost civilization, not the ancestors of present-day indigenous inhabitants of the region. The mysterious history of these former inhabitants gave rise to an extraordinary array of wild hypotheses, demonstrating the human potential of the so-called new world and ancient pedigree of its original inhabitants. The antiquarian-cum-archaeologists who followed in the wake of the settlement frontier generated extraordinary excitement back in Worcester. The first volume of the society's *Transactions* was devoted entirely to their reports.

As antiquarians focused on the ancient history of the Ohio Valley, American antiquarianism lost its distinctive character. Thomas's great collection of printed material illuminated the recent past, enabling patriots to leave a definitive record of their nation-making history for future generations. But the lost civilization of the Ohio Valley drew antiquarians away from the ongoing progress of their own civilization into a distant, obscure, illegible past that could never be fully known. Like their Old World counterparts, American antiquaries increasingly found the unknowable irresistible. Lost in a sea of mute fragments, they spun fabulous stories about mankind's mythic origins. Americans could not draw on the rich literary legacy of the classical world to direct their research or confirm their hypotheses; the Bible was the only text that could help Atwater and other Christian navigators find their way in this newly discovered ancient world. If Thomas's antiquarianism was grounded in the great archive of texts that he and his fellow printers generated, antiquarian research on the western frontier focused on collecting and interpreting unmediated objects in a world without texts. Digging deeper, these antiquaries became archaeologists, applying a rigorous, painstaking, self-consciously scientific methodology to their field of study—and curbing the tendency toward grand and groundless speculation about humankind's history.

Antiquarian speculations about the ancient history of North America betrayed the persistent sense of creole inferiority that spurred Jefferson and other cultural nationalists to exalt the natural capacity of their New World for sustaining the ongoing progress of human civilization. There was an undercurrent of pathos, however, in antiquarian reports from the settlement frontier. Why had this once-flourishing civilization collapsed? Had ancient Americans been overrun by a barbarian horde, plunging them into their own dark and silent age? Were all great empires—and republics—subject to the relentless logic of the life cycle, doomed to decline and fall? Such concerns were compelling to anxious Americans, who were acutely aware of existential threats to the success of their republican experiment and the very survival of their tenuous, radically imperfect union. American patriots loudly proclaimed their faith in themselves and in succeeding generations to keep sacred fires burning. But did they protest too much? The Antiquarian Society was a mighty buttress against the forgetfulness that doomed republics. But what if there were no patriotic antiquarians to man the barricade and the AAS proved to be an empty, abandoned shell, its collections rendered mute?

The mysterious mounds on the Muskingum River in Ohio led Caleb Atwater to contemplate the problem of memory and the ways in which names could be forgotten and the traces of human existence obliterated. "These monuments of ancient manners," he exclaimed, "how simple and yet how sublime!" "Their authors" were "unacquainted with the use of letters," but they spoke "a language as expressive as the most studied inscriptions of latter times upon brass and marble." Now these nameless "authors are gone," and the "events, which they were intended to keep in the memory, are lost in oblivion." Only "their monuments remain." Identifying with those authors and imagining their original intentions, Atwater stipulated a universal human imperative "to perpetuate the memory of those to whose kind care we are so greatly indebted." The mounds, he confidently concluded, were meant to be "lasting monument[s] of filial respect."[83]

The tragedy of this lost civilization was that the generational bonds which sustained memory supposedly were ruptured and its history was obliterated. In 1814, when America was at war and British barbarians were at the gate, Reverend Abiel Holmes underscored the sobering lesson for his own day. "The time may come," he warned, "when, without our care, the monuments of our wars will become unintelligible, like those of Muskingum." Holmes conjured up the antiquarian nightmare of history in reverse, a history without antiquarians to "care" for our monuments. It was easy for an antiquarian to imagine a time "when the antiquities of our [New England] aborigines can no longer be found, and the vestiges of our own pristine settlements, no longer be traced." But how could "the sons of the Pilgrims" forget their fathers without consigning themselves to oblivion? When the ultimate crisis came, they would seek salvation by reverting "to the times of their forefathers for old principles, antiquated manners, and patriarchal examples."[84] Antiquarians would show the way. In doing so they would cultivate a regional patriotism, thus subverting the antiquarian commitment to the nation as a whole.

Isaac Goodwin ruminated on the Muskingum mounds in less troubled times. The lessons he drew were more universal, more personal, less regionally specific. For "many centuries," he explained, the mounds have mutely testified to "the folly of human vanity, and the weakness of human pride." These "interesting mausolea were probably erected" to perpetuate the "fame" and memorialize the achievements of great men. But "the names of those once illustrious heroes . . . have been swept away by the lapse of ages; and even the period m which they existed, is now shrouded in a night of forgetfulness."[85]

The stereotypical antiquary lost himself in his subject, floating free of any meaningful connection to the world in which he lived. In their flights of fantasy about the fate of the lost civilization of the Ohio Valley, American antiquarians contemplated the deeper, personal implications of living in a forgetful world, of being cast away by history, of being disconnected from past and future, fathers and sons. They meditated on what it would be like to *be* nameless, to have all the evidence about who they were and what they had done obliterated. As antiquarians they were fighting the good fight on behalf of their ancestors and those peoples who had preceded them in their New World. They would remember; they desperately wanted to be remembered.

Isaiah Thomas meditated on these problems when he sought to settle accounts with his Maker and those he left behind in his wills. While he lived, he created a society and constructed a building to care for and add to his collections and built a home for them. It was a monument to his antiquarian vision, a great, inclusive, democratic house of names. But, of course, it was also a monument to himself. On the opening of Antiquarian Hall in 1820, twenty-one-year-old William Paine Cabot, scion of a prominent Worcester family, wittily observed that Thomas himself was as "great a curiosity as anything that can possibly be contained" in the new building. Playfully identifying the collector with his collection (a "curiosity" in a monumental cabinet), Cabot rendered a devastating verdict of the old printer's quest for a secular, earth-bound kind of immortality. "It would be a great pity," Cabot wrote, "if Posterity should not have it in their power to view the poor remains of so great, so good, so honest and so upright a man." Thomas of course had other ideas about what posterity would or should remember. But Cabot's premature obituary struck a resonant chord at a troubled moment in the history of the republic. Thomas, quipped Cabot, "would sell—if he has not already sold, his soul to the Arch fiend to hold a place in the memory of future ages."[86]

Yet who would not share the more modest ambition of simply being remembered? Could the republic survive without being conscious of its own history? "The benefits resulting from the American Antiquarian Society will be increasing with time," Thomas wrote in his will. The society "has no local views nor private concerns," he insisted. Antiquarians were instead animated by a "more disinterested, generous & enlarged benevolence" that embraced "all time, past, present & future."[87] Antiquarians were true patriots. They would sacrifice narrow self-interest to save the county's soul, praying that future generations would never forget their predecessors.

Notes

1. Clifford K. Shipton, *Isaiah Thomas: Printer, Patriot and Philanthropist* (Rochester, N.Y., 1948); Isaiah Thomas (hereafter IT), *Three Autobiographical Fragments, Now First Published upon the 150th Anniversary of the Founding of the American Antiquarian Society, October 24, 1812* (Worcester, Mass., 1962).

2. Thomas Jefferson (hereafter TJ), Declaration of Independence as Adopted by Congress, July 4, 1776, Julian P. Boyd et al., eds., *The Papers of Thomas Jefferson*, 44 vols. to date (Princeton, N.J., 1950–), 1:429 (hereafter *PTJ*); Pauline Maier, *American Scripture: Making the Declaration of Independence* (New York, 1997); Jay Fliegelman, *Declaring Independence: Jefferson, Natural Language, and the Culture of Performance* (Stanford, Calif., 1993).

3. Robert M. S. McDonald, "Thomas Jefferson's Changing Reputation as Author of the Declaration of Independence: The First Fifty Years," *Journal of the Early Republic* 19 (1999): 169–95; McDonald, *Confounding Father: Thomas Jefferson's Image in His Own Time* (Charlottesville, Va., 2016).

4. TJ to Henry Lee, May 8, 1825, Merrill D. Peterson, ed., *Thomas Jefferson: Writings* (New York, 1984), 1501.

5. Fliegelman, *Declaring Independence*, 164–67.

6. Mark G. Schmeller, *Invisible Sovereign: Imagining Public Opinion from the Revolution to Reconstruction* (Baltimore, 2016), 7–59. See also Alan Gibson, "Veneration and Vigilance: James Madison and Public Opinion, 1785–1800," *Review of Politics* 67 (2005): 5–35.

7. TJ to David Rittenhouse, July 19, 1778, *PTJ*, 2:203.

8. TJ, *Notes on the State of Virginia*, ed. William Peden (Chapel Hill, N.C., 1954), query XIX ("Manufactures"), 165.

9. Isaac Goodwin, unpublished address, April 1831, Isaiah Thomas Papers, box 7, folder 19, American Antiquarian Society, Worcester, Mass. (hereafter AAS).

10. In accepting membership in the AAS, Jefferson expressed the modest "hope of not being altogether unuseful." TJ to Samuel M. Burnside, January 9, 1814, J. Jefferson Looney et al., eds., *Papers of Thomas Jefferson: Retirement Series*, 13 vols. to date (Princeton, N.J., 2004–), 7:115.

11. Peter N. Miller, *History and Its Objects: Antiquarianism and Material Culture since 1500* (Ithaca, N.Y., 2017); Arnaldo Momigliano, "Ancient History and the Antiquarians," *Journal of the Warburg and Courtauld Institutes* 13 (1950): 285–315.

12. Rosemary Sweet, *Antiquaries: The Discovery of the Past in Eighteenth-Century Britain* (London, 2004), 57–60.

13. Benedict Anderson, *Imagined Communities: Reflections on the Origin and Spread of Nationalism*, rev. ed. (1983; London, 1991).

14. Josiah Flagg wrote to Thomas that Franklin, his great uncle, had told him that "your countryman Mr. Thomas of Worcester, is the Baskerville of America." Flagg to IT, June 28, 1824, AAS Correspondence, box 3, folder 20, AAS.

15. Michael Warner, *The Letters of the Republic: Publication and the Public Sphere in Eighteenth-Century America* (Cambridge, Mass., 1990); Bernard Bailyn, *The Ideological Origins of the American Revolution* (Cambridge, Mass., 1967).

16. James N. Green, "The Rise of Book Publishing," in *An Extensive Republic: Print, Culture, and Society in the New Nation, 1790–1840,* ed. Robert A. Gross and Mary Kelley (Chapel Hill, N.C., 2010), 75–127; Green, "The Rise and Fall of Isaiah Thomas's Bookselling Network," paper presented at the AAS, October 24, 1996, copy in author's possession.

17. Sir Walter Scott, *The Antiquary* (Edinburgh, 1816).

18. Alan Taylor, *William Cooper's Town: Power and Persuasion on the Frontier of the Early American Republic* (New York, 1995).

19. Michael Hattem, *Past and Prologue: History, Culture, and the American Revolution* (New Haven, Conn., 2020); Lester H. Cohen, *The Revolutionary Histories: Contemporary Narratives of the American Revolution* (Ithaca, N.Y., 1980).

20. On stadial theory, see Nicholas Onuf and Peter Onuf, *Nations, Markets, and War: Modern History and the American Civil War* (Charlottesville, Va., 2006), 42–48, 91–95, and Ronald L. Meek, *Social Science and the Ignoble Savage* (Cambridge, U.K., 1976).

21. On Jefferson and history, see Hannah Spahn, *Thomas Jefferson, Time, and History* (Charlottesville, Va., 2011); on his civic humanism, see Matthew Crow, *Thomas Jefferson, Legal History, and the Art of Recollection* (New York, 2017).

22. Sweet, *Antiquaries.*

23. IT, *The History of Printing in America. With a Biography of Printers, and an Account of Newspapers,* 2 vols. (Worcester, Mass., 1810). See also IT, *History of Printing,* 2nd ed., with the author's corrections and additions, and a catalogue of American publications previous to the revolution of 1776, published under the supervision of the AAS (Albany, 1874), and IT, *History of Printing,* ed. Marcus A. McCorison (New York, 1970).

24. IT, *History of Printing* (1810 ed.), 1:368–85.

25. See IT, *History of Printing* (1874 ed.). William McCulloch of Philadelphia congratulated Thomas on his "excellent performance" yet thought "it would be rendered much more valuable, if a few of the craft would transmit you such additional information as may be diffused through different individuals." McCulloch to IT, September 1, 1812, Isaiah Thomas Papers, box 6, folder 12.

26. Isaiah Thomas Papers, box 14, folders 2, 4.

27. IT, "An Account of the American Antiquarian Society, Incorporated. October 24th, 1812," *Proceedings of the American Antiquarian Society, 1812–1849* (Worcester, Mass., 1912), 14 (hereafter *AAS Proceedings*).

28. Green, "Rise and Fall of Isaiah Thomas's Bookselling Network." See Thomas's valuations in "Donations to the AAS with the Names of Its Benefactors," bound volumes (one for books, the other for manuscripts, coins, and miscellaneous curiosities), AAS.

29. Isaac Goodwin, "An Address Delivered at Worcester, August 24, 1820," *AAS Proceedings,* 161.

30. IT, *History of Printing* (1810 ed.), 1:10.

31. Samuel A. Miller, *A Brief Retrospect of the Eighteenth Century; Part the First, in Three Volumes* (London, 1805), 3:chap. 22, "Political Journals."

32. Ibid., 3:131.

33. IT, *History of Printing* (1810 ed.), 2:403, quoting Miller, *Brief Retrospect of the Eighteenth Century.*

34. Ibid.

35. Isaac Goodwin, unpublished address, April 1831, AAS Correspondence, box 7, folder 19.

36. IT, *History of Printing* (1810 ed.), 1:203. The history of "our own country," antiquarian William Paine told the AAS in 1815, "may be accurately traced, from its first discovery to this day, and whatever relates to it may be ascertained by the most authentick documents. Not so the history of ancient nations, which is so much involved in fable." Paine, "An Address to the Members of the American Antiquarian Society, Pronounced in King's Chapel, Boston, on Their Third Anniversary, October 23, 1815," *AAS Proceedings,* 87.

37. IT, *History of Printing* (1810 ed.), 1:10.

38. John Russell, *An Address Presented to the Members of the Faustus Association in Boston, at Their Annual Celebration, Oct. 4, 1808* (Boston, 1808), 20–22.

39. "From long habits of prudence & economy," Isaac Goodwin wrote, Thomas "preserved copies of almost every work that issued from his presses." Goodwin, unpublished address, April 1831.

40. IT, "Communication from the President," October 24, 1814, *AAS Proceedings,* 52–53.

41. IT, "An Account of the American Antiquarian Society," 17–18.

42. Goodwin, "Address Delivered at Worcester," 161.

43. "Half the treasure of information which a complete view of all that concerns" the history of mankind's development "will be lost to the world, unless something shall be done to rescue it from oblivion." Enoch Lincoln to Rejoice Newton, February 20, 1819, AAS Correspondence, box 2, folder 12, AAS.

44. Montesquieu, *The Spirit of the Laws,* trans. and ed. Anne M. Cohler et al. (Cambridge, U.K., 1989), part 1, book 3, chap. 3, pp. 22–24.

45. Samuel Johnson, April 7, 1775, quoted in James Boswell, *Boswell's Life of Johnson,* ed. Charles Grosvenor Osgood (New York, 1917), 246.

46. William Jenks, "An Address to the Members of the American Antiquarian Society, Pronounced in King's Chapel, Boston, on Their First Anniversary, October 23, 1813," *AAS Proceedings,* 37.

47. TJ to James Madison, September 6, 1789, *PTJ,* 15:393, 395. See Herbert Sloan's brilliant essay "'The Earth Belongs in Usufruct to the Living,'" in *Jeffersonian Legacies,* ed. Peter S. Onuf (Charlottesville, Va., 1993), 281–315, and Onuf, *Jefferson and the Virginians: Democracy, Constitutions, and Empire* (Baton Rouge, La., 2018), chap. 3.

48. IT, *History of Printing* (1810 ed.), 1:203.

49. William Bentley, address to the AAS, October 23, 1816, AAS Correspondence, box 1, folder 19. For a rough transcription, see *AAS Proceedings,* 105–22.

50. Montesquieu, *Spirit of the Laws,* part 1, book 3, chap. 9, pp. 28–29.

51. IT, *History of Printing* (1810 ed.), 1:209.

52. IT to William Bentley, August 17, 1814, Isaiah Thomas Papers, box 6, folder 21.

53. George Washington, First Inaugural Address, April 30, 1789, Dorothy Twohig et al., eds., *The Papers of George Washington: Presidential Series,* 19 vols. to date (Charlottesville, Va., 1987–), 2:175.

54. TJ, First Inaugural Address, March 4, 1801, *PTJ,* 33:149.

55. Jenks, "An Address to the Members of the American Antiquarian Society," 26, 37.

56. IT, *History of Printing* (1810 ed.), 1:7.

57. Samantha Harvey, *Reading the Book of Nature: Imagination, Observation, and Preservation* (forthcoming). On natural religion, see Matthew Stewart, *Nature's God: The Heretical Origins of the American Republic* (New York, 2014).

58. Ellen Dunlap, comp., "Members of the American Antiquarian Society Elected from 1812–1831," AAS.

59. Eran Shalev, *American Zion: The Old Testament as a Political Text from the Revolution to the Civil War* (New Haven, Conn., 2013).

60. IT Will, July 24, 1817, Isaiah Thomas Papers, box 4, folder 14.

61. Jenks, "An Address to the Members of the American Antiquarian Society," 26.

62. Samuel Burnside to William Findlay, December 17, 1817, AAS Correspondence, box 1, folder 23.

63. Oliver Fiske, "Address to the Members of the American Antiquarian Society; Together with the Laws and Regulations of the Institution," *AAS Proceedings,* 140.

64. William Bentley, address to the AAS, October 23, 1816.

65. For a typical complaint about the "depredation" of "ancient ruins and relicks" in the West, see Moses Fiske, Fulham, Tenn., April 8, 1815, "Conjectures Respecting the Ancient Inhabitants of North America," *Archaeologia Americana: Transactions and Collections of the American Antiquarian Society* 1 (1820): 307.

66. Goodwin, "Address Delivered at Worcester," 161.

67. John Randolph of Roanoke to Oliver Fiske, September 25, 1815, AAS Correspondence, box 2, folder 23.

68. See, for example, letters in the AAS Correspondence collection from Manasseh Cutler, box 1, folder 29; Timothy Dwight, box 1, folder 31; John Jay, box 2, folder 9; TJ, box 2, folder 9; Andrew Jackson, box 3, folder 30; and Bushrod Washington, box 2, folder 36.

69. James M. Banner, *To the Hartford Convention: The Federalists and the Origins of Party Politics in Massachusetts, 1789–1815* (New York, 1970); Steven Watts, *The Republic Reborn: War and the Making of Liberal America, 1790–1820* (Baltimore, 1987).

70. According to Miller, "American newspapers . . . have been pronounced by travellers the most profligate and scurrilous public prints in the civilised world"; quoted in IT, *History of Printing* (1810 ed.), 2:406–7. For Thomas's response, see his "Observation," ibid., 2:407n.

71. In his first will, dated April 15, 1792, Thomas stipulated that when interest from a bequest of £500 to the town of Boston increased to a total of £4,000, £2,000 should "be appropriated for the purpose of purchasing a piece of Land in said Town, and building thereon an handsome, durable, brick, or Stone building, for an Academy—to be called the Printers Academy, for the purpose of educating the children of poor Printers, Booksellers, and Bookbinders, in reading, writing, Arithmetick, and the English and Latin Languages, &c." He bequeathed the same amount to finance "an Academy—to be called Thomas's Academy, or whatever said town may please to call it, for the purpose of educating children, particularly those of poor Farmers and Mechanicks." For subsequent references to the academies, see wills of 1797 (same provisions); 1800 (with $10,000 designated for each academy); 1803 (with "Thomas's" eliminated from the Worcester academy); 1813 (with $22,000 designated for each academy); and 1813–17? (fragment, with $25,000 for the Printers Academy; nothing for Worcester). Neither academy is mentioned in Thomas's wills beginning with the one he drafted on July 24, 1817. All the wills are in Isaiah Thomas Papers, box 14, folder 4.

72. Isaiah Thomas Papers, box 14, folder 4.

73. See "Donations to the AAS with the Names of Its Benefactors."

74. Thomas recorded twelve donations from Hannah Mather Crocker in 1814–16, including books, manuscripts, portraits, and the family arms of her Mather ancestors; in his will, William Bentley left portraits, maps, and engravings as well as a large portion of his famous library to the AAS. "Donations to the AAS with the Names of Its Benefactors."

75. Francis D. Cogliano, *Thomas Jefferson: Reputation and Legacy* (Edinburgh, 2006).

76. *Archaeologia Americana*, vol. 1.

77. "I greatly desire the pleasure of spending an hour or two with you, and more if it can be," Thomas wrote William Bentley, April 7, 1817: "I hope circumstances will soon favour an interview." Isaiah Thomas Papers, box 7, folder 4.

78. Many members referred to dues as taxes. See, for example, Timothy Dwight to Samuel Burnside, December 13, 1813: "The annual tax I will transmit by the first convenient, private conveyance." AAS Correspondence, box 1, folder 31.

79. On delays in publishing the second volume of *Archaeologia Americana*, see John Farmer to IT, January 24, 1823, and November 11, 1823, AAS Correspondence, box 3, folder 17; and IT to Farmer, June 3, 1824, Isaiah Thomas Papers, letterbook 14, 53–56.

80. Jacob Porter, "Notice of the American Antiquarian Society; Abridged from a Letter Addressed by Dr. Jacob Porter to M. Fursi Laisne, of Paris," *American Journal of Science* 18 (July 1830): 136–39.

81. Last Will of Isaiah Thomas, Executed, November 13, 1820 (bound volume), Isaiah Thomas Papers, box 14, folder 2, 30–32.

82. Goodwin, "Address Delivered at Worcester," 161, 164.

83. Atwater, Letter to the president of the AAS, January 20, 1820, *Archaeologia Americana*, 1:144, 165.

84. Abiel Holmes, "An Address Delivered before the American Antiquarian Society, in King's Chapel, Boston, on Their Second Anniversary, October 24, 1814," *AAS Proceedings,* 57–70, 68–69 (quotations).

85. Goodwin, "Address Delivered at Worcester," 155. See also Goodwin, unpublished address, April 1831: "What acts they performed to entitle them to empty honors now baffles the wisdom of the learned and the researches of the antiquary."

86. Quoted in Philip F. Gura, *The American Antiquarian Society, 1812–2012: A Bicentennial History* (Worcester, Mass., 2012), 43–44.

87. IT Will, November 13, 1820, 31.

Afterword

The Contradictions and Paradoxes of American Future-Gazing

This is a book of contradictions and paradoxes. It shows how a group of provincials thought continentally; how a cluster of idealists remained true to hard realities; how a people looking forward anchored themselves in the past. It shows how early Americans imagined themselves.

There were big questions yet to be decided that loomed large on their horizons following the Revolution. Would Americans' experiment in self-government function? Could a republic survive in the modern day? Would the New World rise above Old World corruption? And what of the nation's original sin: slavery? Where would it be in America's future? Looking forward in time, the people in this book saw different answers to those questions. There was no one vision of a future America, no joint prophecy of things to come. Indeed, there was no single founding. American nationhood was launched by a broad spectrum of hopes and expectations. In exploring how the founding generation envisioned America, this book tells a tale of a thousand tales and more.

Some things—like the spirit of the moment—remained constant. Founding periods are fraught with opportunity and risk. Embracing change requires asking and answering questions; each answer has unknown and potentially dire implications. The spirit of the Enlightenment contained both sides of this equation. It suggested that people could understand humanity and improve humankind, but in doing so, it exposed the countless ways that people could—and would—fall short.

The institution of slavery represented a massive, unforgiveable shortcoming. Despite the soaring rhetoric—indeed, *because* of the soaring rhetoric—the anchoring weight of slavery befouled the founding and the founders, their hypocrisy exposed. As the essays in this volume show, some people freely, even aggressively, projected slavery into America's future. Others dreamed of its demise but did little more. Regardless, there was no way to ignore the issue of slavery. Any attempt to do so was a choice within itself.

This was the climate in which the founding generation struggled with nationhood, and it underlies all of the essays here. The people in these pages were in a nation-in-formation, and they knew it. Their thoughts for the future were not mere abstractions. They had an immediacy that made them important—and for some, that immediacy was a matter of life and death. "Founders" often had the money or leisure to project a distant future. More "common" folk did not have that privilege. Artisans and sailors, farmers and manufacturers: their existence was often hand to mouth, so they needed to see the promise of the future in the present. They needed results. For Native Americans and enslaved people, this truth was even more pressing: they were engaged in a life-and-death struggle for survival, day by day. The promise of the future needed to take effect now, and yet it did not—a fact that reveals much about our nation's past and present. "Equality" was an amorphous and limited ideal in the founding period; powerholders pushed for a future in which they remained on top.

But the people in these pages weren't only looking to the future. In the midst of a deliberate, self-aware founding moment, they understood the pull and power of the past. New nations need histories and identities. They need principles and ideals and processes and rituals and myths to join peoples (or at least some of them) in shared cause. The resulting historical consciousness of the founding generation of Americans—their awareness that they needed to create and preserve a narrative of a shared past so they could move into the future—was at the core of their prophecies of what the nation would become.

Some of them structured a national narrative with words. The printer Isaiah Thomas dedicated much of his energies to this task, collecting, preserving, and thereby constructing a documented past aimed at serving the future. The American Antiquarian Society was founded as a touchstone of America's identity for "a remote and distant posterity." Without such efforts, what would future generations share as a standard? As Peter S. Onuf aptly puts it, Thomas's efforts to create a past were a "prayer for future remembrance."

Benjamin Franklin—so admired by Thomas—also used words to speak to future Americans. In narrating and exploring Franklin's youth and lessons learned, his *Autobiography* created a portrait of a "Young America" for the future, its lessons passed along with wit, humor, and the practicality of the self-made man. Indeed, Franklin crafted a national narrative in much the same way he fashioned himself. For both Franklin and Thomas, the past had a practical utility that they used to full effect.

Others in this volume reached toward the future through their actions. Alexander Hamilton's political trajectory shows this bluntly. Never fully trusting in democratic governance, he nevertheless proved willing to adopt democratic methods to advance his cause. He may not have liked it, but he was struggling to move forward in time toward an unknown but more democratic future. Most Federalists did not join him, thereby prefiguring their ultimate collapse. John Adams was a man of action too, gearing his politics toward a future America that would be newly continental yet familiarly provincial. As J. Patrick Mullins puts it, Adams was a "practical idealist," a man whose national ideals were linked with provincial realities. His future America was national in scope but had the character and flavor of his New England home.

Of course, Hamilton and Adams were not alone. Entire groups of people actively reached for their futures. Agrarian founders understood the seeming promise of the Revolution and took action to move from a colonial past to that far more promising future. Their petitions, demonstrations, and mob actions were demands for the America they felt entitled to—the future they had fought for. Along similar lines, Native Americans reimagined their future through their actions, learning to think of their tribes as state-like entities through treaty-making with the United States—a nation that did not share their vision, and in time created a future far darker than they may have imagined. Women, too, emerged from the Revolution with a reimagined future. Politically active during the war—writing, petitioning, printing, equipping troops, and managing businesses and farms in the absence of their legal owners—women carried their political entitlement into the postwar years but were soon stripped of their illusions. The future they envisioned remained distant in time.

Not all formulations of the future required actions or even words. James Monroe and James Madison envisioned an America-to-come that grew from their assumptions about America-as-it-was. For Monroe, that meant a nation that would continue to protect slavery and the slaveholding gentry; looking at America's future, Monroe cast his eyes south. Madison had a more national outlook. He envisioned some of Virginia's bounties spreading nationwide. His focus on agriculture in his old age was grounded on an assumption that it would be a unifying factor for the nation at large. Agrarian growth would encourage the growth of national sentiment—a promise that ultimately proved both true and false. Agrarianism was a widespread bond that seemed inherently "American" to some. It was also inextricably bound with the problem of slavery and led to a bloody civil war.

In one way or another, all of these people were using past and present to build toward the future through words, actions, and assumptions. George Washington did something more. Already the "Father of his Country" during his lifetime, he actively worked to preserve his founder status, preserving his reputation not only for himself but for future generations. Standing at center stage during the Revolution and its aftermath, Washington became a symbol of nationhood in and of himself, as he was all too well aware. As he grew to think nationally, his vision of the future grew; his widespread travels around the nation informed his thoughts. Like many, he believed in the "Rising Glory of America," as amorphous as that glory might be.

That vision of America was grounded on a profound belief in American exceptionalism, a belief with deep roots in history that survives even today. However diverse their predictions of things to come, most Americans believed that their experiment in government was special, a providential beacon that would light the way for the world. In a sense, they were doing something *beyond* history—something that had never been done before.

This mindset has a high price, as our nation's history has taught us. An "exceptional" people does not necessarily engage with other nations or peoples in good faith. They assume that their self-defined virtue and glory justify their actions. They value themselves above those who are unlike them or less fortunate; their strutting on the world stage often has grave implications. As unifying as it can be, a sense of exceptionalism can crush competing peoples and cultures with nary a second thought. As shown in this book, that dangerous kind of magical thinking started early—very early—as early as the nation itself.

It is difficult to imagine the people of a newborn republic in a world of monarchies imagining themselves this grandly and with such confidence. How was it possible? What built their convictions? This book offers a fascinating but paradoxical answer—perhaps the biggest paradox in its pages. It reminds us that Americans in this period were provincials. And precisely *because* their world was small, they could dream big for the future, unaware of many of the challenges to come. As Mullins explains regarding John Adams, his "very provincialism insulated him from early doubts" about the size, scope, and mission of the American experiment. The smallness of their worlds enabled them to think big.

The authors in this volume describe that mindset in several ways, each construction of it capturing this paradox: "Yankee continentalism," "enlightened provincialism," "democratic antiquarianism." People envisioned their nation's future through complex lenses, this volume teaches. To fully understand their mindset, we have to take these contradictions and paradoxes into account.

Which brings us to the present, in all its complexity, and the many ways in which we forecast our nation's future. Like the founding generation, we see it through different lenses. Like them, more often than not, those lenses are clouded; our understanding of our past and present structures our sense of things to come. Provincial continentalists no more, we are national globalists, our worldwide gaze framed within the limits of our nation. This book teaches us to recognize that gaze and consider its implications. It invites us to consider how we imagine ourselves. We move toward our future ever crafting national narratives of contradictions and paradoxes, ever wrestling with who we are as a people, and who we will become.

Contributors

KENNETH R. BOWLING is the retired co-editor of the *Documentary History of the First Federal Congress, 1789–1791* and Adjunct Professor of History at George Washington University. He received his Ph.D. in history from the University of Wisconsin in 1968. He specializes in the study of the creation of the federal government during the American Revolution and particularly in the establishment of Washington, D.C., as the nation's capital.

TODD ESTES is Professor of History at Oakland University in Rochester, Michigan. He is the author of *The Jay Treaty Debate, Public Opinion, and the Evolution of Early American Political Culture* (2006) and the editor of *Founding Visions: The Ideas, Individuals, and Intersections That Created America* (2014). He is currently at work on a book manuscript about the role of political moderation in the ratification debate of 1787–88.

ROBERT A. FERGUSON was George Edward Woodberry Professor of Law, Literature, and Criticism Emeritus at Columbia University. He was affiliated with law schools, English departments, history departments, and American Studies programs and taught at Columbia University, Harvard University, the University of Chicago, Stanford University, Princeton University, and Yale University. His books included *Law and Letters in American Culture* (1987); *The American Enlightenment, 1750–1820* (1997); *Reading the Early Republic* (2004); an annotated edition of *The Federalist* (2006); *The Trial in American Life* (2007); *Alone in America* (2013); *Inferno: An Anatomy of American Punishment* (2014); and *Practice Extended: Beyond Law and Literature* (2016).

JOANNE B. FREEMAN is the Class of 1954 Professor of History and American Studies at Yale University. Freeman's scholarship centers on early American political culture, partisanship, and political violence. She is the author of *Affairs of Honor: National Politics in the New Republic* (2001) and *The Field of Blood: Violence in Congress and the Road to Civil War* (2018), as well as the editor of *Alexander Hamilton: Writings* (2001) and *The Essential Hamilton* (2017). She co-hosted the popular American history podcast *BackStory.*

JOHN CRAIG HAMMOND is Associate Professor of History at Penn State University and Assistant Director of Academic Affairs at Penn State New Kensington. The author of numerous articles, chapters, and books on slavery in the early American republic, he is currently at work on a co-edited volume on the Missouri Crisis and a monograph that examines the politics of slavery between 1815 and 1825.

DREW R. MCCOY is the Jacob and Frances Hiatt Professor of History at Clark University. He is the author of *The Elusive Republic: Political Economy in Jeffersonian America* (1980) and *The Last of the Fathers: James Madison and the Republican Legacy* (1989), the latter of which was awarded the John H. Dunning Prize by the American Historical Association. His more recent research focuses on the early life of Abraham Lincoln in relation to the transformative developments of the early nineteenth century.

ROBERT M. S. MCDONALD is Professor of History at the United States Military Academy. He is author of *Confounding Father: Thomas Jefferson's Image in His Own Time* (2016) and editor of several collections of essays including, most recently, *Thomas Jefferson's Lives: Biographers and the Battle for History* (2019).

J. PATRICK MULLINS is an American cultural and intellectual historian. He serves as Assistant Professor of History and Public History Director at Marquette University. He received his Ph.D. in history from the University of Kentucky in 2005, where his dissertation was directed by Professor Lance Banning. He is author of *Father of Liberty: Jonathan Mayhew and the Principles of the American Revolution* (2017). His next book project explores how public memory of the execution of King Charles I contributed to the cultural origins of the American Revolution.

Paul Douglas Newman is Professor of History at the University of Pittsburgh at Johnstown where he has taught for twenty-five years since studying with Lance Banning for his Ph.D. at the University of Kentucky. He is the author of *Fries's Rebellion: The Enduring Struggle for the American Revolution* (2004) and past editor of *Pennsylvania History: A Journal of Mid-Atlantic Studies* (2000–2010). He is currently studying political and diplomatic identity formation, independence, and struggles for sovereignty among Pennsylvania's eighteenth-century multiethnic Indian communities.

David Andrew Nichols is Professor of History at Indiana State University. He is the author of *Red Gentlemen and White Savages: Indians, Federalists, and the Search for Order on the American Frontier* (2008); *Engines of Diplomacy: Indian Trading Factories and the Negotiation of American Empire* (2016); and *Peoples of the Inland Sea: Native Americans and Newcomers in the Great Lakes Region, 1600–1870* (2018).

Peter S. Onuf is Thomas Jefferson Foundation Professor of History Emeritus at the University of Virginia. He is the author of numerous works on the history of the early American republic, including *The Origins of the Federal Republic: Jurisdictional Controversies in the United States, 1775–1787* (1983), *Jefferson's Empire: The Language of American Nationhood* (2000), and, with Annette Gordon-Reed, *"Most Blessed of the Patriarchs": Thomas Jefferson and the Empire of the Imagination* (2016).

Index

abolition movement/abolitionists, 11, 99–100, 195–96, 199–200, 204. *See also* colonization; emancipation

Adams, Abigail, 51–52

Adams, Henry, 161

Adams, John: admirer of monarchy and aristocracy, 58; appointment to Continental Congress, 53, 65–66; commentary on nature of government, 59–64, 74–75; delegate to Provincial Congress, 66; drafting the Declaration of Independence, 76–77; drafting the Declaration of Rights and Grievances, 65, 66; drafting a template for state governments, 73–75; election of 1800, 155; experiences that shaped, 8–10; observations on human nature and reason, 56–59; support of union and war with Britain, 68–73; teaching school in Worcester, Mass., 55; views on common people to govern, 58–64, 76–78; vision of America, 51–56, 77–78, 261, 263; writing under "Novanglus" pseudonym, 66–67

Adams, John, Sr., 65

Adams, John Quincy, 93, 176, 186–87, 193n42

Adams, Louisa Catherine, 187

Adams, Samuel Quincy, 58, 69, 78

Addison, Alexander, 115, 119, 120–21

agrarianism/agriculture/farming: conversion of Indians to, 97–98; Madison's support of, 181–86; as unifying force in America, 262; vision of America, 261–62; Washington's promotion of, 90–91, 93–94

agrarian rebellion (1786–99), 12–13, 107–29, 261. *See also* Fries's Rebellion (1786–87); Shays's Rebellion (Shaysite "Regulators," 1786–87); Whiskey Rebellion (1791–94)

ahistoricism, 27, 33

Albany Plan for Union, 38, 39, 55

Alexandria, Va., 86–87

Alien and Sedition Acts, 13, 122, 124, 127, 129, 157

"all men are created equal." *See* equality (principle of being "created equal")

America (Dwight), 83

American Antiquarian Society (AAS): antiquarianism as field of study, 226–30; author's gratitude for assistance, 129n; creating/preserving a collection of works, 230–44; donations/contributions to, 245, 253n25, 256n74; founding, 19, 225–28, 235, 242; insuring the financial future, 244–48; Jefferson as member, 252n10; publication of *Transactions*, 245–46, 256n79; research into "ancient America," 248–51, 254n36; as touchstone of America's identity, 260. *See also* Thomas, Isaiah

RECENT BOOKS IN THE SERIES
Jeffersonian America

The Founding of Thomas Jefferson's University
JOHN A. RAGOSTA, PETER S. ONUF, AND
ANDREW J. O'SHAUGHNESSY, EDITORS

Thomas Jefferson's Lives: Biographers and the Battle for History
ROBERT M. S. McDONALD, EDITOR

Jeffersonians in Power: The Rhetoric of Opposition
Meets the Realities of Governing
JOANNE B. FREEMAN AND JOHANN N. NEEM, EDITORS

Jefferson on Display: Attire, Etiquette, and the Art of Presentation
G. S. WILSON

Jefferson's Body: A Corporeal Biography
MAURIZIO VALSANIA

Pulpit and Nation: Clergymen and the Politics of Revolutionary America
SPENCER W. McBRIDE

Blood from the Sky: Miracles and Politics in the Early American Republic
ADAM JORTNER

Confounding Father: Thomas Jefferson's Image in His Own Time
ROBERT M. S. McDONALD

The Haitian Declaration of Independence: Creation, Context, and Legacy
JULIA GAFFIELD, EDITOR

Citizens of a Common Intellectual Homeland: The Transatlantic
Origins of American Democracy and Nationhood
ARMIN MATTES